The Other Muslims

WITHDRAWN

The Other Muslims

Moderate and Secular

Edited by
Zeyno Baran

THE OTHER MUSLIMS

Copyright © Zeyno Baran, 2010.

First published in 2010 by
PALGRAVE MACMILLAN®
in the United States—a division of St. Martin's Press LLC,
175 Fifth Avenue, New York, NY 10010.

Where this book is distributed in the UK, Europe and the rest of the
world, this is by Palgrave Macmillan, a division of Macmillan Publishers
Limited, registered in England, company number 785998, of Houndmills,
Basingstoke, Hampshire RG21 6XS.

Palgrave Macmillan is the global academic imprint of the above
companies and has companies and representatives throughout the world.

Palgrave® and Macmillan® are registered trademarks in the United States,
the United Kingdom, Europe and other countries.

ISBN: 978–0–230–62188–6 (pbk)
ISBN: 978–0–230–62187–9 (hc)

Library of Congress Cataloging-in-Publication Data is available from the
Library of Congress.

A catalogue record of the book is available from the British Library.

Design by Newgen Imaging Systems (P) Ltd., Chennai, India.

First edition: March 2010

10 9 8 7 6 5 4 3 2 1

Printed in the United States of America.

CONTENTS

Part III Looking Ahead: Islam's Renaissance and Coexistence with Secular Democracy

NOTE ON THE COVER PICTURE

The *cover picture,* taken by Lala Abdurahimova of Azerbaijan, depicts students in the garden of the Ulugh Beg Madrasa in Samarkand, Uzbekistan. This *madrasa* (Islamic university), built in the fifteenth century under the Central Asian ruler Ulugh Beg, became a center of tolerant faith and scientific learning. Ulugh Beg, a grandson of Emperor Timur (known in the West as Tamerlane), was revered throughout his empire that encompassed present-day Central Asia, South Asia, and large parts of the Middle East as a great political leader and scientist. His astronomical discoveries rivaled those of Copernicus and Galileo; Ulugh Beg plotted the positions of the moon, the planets, and over a thousand stars, and calculated the length of the year to within fifty-eight seconds. Under his patronage, this *madrasa* became one of the foremost universities in the Muslim world, focusing equally on secular and spiritual studies, which helped usher in a period of Islamic enlightenment. These developments were in the tradition of earlier Central Asian theologian scientists, such as Ibn Sina (known to Westerners as Avicenna), whom Italian Renaissance scholars considered a forefather of modern medicine, and al-Khwarizmi, who coined the terms "algebra" and "algorithm" and helped establish the Indian number system and use of decimal notation.

ACKNOWLEDGMENTS

I express my deep gratitude to my co-authors of this book not only for their superb contributions, but also for sharing my trust in our ability to make a difference as we defend our beautiful religion against those who seek to distort and misuse it to undermine our universal values. I am also honored by their faith in me as the coordinator of this project.

I am grateful to my husband, Matthew Bryza, for his constant inspiration in helping me develop the fundamental concepts about which I have written, in honing these thoughts, and in expressing them (I hope) clearly and convincingly.

My research assistants at the Hudson Institute also made crucial contributions. Emmet C. Tuohy translated into English articles originally written in French, German, and Italian and carefully edited all of them. His insightful thinking and diligent drafting efforts became intellectual sinews that helped hold this project together. Onur Sazak helped sustain the project's momentum by reviewing the articles, offering sharp insights, and meticulously ensuring the final drafts were ready for publication. Robert A. Smith helped organize our initial gathering of co-authors in the Netherlands, and provided thoughtful views on general themes of the book.

I am also grateful to Hudson Institute interns Diana Marongiu, Henrik Bliddal, Catherine de Vulder, Jordan Daniels, and Aislinn Hettyey for their help over the course of the project.

I thank Miriam Himmelfarb for assisting with the editing of this collection of diverse essays.

Finally, I am grateful to Farideh Koohi-Kamali of Palgrave Macmillan for accepting our belief as authors and thinkers in the importance of this book, and giving us a chance to publish it. I thank Farideh's editorial assistant Robyn Curtis, for helping to shepherd us through the publication process.

Introduction and Overview

Zeyno Baran

The most important ideological struggle in the world today is within Islam. Moderate and secular Muslims, who embrace the compatibility of Islam and democracy and the individual freedoms we all cherish in the West, are being confronted by Islamists, who are extremist activists that hijack Islam and seek to gain political power and reshape societies. Islamists pursue these ends out of a firm conviction in their narrow interpretation of Islam, which holds that all authority derives from God alone, and which highlights the supremacy of the community over the individual. This Islamist conviction undermines the rights of the individual, and thus, universal human rights, and is emerging in much of Europe and the United States as the mainstream.

This book is a collection of Muslim voices from Europe and the United States that oppose the Islamists. The contributors are individuals from a variety of backgrounds—academia, theology, theater, activism, military, and others. Some live according to the strict dictates of Islam, while others eschew formal religious practice and identify as culturally Muslim. Some were born in the West, while others have come as immigrants or divide their time between Europe and the Middle East or North Africa. Many do not like to be labeled merely as "Muslim"; they want to be recognized as European and American.

The authors do not agree on all the points, but all ten authors are united in their belief that Islam is fully compatible with the Western understanding of democracy. Moreover, they believe that this compatibility does not—and should not—require Western societies to make "exceptions" or concessions in civil liberties. They contend that such concessions will lead to the creation of "parallel societies" in which Muslims will lead an entirely separate existence governed not by the laws of the countries in which they live, but instead by *sharia*, the legal code of the Qur'an.

Though sharia means "the path" (to truth or to the divine)—a path that individuals are supposed to find on their own—over the centuries this notion has hardened into a harsh legal system. Today, Islamists seek to extend *sharia* to regulate all aspects of life, from politics and economics, to science, social issues, interpersonal relationships, and even sexuality. *Sharia's* starting point in society is to restrict women's freedoms and individual human rights. In the extreme, *sharia* demands that those who leave the religion or are deemed non-religious be killed. Instead of providing the freedom for people to find their way to God, *sharia* has become the chief instrument in the hands of repressive clerical regimes who claim that their all-encompassing authority derives from their connection to the supreme authority, God.

In the same way, Islamist extremists in Europe and the United States seek to undermine democratic societies that are based on the authority of "mere" people rather than of God. Some Islamists speak openly about wanting to impose *sharia*, not just in Muslim-majority countries, but also in the West. Other Islamists have learned over the years to be more circumspect. They deceptively talk about "democracy," "human rights," and "religious freedom," but instead have in mind limited definitions of these concepts, in which individuals' rights and freedoms are subverted to *sharia* and flow only from God, not from the principle that "all men are created equal." They use the Islamic concept of *taqiyyah*, or "concealment," which permits the believer to lie about his or her faith when deemed necessary.

Islamists also take advantage of Western ideals of tolerance and diversity, seeking—and receiving—special treatment for Muslims. This encourages "us versus them" mentalities, and exacerbates extremism and intolerance among Muslims and non-Muslims alike. These demands have already led to the reduction of civil liberties in Western societies. For example, self-censorship is slowly replacing the freedom of expression in the West since the "Danish cartoon crisis." The protests directed at a Danish newspaper for publishing tasteless caricatures of the Prophet Muhammad in 2006, quickly turned into a tool in the hands of Islamists to undermine free speech while disseminating hatred against the West. Since then, many authors, artists, and playwrights who have drawn their inspiration from Islam have either pulled their own work from publication or been rejected by publishers and producers lest they ignite another "cartoon crisis." By tolerating intolerance, many in the West make it harder for moderate and reformist Muslims to succeed.

That is why this book's authors are critical of Islamists and of those in the West who support them. Ignoring the Islamist efforts to construct parallel Muslim communities that isolate themselves from our broader societies will allow the Islamist messages of hatred and rejection of secular authority to fester. Left unchecked, these subversive undercurrents risk further emboldening Islamists who seek to undermine the fundamental rights and freedoms that define our civilization. While this may sound alarmist, many in the West ignored analogous warnings in pre-revolution Iran, not to mention pre-communist and pre-Nazi Europe.

The way forward is to bolster connectivity between Muslim and non-Muslim populations in the West. This will require aggressive education initiatives, which transcend efforts to date that have focused merely on governments' "outreach" or "engagement" with Muslim populations, and instead, deepen mutual knowledge and respect between Muslim and non-Muslim cultures. As non-Muslims deepen their appreciation of the profound contributions Muslims have brought to Western civilization, their own intolerance will decline—thereby propelling fewer Muslims toward the Islamist objective of parallel societies. Moreover, as Muslims find a dignified place in the West, they will increasingly seek to integrate fully into the secular societies that surround them.

A key element in this effort must be education. The general public both in Europe and the United States needs a basic understanding of Islam as a religion whose followers have achieved more than military conquests. Islamic heritage includes significant advances in science and philosophy, including: Avicenna, the Bukharan [from modern-day Uzbekistan] theologian and scientist whose medical texts were closely studied during the Italian Renaissance; Averroës, the medieval philosopher largely responsible for Europe's rediscovery of Aristotle; and Piri Reis, the Ottoman admiral whose sixteenth-century map of the world is now understood as possibly the most accurate produced until that time. Such knowledge is important not only to advance European acceptance of Muslims, but also to help Muslims understand that their own heritage is deeply connected to the development of Europe's scientific knowledge and societal values.

As this mutual understanding of how "European" and "Muslim" thought is inter-connected grows, Europeans will more readily embrace Muslims as full citizens, and Muslims will seek full integration into mainstream European societies rather than isolation in parallel communities.

This mutual acceptance will counter Islamist efforts to establish a separate global community, or *umma*, to which Muslims will offer their primary loyalty, rather than to their countries of citizenship. Like most concepts of Islam, Islamists have distorted the understanding of *umma*, which means "community," that is, all the people who live around us. In the hands of Islamist groups, *umma* has come to be understood only as "the community of Muslims." Consequently, some Muslims living in Europe care more—and, thanks to modern communications and satellite broadcasting, know more—about the affairs of other Muslims on the other side of the globe than about what happens around the corner from where they actually live.

The three key concepts—*sharia, taqiyyah,* and *umma*—have been used by Islamists to propagate their narrow interpretation of Islam as an ideology that can and should aim to reshape societies around the globe to in order for secular democracies to be replaced with Islamic rule. This Islamist ideology is *the* singular root cause of radicalization, and radicalization, as I have written on other occasions, is the conveyor belt to terrorism.

Tony Blair was right when in the aftermath of the 7/7 London bombings he declared that "[w]hat we are confronting here is an evil ideology.... This is the battle that must be won, a battle not just about the terrorist methods but their views. Not just their barbaric acts, but their barbaric ideas. Not only what they do but what they think and the thinking they would impose on others."

Unfortunately, many in the West deem non-violent Islamists "moderate," and seek to partner with them against violent Islamists, believing that only Islamists can stop other Islamists from using violence. They fail to recognize Islamism as the ideology that generates the pool of alienated and extremist individuals from which eventual terrorists emerge. In the 1980s, the United States allied with Islamist *mujahedeen* against the Soviets in Afghanistan. Those same jihadists cleared the way for, or even later personally became, the Taliban. Today, after nearly a decade of war against many of those same jihadists, the United States and its allies are again considering partnership with some of these Islamists against others, thereby perpetuating a cycle of radicalization that undermines our fundamental objectives in Afghanistan, Pakistan, and the broader region. Similarly, in Europe and the United States, our leaders are again ignoring the risk of Islamists' destructive ideology, as they search for "non-violent" Islamist partners to counter "violent" Islamists. The West has lost sight of a fundamental truth: empowering Islamists, regardless of whether or not they are violent, sows the seeds for future radicalization that undermines our civilizational structures and breeds terrorism.

Islamism has much in common with totalitarian ideologies such as Nazism, Fascism, and Marxism-Leninism, including anti-Semitism, ethno-religious hatred, ambition to restructure the world, and an embrace of violence. Islamism has not emerged simply due to the lack of economic development or freedom of expression. Islamism has developed because its extremist proponents have deceived and co-opted government leaders and common citizens through active and sophisticated propaganda, indoctrination, and infiltration. However, unlike purely political totalitarian movements, Islamism has a profound and deeper appeal that derives from its claim to stem from the will of God.

Since the U.S. attacks on Afghanistan and Iraq, Islamism has increased significantly, due in large part to the prominent role of anti-Americanism in Islamist ideology. Islamists exploit the Internet, including Facebook and similar networking tools, to recruit Muslims who are angered by the racism, intolerance, and perceived injustices they face in many Western societies. Western governments exacerbate the Islamist appeal by treating Muslims not as normal citizens with regular needs, but as "Muslims" first and foremost—thus alienating them from the start.

Even in the United States, which traditionally derives strength from its integration of people of diverse nationalities and religions, Islamism is spreading at an alarming rate. The U.S. government is increasingly concerned about "homegrown" and immigrant terrorists, who became radicalized by Islamism. The spread of Islamist ideology is making it harder not only for newer immigrants to "become American," but also for American-born Muslims and converts to "remain American," as their loyalty shifts from the United States to the *umma*.

So much has been written in the West about Islam and Islamism that deciding whom to believe can be difficult. Worn slogans like "Islam is a religion of peace" seem to contradict daily news reports of Muslims killing other Muslims, fathers murdering their daughters to protect their family's "honor," riots against statements or drawings deemed "offensive" to Islam, and Islamist leaders exhorting their huge followings to hate—and kill—Jews, Christians, Hindus, and Muslims who do not follow the *sharia*. Every day we hear headlines from a seemingly bygone era: women covering themselves from head to toe (and not in faraway Afghan villages, but in the downtown areas of major Western cities) or *sharia*-mandated public stonings and amputations. It is difficult to understand that "nice people" who may even share an outwardly secular lifestyle still firmly believe that their lives should be governed according to a legal code of seventh-century Arabia.

Three transnational movements stand out as the most influential and effective in advancing Islamism globally, as they try to restore *sharia* using the tactic of *taqiyyah* to establish the *umma* as the substitute for modern societies. The Wahhabis are Saudi Arabian extremists who practice Wahhabism, a religious movement born in the eighteenth century that seeks to resurrect "true" Islam as they perceive to have existed in seventh-century Arabia. In the West, Wahhabism has successfully repackaged itself as "mainstream" as a result of a massive diplomatic and propaganda effort financed by Saudi Arabia's extensive oil revenues. Claiming to be the "Salafis," that is, "followers" of the first Muslims, the Wahhabis have succeeded in presenting themselves as the most authentic and "true" of all Muslims. In their attempt to redefine Islam on their own terms, they seek to limit access to the actual legacy of the Prophet Muhammad by demolishing the homes of Prophet Muhammad and his family, and denouncing many of the Prophet's teachings as "not Islamic."

The second significant movement is al-Ikhwan al-Muslimun, or the Muslim Brotherhood (MB). The MB was founded in Egypt in 1928 as a political organization and now widely present around the world. Opposed to secular rule, many of its leaders were exiled from Muslim lands, finding refuge in the open societies of the West. They exercise enormous influence over Islamic affairs in many countries, where they seek to establish their interpretation of *sharia* as the fundamental determinant of cultural, political, and legal norms. Yet, despite this agenda that aims to undermine Western civilization, some MB leaders have been accepted by Western governments as advisors on "anti-radicalization."

MB's most important theorist and strategist was Sayyid Qutb. In 1964, his *Milestones* gave Islamists a "how-to guide" for creating an Islamist state and defeating the West in a long-term struggle that begins with Islamization of the individual, then progressively expands to the individual's family, community, and entire society. Eventually, Islamized countries will unify into a single caliphate and replace secular governments in a new world order.

Today, MB's most prominent figure is the Qatar-based jurist Yusuf al-Qaradawi, who has gained a wide following with his *fatwas*, or religious legal opinions on how Muslims (including citizens of Europe) should lead their lives. Several contributors to this book mention Tariq Ramadan, the grandson of MB founder Hasan al-Banna, as another prominent MB figure. Ramadan denies any affiliation with the MB, and has developed a reputation in Europe as a moderate reformer seeking integration of Muslims into Europe. Using the term "European Islam," Ramadan has convinced many Europeans he is "Islam's Martin Luther," who can lead Muslims to live as loyal citizens in Europe. Instead, as several of the authors of this book argue, Ramadan seems to favor creating parallel and separate Muslim communities within mainstream European societies; Ramadan masks these apparent objectives by exploiting his knowledge of European culture and freedoms.

The third prominent Islamist group is Hizb ut-Tahrir, the Party of Liberation. The founder of Hizb ut-Tahrir (HT), Sheikh Taqiuddin al-Nabhani al-Falastani, was a Muslim Brotherhood member who broke with the MB after deciding on the need for more radical movement that could "liberate" Muslims from Western-dominated global political and economic structures. Since its founding in 1953, HT has been at the forefront of Islamist efforts to unite all Muslims under the redefined concept of the *umma*. It hopes to create a global Islamist state, or caliphate, ruled by *sharia*, which will replace secular governments, whose authority derives from voters rather than God. Organized as a secretive network of cells, HT seeks to subvert elected governments by infiltrating societal elites and co-opting them as fellow conspirators. HT condones terrorism as a legitimate tool in reestablishing the caliphate, but wins Western supporters through deceptive claims that it does not itself conduct terrorism. Though outlawed in Germany, HT remains a legal organization in the rest of Europe and the United States and is headquartered in the UK.

These three movements reinforce each other through separate but related efforts. Wahhabis provide the Islamic credentials, given the Saudi Government's sovereignty over Islam's holiest places (Mecca and Medina), and its claim of restoring Islam to its origins; Saudis also provide massive funding from oil revenues. The MB advances *sharia* rule wherever possible by infiltrating civilian and military structures. HT lays the ground for a new caliphate by infiltrating secular governments while persuading Muslim citizens to direct their allegiance to the *umma* rather than their country.

This book gathers together a group of Western Muslim theorists and activists who are working in different ways to counter these three movements and their allies, who are engaged in an Islamist offensive. The authors of this book do not have all the answers, but our combined personal and professional experiences collectively afford us a uniquely insightful perspective on Islam and Islamism. Many people wonder why moderate Muslims do not speak out, and doubt that we even exist. Moderate voices are regularly drowned out by two camps. A pro-Islam camp consists of clerics and scholars, who formulate excuses for Islamist behavior, focusing on Israeli actions, European xenophobia, or U.S. foreign policy as pretexts for Islamists' extremism. The second camp looks critically at Islam, and includes ex-Muslims who believe Islam is inherently flawed. While they enjoy media attention and support from anti-Muslim groups, they offer little hope for faithful Muslims who seek integration into mainstream society.

This book fully embraces the beauty and peacefulness that is at the heart of Islam, and attempts to defend this great religion against those who seek to harness it for their selfish political purposes. This is not intended to be a purely academic work. The audience we seek to reach includes concerned parents seeking to help shield their children from Islamist ideology; confused and alienated individuals of all ages, ethnic, and religious backgrounds; policymakers, journalists, academics; religious and civil rights groups; and general readers. This book addresses, often in very personal ways, the crises of identity that set many people along the path to radicalization.

The Authors

The authors of this book are moderate and secular Muslims. As "moderates," we defend the compatibility of Islam and universal human rights. Maintaining and strengthening this vital connection between Islam and universal values is crucial to forestalling Islamists' efforts to radicalize and recruit a new generation of religious extremists who aim to undermine secular democracy, and who can devolve into terrorists. For many in the West, a moderate Muslim is simply one who does not engage in terrorism or other violence against Western interests. This conception is too broad, as it encompasses the vast number of outwardly non-violent but ideologically extremist Muslims who are tightly wedded to an Islamist agenda and who provide the pool from which terrorists emerge. Islamists are at ideological war with moderates, and dismiss us as opponents of "true Islam" and servants of Western interests. Yet, many non-violent Islamists call themselves moderates, recognizing that Westerners have been searching for moderate Muslims to counter extremists—even though it is these very same Islamists who are producing the extremists the West seeks to counter.

As "secularists," we believe in the separation of earthly and spiritual powers. As in many other faith traditions, we hold that a Muslim can be both pious *and* secular. Thus, the leader of a democratic government can believe in God, but derive authority from his/her surrounding society and voters. Islamists, in contrast, interpret Islam as an all-encompassing system of life, which governs family relations, politics, economics, business, and culture. Moreover, Islamists insist their ideology alone has unlocked the secrets of God's plan for human beings. From the Islamist perspective, secularists cannot be true Muslims, as secularists recognize individual freedom, including the rights of individual Muslims to determine their own relationships with God and with the world around them. Using this logic, Islamists have called many Muslims "apostates," a charge that according to *sharia* is punishable by death—thereby justifying the assassination of political leaders and other heinous crimes. Sadly, they have also convinced many Muslims, especially those young people with little or no knowledge of pre-1950s Islam, that the concepts of secular and democratic rule are alien Western ideals that are being imposed on Muslim societies to destroy Islam.

Our moderate and secular voices are not as loud as those of the Islamists. We lack media support and financial resources to garner public attention. But, ours are the voices of "the other Muslims," who offer a vision of Islam that is fully compatible with, and indeed, thrives in and strengthens the secular democracies in which we live.

The book's authors are realistic and idealistic at the same time. We know we are up against decades of funding, networking, and indoctrination that have turned Islam into a political instrument of limited, harsh Islamist doctrines. We also know the West has been an accomplice in this process, due to its failure to press Saudi Arabia and some other oil-rich countries to cease their massive propagation of Islamism. The West has also failed by repeatedly working with a "lesser evil" of non-violent Islamism against a "greater evil" of violent Islamism. Reversing these trends will take not only time, money, and support from Western governments and societies, but will also require all of us to recognize we have an obligation to do whatever we can to ensure that the most significant ideological struggle in the world today results in the triumph of the forces of tolerant faith and scientific thought. The good news is, as this book's authors convey, these hopeful concepts lie at the foundation of Islam.

In light of the demographic trends that predict a significant increase in Muslim populations in the West and worldwide over the next decade, it is critical that a more humanistic understanding of Islam be made more widely available. Several authors are working on this historic task—albeit with little support from their own governments or societies. This book seeks to increase their visibility and inspire others to develop into vanguards of an Islamic renaissance. While our predecessors were repressed, we now have an unprecedented chance to overcome centuries of silencing attacks that distorted Islam's fundamental messages of peace, justice, and self-improvement. Mass communication in our modern era can provide a platform for advancing such a renaissance, but only if moderate voices can obtain the support of the West and overcome the din of Islamists' mass propaganda and pressure tactics.

Despite their different backgrounds, the authors of this book have reached a similar conclusion, namely, that Islamism poses a profound threat to our fundamental values and political systems, and that few people—and even fewer political leaders—in the West recognize this brewing danger. While all of the authors were educated in Western institutions, many have had some form of Islamic education as well. They have tested their Muslim faith and chosen to stay with it; one author converted to Islam from Roman Catholicism.

Some of the authors of this book have drifted toward, then away from Islamism. Their personal explorations of their faith mirror those of hundreds of millions of Muslims from an enormously diverse mixture of culture and geography, who constantly seek the proper balance between God and the individual in everyday life. For people of all faiths, this quest requires profound thought and continuous adjustment. In the West, the Catholic Church and its interpretation of Christianity were at the center of European life for several centuries during the Middle Ages. Then, at the start of the Renaissance, European thought adjusted, and Humanism placed the individual at the center of life.

As several authors point out in this book, Muslim jurists and other scholars made important contributions to the development of Humanism in Italy. In this same spirit, the authors of this book call for an analogous renaissance in Islam. While we do not attempt to define a precise action plan to catalyze this profound evolution of Islamic thought, we agree on the need for jihad in the classical sense, meaning, an internal struggle for self-improvement by restraining our material impulses to deepen our individual connections with God.

The spiritual confidence of several of this book's authors derives from Sufi teachings. Sufis organize their beliefs around the concept of *tasawwuf*, a deeply individualistic quest to rediscover the heart, soul, and mind of Islam. *Tasawwuf* defines general ethical and moral guidelines for individual Muslims to define their personal relationships with God based on love and acceptance. Among older generations of Muslims, Sufism and the philosophy of *tasawwuf* are still part of mainstream Islamic understanding. However, younger generations are often unfamiliar with Sufism, since Islamists dominate Islamic media sources, academic institutions, theological schools, and other sources of religious knowledge. Islamists oppose *tasawwuf's* focus on love, tolerance, and the individual, which they fear will undercut their domination over the interpretation of Islam. Indeed, the ideals of *tasawwuf* can lay the foundation of a new Islamic humanism and renaissance.

Some of the authors of this book are dismissed by Islamists as "not real Muslims." Massive lobbying efforts by Islamists in the United States and Europe sometimes find receptivity among Western officials. I was shocked the first time an American official told me, "You are not a real Muslim." But all of us who contributed to this book know who we are, regardless of the Islamist demands that we accept their version of Islam.

The book is organized into three parts. Part I describes the challenge Islamism poses to other interpretations of Islam and to secular societies in the United States, Europe, and the Maghreb. Part II consists of personal stories recounting the authors' (whether actual or potential) drift toward Islamism, their reaffirmation of their own Islamic traditions, and/or their varied efforts to blunt Islamists' extremist inroads in Europe. Part III looks to the future, identifying ways to catalyze a renaissance within Islam that allows Islam and secular democracy to coexist and thrive in Europe and the United States.

Part I opens with a chapter by **Hedieh Mirahmadi**, an Iranian-American lawyer and activist, who writes about her own experiences within the American Muslim community. She begins with a discussion of the main principles and teachings of classical Islam, which emphasizes an individual's personal and internal relationship with God, which she contrasts with later Wahhabi and Salafi movements that emphasize *jihad* as an external struggle against infidels. Mirahmadi demonstrates how the partnership between Saudi Arabia and the Muslim Brotherhood spread Wahhabi ideas through schools, mosques, and religious institutions "from California to Calcutta," thereby indoctrinating millions. Before concluding with suggestions on how to counter this trend, Mirahmadi discusses Islamist groups in the United States.

Chapter two (translated from German) is by **Yunis Qandil**, a Palestinian French researcher and public lecturer who identifies Islamist tactics to dissuade Muslims from integrating spiritually into mainstream European societies and clear the way for a parallel spiritual society that Islamists will lead. Qandil is especially concerned about the Muslim Brotherhood with which he once was affiliated, and which, he warns, has infiltrated secular society in Europe by encouraging outward integration by Muslims while demanding their inner and spiritual loyalty to their Islamist interpretation of Islam. He cautions that Islamists have taken over Muslim organizations in Europe, from which they proclaim the sole right to interpret Islam for European Muslims. Qandil criticizes European governments for treating these "Euro-Islamists" as moderates rather than as opponents of secular democracy. He further criticizes European leaders for choosing to work with non-violent Islamists against violent ones, rather than adopting the politically difficult path of confronting Islamists' extremist mode of thinking.

Chapter three (translated from Italian), by Italian professor, government advisor, and convert to Islam, **Ahmad Gianpiero Vincenzo**, outlines Islam's rich contributions to Italian culture, beginning with the arrival of Muslims in Sicily in the ninth century and extending through the Renaissance. Vincenzo describes Italy's enduring effort to demarcate relations between its secular government and the Vatican, which, following the success of the Italian *Risorgimento* (unification movement) in the 1870s, required five decades to complete. He calls for an analogous mechanism to separate mosque and state. At the same time, he warns Italian officials against developing such a mechanism together with Islamists, who increasingly dominate Italy's Muslim organizations and ultimately seek to undermine Italy's secular democracy. Vincenzo is also concerned about anti-immigrant and anti-Muslim sentiment in Italy, and calls on Italians to resurrect the spirit of the *Risorgimento* to strengthen societal unity between Italy's mainstream and Muslim populations.

Chapter four, by Moroccan-born Netherlands researcher **Fouad Laroui**, warns that Islamists' attempts to undermine secular democracy in the Maghreb are echoing in Europe through North African immigrant communities. Laroui pleads for European support of secular democrats against Islamists to protect universal freedoms in both North Africa and Europe. Laroui further cautions that Moroccan Islamists learned to practice *taqiyyah* from the failure of their Algerian counterparts to consolidate their 1992 electoral victory; they learned to obtain Western support by falsely claiming to espouse secular democracy even while working to undermine it. He also worries that many of Europe's second-generation Muslims are being driven by Islamists to think of themselves as members of the *umma* rather than of their European society.

Part II opens with **Cosh Omar's** chapter five, in which the British actor and playwright of Turkish Cypriot descent describes how Hizb ut-Tahrir (HT) exploited his confusion about his multiple identities. Omar's upbringing was shaped by his immigrant parents' Sufism and his alienation from both the Turkish Cypriot and British societies, which laid the foundation for his radicalization. The proximate cause of his recruitment by HT was repulsive images of atrocities against Bosnian Muslims in the early 1990s. Omar later broke with HT, when the Islamist organization told him that acting was a sin and that his Sufi beliefs were heretical. Omar's split with HT was boosted by his love for American culture. Eventually, he realized he had been exploited by HT to infiltrate the United Kingdom's Cypriot community through his father, a local spiritual leader. Omar's story underscores the importance of culture in fighting Islamist efforts to undermine Western society.

In chapter six (translated from French), Tunisian French author and pro-reform activist **Samia Labidi** condemns Islamists' restriction of women's individual freedoms. She writes about how her free and peaceful childhood rooted in the traditional Islam of her mother and grandmother was disrupted when her sister married an Islamist who thrust his intolerant views on his new family. Labidi's father adopted the oppressive views of his new son-in-law, restricting the family's access to music as well as a range of other freedoms. While Labidi's mother fled to France after obtaining a divorce, the author succumbed to this Islamist pressure, donning the veil and convincing hundreds of other girls to follow her example in a supposed show of "Islamic freedom" that liberates girls and women from men's objectification of females. Labidi eventually abandoned Islamism, after concluding that the veil oppresses rather than liberates women. She worries that many of her fellow French citizens fail to recognize that the same individual freedoms they derive from their country's strong tradition of secularism are as important to many Muslims as to non-Muslims.

Mostafa Hilali explains in chapter seven how he, a Moroccan immigrant to the Netherlands, serves proudly as a Dutch military officer, though he grew up just steps away from Mohammed Bouyeri, another Moroccan (second-generation) immigrant who murdered Dutch filmmaker Theo van Gogh in the name of Islam. Hilali credits his parents' teachings about Islam for his resistance to extremist recruiters. His comfort with his own Dutch Muslim identity allowed him to withstand cultural insults (including a brutal beating by Dutch youths for dating a Christian woman) that transform neighbors into Islamists. With his parents' encouragement, Hilali joined the Royal Netherlands Army, served in operations in Bosnia, Afghanistan, and Iraq, and helped his Dutch military colleagues better understand not just these Islamic cultures, but also the developing Islamic culture of their homeland.

Part III opens with chapter eight (translated from French) by Algerian French professor and essayist **Ghaleb Bencheikh,** who makes a strong case for secularism as the most legitimate, effective, and moral form of government. He explains that although separation of church and state are rooted in the Gospel teachings of Jesus, this distinction was not fully accepted by the Vatican until the 1960s. Similarly, many religious and political leaders within Islam have resisted separation of mosque and state, though this principle can be found in the Qur'an as well. At the same time, to defend against Islamists who will find other Qur'anic passages to justify their opposition to secular government, those who seek to "update" Islam must look beyond religious scripture and trust their intuitive grasp of universal morals and values. Bencheikh calls for France to help catalyze this Islamic renaissance through key educational initiatives to: win over disaffected Muslim youth; help France's Muslim and non-Muslim populations appreciate Islam's contributions to European civilization; and train France's imams so they can advocate humanism and counter extremist preaching. Bencheikh also argues for France to work harder to establish an "inclusive citizenship" that ensures all Muslim citizens of France are accepted as fully French.

In chapter nine, Syrian German professor **Bassam Tibi** presses for Muslims in Europe to adapt to European values and develop a "Euro-Islam," rather than expect Europe to adapt to Islamist demands. Human rights, separation of religion and politics, and respect for the individual are not just European values, but universal ones that Islam shares. Moreover, united Europe's new ideal of inclusiveness provides European Muslims with the best opportunity to integrate into mainstream society, provided that Europeans (and Germany in particular) broaden their concept of citizenship to include more than just ethnicity and country of birth. Other challenges remain: Europe's post-religious society has difficulty embracing devout Muslims for whom religion remains at the center of life, while racism and intolerance also inhibit acceptance of Muslims as wholly European. Further difficulty results from Islamist activists like Tariq Ramadan, who seem to advocate a Muslim rather than European identity for Europe's Muslims.

Chapter ten is authored by **M. Zuhdi Jasser**, a Syrian-American medical doctor, former military officer, and activist, whose Syrian political refugee parents raised him with a profound love for both Islam and the United States. Jasser warns that Islamists who tried to undermine secular regimes in their homelands have taken over major Islamic organizations and mosques in the United States. These Islamists are using American freedoms to undermine these very same values and establish a parallel Muslim society in the hope that, over time, *sharia* rule might replace secular democracy. To defend America, he proposes an "anti-Islamist Islam," which places the free individual at the apex of Muslim morality, thereby ensuring the compatibility of Islam and democracy.

PART I

Islamism's Threat to Islam and the West

CHAPTER ONE

Navigating Islam in America

HEDIEH MIRAHMADI

I will never forget that beautiful summer night, in the elegant Hollywood Hills eatery, where I first met a Saudi prince. Having grown up in a staunchly secular, yet culturally Muslim family, it was fascinating for me to meet an official member of the Saudi royal family. That title carries a mystique and an air of superiority, conferring on its holder the role of official representative of Islam, a topic I then knew very little about. The night progressed, with countless bottles of champagne and unimaginably priced bottles of wine, until I could no longer restrain myself from posing the question that had been on my mind all evening: "Sorry to ask this," I turned to my gracious host and said, "but isn't it forbidden to drink alcohol?" With a coy smile, and the utmost seriousness in his voice, · Prince Ahmed responded, "Oh Hedieh, don't you know? Allah doesn't live here. This [America] is *dar al-harb* [land of war], and Allah doesn't turn his gaze to this land." That statement thrust me directly into the curious and contentious debate over the true understanding of Islam, an issue that I—and many others—would spend the next decades trying to decipher.

In order to understand how we should engage the Muslim community today, it is critical to begin with a discussion of how the study and practice of Islam has changed over time. A brief analysis of over fourteen centuries of history is essential to understanding the diversity in thought and beliefs of Muslims around the world. While this diversity is at times a cause of great conflict among Muslims, at other times it has been a source of great strength—and not just for Muslims. As the West continues its long-term struggle against radical extremism, this diversity makes clear just who its real allies are among Muslims.

Today, Americans want to know how a religion whose very name is derived from the Arabic word for "peace" could become a rallying point for terrorists. They want to know how a faith that teaches tolerance and compassion could provide the moral impetus for hijackings and suicide bombings. And they want to know why men who claim to act in the name of Islam could have declared war against their way of life.

These questions should be asked, for they go to the very heart of the present conflict. In answering them, America will learn that its real enemy is not Islam or Muslims, but rather a small sect that has been working for centuries to subvert Islam and transform it into a weapon of war. This enemy is not an individual or group, but rather a complex transnational network of organizations that share a common ideology and that are united by their hatred of the West, and their determination to create a new world order.

While most of the world began to appreciate the full magnitude and nature of this threat only after the terrorist attacks on New York and Washington, the Muslim world has been aware of its existence for some time. There is no umbrella term that defines all the adherents to this extremist movement, but a couple of terms applied to them should be familiar. Many use the term "Wahhabi," after the founder of their sect, but they prefer to call themselves "Salafis," which translates as "pure ones." Unlike classical Muslims, whose focus is on an individual's personal relationship with God, the focus of Wahhabis and Salafis is on military combat, which they call *jihad*. The catch-all term "Islamist" is also commonly used to describe various factions of Islamic movements that, despite their differences, are all united in the drive to establish a new world order dominated by a rigid interpretation of Islamic law.

Classical Islamic Roots

History reveals that some companions of the Prophet Muhammad brought Islam to the Far East and the West not only through trade, but also through directed social outreach. Ascetic scholars of classical Islam taught—and lived by—teachings of goodwill toward others, respect, compassion, and purity of heart, thereby helping Islam to flourish and develop into four main Sunni schools of thought (*madhabs*) based on divine law and the examples of the Prophet. The names of these pious scholars still resound throughout the Muslim world, where judicial systems and disciplines of academic legal study remain based on the four major schools of Islamic thought they founded.

The Qur'an teaches that "among God's signs are the variations in your languages and your colors," reminding us that diversity and multiplicity are God's way. Diversity in religious interpretation and practice strengthens all religions, just as a multiplicity of political parties strengthens democracy. A strong intellect requires competing stimuli and the exchange of ideas in order to develop; when people are forced to follow a single opinion, the result is the death of reason, invention, and growth. The founding of different schools of Islamic thought was the fruit of the mental and spiritual labor of believers; this labor was directed towards the goal of creating interpretations of divine law that evolve in each era and reflect changing cultural dynamics while retaining the spirit of religious scriptures.

Throughout Islamic history, we find hundreds of interpretations of religious texts introduced in different eras. This plethora of competing ideas tremendously enriched traditional Islam and gave individuals the means to seek security, peace, and tranquility through their own beliefs and practices.

Unity in Principles

Though the interpretations of Islamic texts vary widely, all Muslims agree on certain basic principles of their faith. These include: the oneness of God, the validity of the prophecy of the Prophet Muhammad and of all earlier prophets, and the divine perfection of the Qur'an as God's final revealed word to humankind. There is a similar lack of disagreement among Muslims on what constitutes Islam's pillars of worship: the profession of faith ("There is no god but God, and Muhammad is His Prophet"), the set amount of mandatory prayer, and the universal requirements to fast, to give alms, and to make the pilgrimage (*Hajj*) to Mecca. These fundamentals—identical to all schools of Islamic thought—constitute the "trunk" of the tree of faith; different opinions and practices exist only in its "branches."

The greatest traditional Muslim legal scholars did not neglect the spiritual dimension of their religion: as Imam Malik, the founder of the Maliki *madhab*, declared, "Whoever studies spirituality without observing the divine law is a heretic, and whoever studies divine law without spiritual teachings is corrupted, and whoever studies spirituality and divine law together will find the truth and reality of Islam."

In the Middle Ages, classical Islam flourished through the teachings of these spiritual masters. Their lives were based on refined manners, generosity, service to others, and humility. Their spiritual nourishment was remembering God by chanting and singing His praises. They asked their students simply to accept God as their Creator and the Prophet Muhammad as His messenger, to worship God without ascribing any partner to Him, and to abandon idolatry. They taught the importance of repentance, of purifying the ego of arrogance and lower desires, and of honesty and trustworthiness in all matters. They emphasized the need to be patient and God-fearing and to love others selflessly, depending only on God for one's reward. They rejected fame and high positions because they did not seek a materialist life.

They convinced the wealthy to build mosques, dormitories, and soup kitchens for the poor, offering free room and board, and stressing charitable work. Based on the teachings of the Prophet Muhammad (who said, "There is no difference between Arabs and non-Arabs, except through righteousness") such institutions joined together rich and poor, black and white, and

Arab and non-Arab. Furthermore, they saw everyone as equal, especially women, who were included as full partners in community building.

Wahhabi Roots

At the same time as this vibrant traditional Islam developed and flourished, another approach to religion began to evolve: Islamic extremism. Even in the early years, some Muslims took an extreme approach—misusing the name of Islam and pretending to be like their tolerant contemporaries while spreading intolerant—and intolerable—doctrines of oppression and fanaticism.

What is often referred to as the "Islamist movement" is, more specifically, the modern outgrowth of an eighteenth-century heresy spawned by a radical Bedouin named Mohammed ibn Abdul Wahhab (1703–1792). Claiming that Islam had been corrupted by countless innovations, he set out with puritanical zeal to eliminate all these "new" elements from the faith. Dogmatic and narrow in his view of religion, Wahhab denounced intellectualism, mysticism, and classical Islam (especially its spiritual aspects), labeled earlier Islamic scholars "heretics," and rejected the teachings of the four *madhabs* that for centuries had fostered justice and moderation in Muslim society.

His strategy allowed the members of his sect, known as "Wahhabis," to interpret Islam according to their own whims; they accepted whatever supported their ambitions, and rejected what stood in their way. Those who rejected the new doctrine were summarily declared "apostates." The "enemies of Islam"—that is, Jews, Christians, and people of other faiths as well as traditional Muslims—were targeted by a vicious crusade to "purify the faith."

Ibn Abdul Wahhab believed that Islam must be reformed through violence and insurrection. By opening the entire faith to reinterpretation, he was able to provide a theological justification for his call to arms. His ideology is in direct conflict with the cooperative, tolerant nature of classical Islam. Wahhabism was imposed by force throughout local tribes, but because it initially lacked economic and political power Wahhabism failed to take root beyond Arabia—although this would change when conditions became more favorable in the twentieth century. To give false credibility to their new sect, Wahhabis refer to themselves as "Salafi," which translates as "the pure ones" and most policy analysts prefer to use that term. Despite this attempt at false credibility, Salafis are still called Wahhabis by the majority of Muslims who resent their oppressive and deviant amalgamation of Islam.

Irrational Fears Forbid the Permissible

Some examples of the rigid Wahhabi-Salafi doctrine include its prohibition on the use of tobacco or the consumption of coffee. Wahhabism became so extreme that some sect members consider *anyone* who smokes or drinks coffee a disbeliever. One of the Wahhabis' most-revered scholars, Shaykh bin Baz, declared that the West was ignorant for considering the Earth to be round; only in 1985, when a Saudi astronaut flew aboard the space shuttle Discovery, did he accept that the Earth was not flat. This narrow view of the world—and the corresponding attitude of dismissiveness toward other perspectives—is a hallmark of Wahhabism.

Salafis destroy ancient relics and shrines based on their irrational fear that they promote idol worship, as seen in 2001 when the Salafi-Taliban regime in Afghanistan destroyed two priceless third-century statues of the Buddha. Salafis also prohibit the visitation of graves and, even destroyed the burial place of the Prophet Muhammad and his loved ones, despite their hugely sacred significance to traditional Muslims everywhere. For decades, Wahhabis prohibited photography—even for purposes of identification—on the grounds that it was also a form of idolatry.

Before the relatively recent rise of Wahhabism, for centuries women had freely pursued careers as teachers of religious texts, physicians and healers, leadership advisers, and social activists. Muslim women owned property, ran businesses, and maintained financial independence—in short, they enjoyed rights that Western women would not obtain until the twentieth century. In sharp contrast, Wahhabism has systematically disenfranchised Muslim women by denying them the freedom to think and operate as independent beings. Strict Wahhabi clerics preach that women must stay at home and obey the men of the family. They deny women education, jobs, the freedom to move about in society, and even the right to choose a husband. Centuries of women's contributions to classical Islamic societies have been excised from history by Wahhabis and their teachings.

Yet, the most damaging aspect of Wahhabi doctrine is the insistence that only its interpretation of Islamic law is correct, and that those who refute it—especially other Muslims—are apostates, making it legal to fight, torture, or kill them as enemies of the faith.

Initial Failure and Subsequent Success

Wahhabism remained confined to its humble tribal origins for years after Wahhab's death until the founder of the Saudi family, Mohammed ibn Saud, converted to Wahhabism and spread it by force. It was a merger of religious hegemony and military might that helped both Wahhab and Ibn Saud realize their dream of power, and soon they established the Kingdom of Saudi Arabia. Wahhab's descendants still preside over some Saudi religious institutions, thus providing a theological foundation for their existence; in return, the Saudi dynasty provides military power, financial support, and political leadership to the Wahhabi clerical structures.

In the rest of the Middle East, the end of European colonialism gave rise to corrupt and despotic new regimes, which only fueled further social and political unrest throughout the region. As traditional Islamic institutions formally collapsed with the dissolution of the Ottoman Empire after World War I, a dangerous void was created. Initially, it was filled by a socio–political paradigm that drew heavily on modernist notions of nationalism and Marxist concepts of class struggle and world revolution.

However, from the late 1970s through the 1990s, Islamism as a political movement began to supplant the failed Marxist liberation movements and Arab nationalism. In some countries, left-wing leaders reinvented themselves as Islamist revolutionaries after calls for popular revolt went unheeded by the masses. Islamist scholars falsified grounds on which revolutionaries could overcome traditional Islamic prohibitions against civil insurrection. While traditional Islamic law categorically forbids uprisings against Muslim rulers, the Islamist scholars declared the leaders of countries such as Egypt and Algeria to be "unbelievers," allowing the masses to revolt.

This led to Islamist opposition movements and insurrections in Algeria, Yemen, Libya, Jordan, Syria, Egypt, and elsewhere. It has also fragmented the movement, since some Islamist leaders urged immediate rebellion while others called for a more gradual approach to social change. The most successful of these movements, known as the Muslim Brotherhood (MB), spread like wildfire across the Muslim world from its origins in Egypt. Though it maintains its base there, and continues to operate to a certain degree as an opposition political party, the repression its members faced under the Nasserite Egyptian government soon forced many MB members abroad. For a significant number of these "political refugees" fleeing Lebanon, Iraq, Jordan, and Syria as well as Egypt, Saudi Arabia was the destination of choice.

With this sudden injection of proselytizing fervor, organizational expertise, and intellectual talent, the Saudi Wahhabi regime developed the ideological infrastructure that—together with considerable sums of money from oil sales—enabled Wahhabism to establish itself in the mainstream across the Muslim world.

Petrodollars in hand, Wahhabis have financed the construction of Islamist schools and the distribution of free Islamist literature all over the globe, in every language and in every country. Muslim students from around the globe flocked to the kingdom, where they received a free education in Islamism along with guarantees of jobs at Saudi-funded mosques and religious institutions from California to Calcutta.

Wahhabi Saudis have built and financed more than 1,500 mosques, 200 colleges, and nearly 2,000 religious schools, most of which are in Europe and North America. Today, Salafis have indoctrinated millions of youth to embrace their puritanical views as a means toward world supremacy.

It is important to note that not all Saudi subjects are Wahhabis. In fact, Saudi Arabia is an ideologically diverse society, and while many of its citizens are adherents of traditional Islam, they are overshadowed by the power and influence of Wahhabi officials. Recently, under King Abdullah's reign, observers have detected attempts to shift the balance of power away from the Salafis so as to allow this diversity of opinion to emerge. It will be important to see whether this internal shift has an effect on the version of Islam that the Saudis propagate abroad.

While Islamists now enjoy a global reach as perhaps the religion's most powerful movement, they constitute only a fraction of the world's 1.3 billion Muslims. It is the special relationship between the Islamist movement and the Gulf Arabs that makes the voice of Islamist extremism resound so loudly through the world today. For over two centuries, traditional Muslims have stood powerless against the unlimited oil wealth that funds the Islamist influence on nearly every Islamic institution throughout the world.

The Globalization of Islamism

Islamists have formed numerous political groups and revolutionary organizations, including Palestine's Hamas, with its legions of suicide bombers, and Algeria's Armed Islamic Movement, which has a penchant for wiping out whole villages with machetes. Salafism motivates political parties such as Algeria's Islamic Salvation Front, which tried to come to power through elections, and Jamaat-e-Islami, a highly influential politico-religious group in Pakistan. Yet despite differences in methods and tactics, all Islamist groups are united by the aim of establishing a theocracy based on a puritanical interpretation of Islam.

The Reinvention of Military Jihad

While traditional Islam rejects the tactics of terror, many Islamists firmly believe that violence is the primary means of reforming religion, society, and the world as a whole. While the majority of traditional Muslim scholars have long held that waging jihad (military combat) against non-Muslims was justified only in response to aggression—as defined collectively by all Muslim nations, not just by one Muslim country—the radical Islamists view war against the West as a religious obligation, with those who participate in it being rewarded with eternal paradise. They give such priority to jihad that they have added it as the sixth pillar of Islam.

Islamists have always been linked to extremism and violence, but the movement did not become a serious threat to the West until the 1970s when the Soviet invasion of Afghanistan sparked a revival of the concept of jihad. Islamist organizations stepped up, calling for volunteers for the "holy war" in Afghanistan and opening recruitment offices and training camps throughout the world. Most volunteers were Arab, but recruits came from as far away as the Philippines and the United States. In addition to military training, each of these volunteers received intensive indoctrination in Salafi Islam, a tactic that did much to facilitate the spread of extremist ideology.

As the conflict in Afghanistan ended, these militants sought new battles. They moved to Bosnia, Somalia, and Chechnya, and are now in Iraq. This, in turn, created a vast international network of jihadis, many of whom later joined al-Qaeda. In many of these regions, Salafis encountered stiff resistance from indigenous Muslims. Wherever traditional Sunni practices predominate, Salafi ideology conflicted directly with the prevailing local understanding of Islamic spirituality and ethics. Until the present day, traditional Muslim leaders are able to distinguish intruding Wahhabi ideologues and their adherents from the rest of their community.

Though all of this history may appear to be relevant only to Muslim nations trapped in an endless factional struggle, nothing could be further from the truth. In fact, it is here in my own country, the United States, that this battle is waged most dangerously.

Islamists in the United States

Islamists first came to the United States in the 1950s and 1960s as students, intending to return home after completing their studies. Many of them remained in the United States; with support from wealthy backers in the Gulf, they established themselves as successful businessmen, engineers, and academics, and began to acquire power and influence in the growing American Muslim community. Thanks to their relentless activism, over time Islamists took control of many existing mosques and Muslim charities, and (again with the help of petrodollars) built hundreds of new mosques, religious schools, and community centers across the United States. Using tactics similar to the communists, they organized domestic organizations to speak for American Muslims, making sure that their voice was the only one heard.

Today, the Islamist movement's influence can be felt in a majority of American Muslim communities. Islamist clerics and activists set the tone for weekly sermons, organize the training and selection of clerics, and may even decide which books will be sold in mosques and Islamic centers. While the Islamists are successful in taking over leadership of many major Islamic organizations and institutions, their views do not represent the vast majority of moderate, mainstream American Muslims. It is important to stress here that these are self-appointed leaders who do not represent the will of the Muslim masses.

Though mainstream American Muslims reject the uncompromising nature of Islamist doctrine and abhor the terrorist violence it sometimes promotes, they lack the financial and political resources, as well as the requisite religious training, to mount a serious defense against their powerful, well-funded, and sophisticated Islamist adversaries.

The traditional Muslim, with his basic understanding of Islam as a way of life based on tolerance and respect, was and is the average worshipper in most mosques. Yet without major outside support, these common Muslims do not have the capacity to retain leadership control, and are thereby consigned to remain "average worshippers" for the foreseeable future. Mosque politics are left to those whose voices are the loudest and to those who can best manipulate the ballot boxes to their advantage. The average Muslim, far more concerned with earning his daily bread and educating his children, has no interest in the bitter political battles waged in mosques, and avoids that whole confrontation. Traditional Islamic leaders are so rare in the United States, and are so lacking in formal support, that they have little or no effect on the American Muslim scene.

The Islamists' tactical focus in the United States is concentrated on the creation of a series of organizations and institutions, each with its own unique function, controlled by a complicated web of interlocking directorates. Some groups are fronts for subversive activities, while others conduct legitimate operations. One group of organizations focuses on Islamic academic institutions, aiming to replace traditional Islamic scholarship with a program of indoctrination that promotes Islamist ideology.

Another group targets the Muslim community as a whole, establishing umbrella organizations that claim to speak for all Muslims, and seizing control of houses of worship. These groups control what is—and is not—preached from the pulpit. They represent Islam to the broader society, attempting to deflect the suspicions of law-enforcement authorities and influence the country's political processes to support the Islamist agenda.

A third group, composed of charities and shell companies, manages the movement's finances and raises funds to support its extremist causes overseas. The entire process is intended to foster rapid ideological change, one that affects entire communities and, in some cases, whole societies.

Again, the strategy is similar to that used by the communists to organize dissent and control socio-political movements, with the targets instead being mosques, religious schools, and Islamic centers. Perhaps a more accurate analogy is the way the Mafia runs a neighborhood or industry. It survives based on economic control, intimidation, and fear.

Salafi Control of U.S. Islamist Organizations

The complex edifice of Salafi control is founded on its ideological principles, created and propagated by the Muslim Brotherhood and its offshoots, and supported by Gulf oil wealth.

During the 2007 trial of an Islamist charitable organization in the United States, prosecutors read into the record a document that outlines the Muslim Brotherhood's grand strategy in the West "to destroy Western civilization from within so Islam is made victorious over all religions." To implement this strategy, organized Islamist groups focus their activity on infiltrating, influencing, and assimilating into the American political system. This was clearly designed to be a long-term social engineering project, and millions of dollars were invested to accomplish these goals. The same document further revealed fundraising in America for terrorist organizations such as Hamas.

The International Institute of Islamic Thought (IIIT, founded 1981) has had a tremendous impact on the development of Islamist organizations throughout the world. Headquartered in Virginia, with offices around the globe, IIIT is believed to have been founded with Brotherhood seed money in order to further propagate the Islamist agenda through publications, short-term continuing education courses, and chaplain training for the U.S. military. Its offices were raided in 2003, along with nineteen other businesses and related non-profit organizations, and its founders, board members, and finances remain under investigation by the U.S. government. IIIT's most troublesome subsidiary is also its best known: the Graduate School of Islamic and Social Sciences, the largest Islamic seminary in the United States. It is one of the only U.S. institutions authorized to certify Muslim chaplains for the American military.

As new Muslim immigrants came to the United States, they integrated into these existing Islamist structures, created separate local mosques to serve their religious needs, or dropped out of Islamic activism entirely. A notable difference between American and British Islam is that American Muslims did not immigrate together with their religious leaders, which left the community very vulnerable to whichever version of Islam was taught by the institutions they found already existing in America—which were invariably Islamist and staffed by imported Salafi and Muslim Brotherhood teachers.

Public Diplomacy Blunders Involving Islamists

The U.S. government continues to make policy blunders when working with American Muslims—despite the overwhelming media attention on the community after 9/11—because of a regrettable lack of understanding of the prevailing currents within Islam. These blunders give credibility to the Islamists and their organizations, rather than empowering the real mainstream voices of the community. A few specific examples will prove illustrative:

- In 2000, the son of an Islamist leader was appointed to the White House Office of Public Liaison. Using the powers of his position, he authorized radical Islamists to meet with President Bush. Following revelations of his Islamist background he was quietly moved to another position—but his successor was also someone of Islamist convictions.

- In 2002, the spokesman for FBI Director Robert Mueller memorably described the American Muslim Council as "the most mainstream Muslim group in the United States." Its founder was sent abroad on numerous missions by the State Department, and once joined President Bush at a prayer service dedicated to the victims of the 9/11 attacks. He is now serving time in a federal prison for an assassination plot and for lying to Federal agents.
- In March 2006, the U.S. Department of Defense helped fund a conference sponsored by the IIIT, which featured an address by the State Department's head of counterterrorism, even though the IIIT was still under investigation by law enforcement agencies.

This is a relatively small sampling of the numerous occasions on which Islamist organizations and speakers have been lauded by the U.S. government. The controversy raises the broader, more troubling question of why the U.S. government uses Muslim employees as "gatekeepers."

As a Muslim community activist for over a decade, I have seen many such gatekeepers throughout the U.S. government. These are often Muslims on different levels who have been working at various jobs unconnected to "Muslim issues," but who, in the aftermath of 9/11, have been asked to take on the "Muslim portfolio." In their new capacity, they are asked to ensure that only "credible Muslims" are allowed into meetings with high-level U.S. government officials. These gatekeepers are also given the authority to determine who is and who is not worthy of the government's various outreach initiatives. Putting it bluntly, these gatekeepers decide who qualifies as a "real" Muslim. I was born a Muslim, live my life as a devout Muslim, and have worked against the Islamist encroachment into American society for over a decade. Having been barred from entry by some of these gatekeepers, I take offense that anyone, let alone someone in the U.S. government, has the right to consider me a "fake" Muslim.

But this is about much more than personal outrage; these gatekeepers are allowed to determine who participates in the debate about American foreign policy, law enforcement, and national security. Many of us have seen the U.S. government repeatedly embarrassed by the media for cozying up to known Islamic extremists, but no one seems to ask why those meetings and relationships continue.

At the same time, individual Muslim leaders and scholars who truly are moderate rarely have the opportunity to meet with politicians, since they are characterized by these organizations and gatekeepers as either "outsiders" or "deviants" with "no credibility" in the Muslim community. This tactic effectively silences the moderate majority and prevents them from reaching policymakers who are willing and able to make a difference. Islamists are fierce opponents of any individual or group who dares to challenge their policies, using strong-arm tactics of slander, threats, and even physical attacks or boycotts to prevent any Muslim straying from the Islamist course. Even public discussion of the orientation of Islamist groups is met with fierce opposition. Their critics are either publicly humiliated or intimidated into silence by well-financed lawsuits designed to prevent anyone from questioning their background.

American Muslim Youth Accept Salafism as "True Islam"

Since Islamists control many of the Islamic primary schools, national organizations, and mosques, a large percentage of the Muslim youth are a product of this ideology. Most have no awareness of the diversity of classical Islam, with its numerous schools of thought and its openness to change, innovation, and integration. Many young Muslims are indoctrinated into believing that Islam is monolithic, and that all Muslims should be united in working toward one political outcome: the world domination of Islam. Currently, we see the national Islamist organizations giving positions of authority to their new generation of leaders, which only perpetuates the problem. Though not official members of the Muslim Brotherhood, they are taught to believe in the same goals.

I tell you this tragic account of Islamism in America not as a researcher for a book, or because of some grudge against Muslims, but as a victim of its aggressors. In the early 1990s, I was naïve about the different sects in Islam and eager to join American Muslim activism. The Islamist leaders took me under their wing and tried to inculcate me with their anti-Semitic prejudices and with their insatiable desire to make America a Muslim nation. When I rejected their dogma and sought a path of spirituality instead, they vilified me in the community and have waged a campaign of slander against me ever since. Islamist oppression is a reality I live with every day, and I can say that it threatens the sanctity of all our lives.

Where Is the Solution?

Unfortunately, traditional anti-Islamist Muslims have had little or no support to build an infrastructure in the United States. Though they form the silent majority, they are not well organized; most have stayed out of national movements because they wanted to concentrate on work and family, and have no interest in community politics and power grabs.

While Islamists have enjoyed massive funding of organizations and mosques, moderates have relied on intra-community resources which are often scarce. By nature, they modestly assimilate into and have respect for the culture in which they live as normal citizens. They fully appreciate the ability to live peaceful lives in America, and keep away from any conflict with aggressive Islamists. They are not power-hungry, and are content to manage their local mosques and cultural associations. Their mosques and prayer halls tend to be simple, unspectacular, and hidden away.

Within these communities there often is great openness to democratic values, as well as a tendency to participate in the U.S. mainstream rather than to isolate themselves from it. This can be seen in the Bosnian, Indonesian, Turkish, Indian, and Moroccan communities. It is further seen—to a great extent within the very large Pakistani community (most significantly, in its cultural associations), and in the Urdu- and English-language press. While some Pakistani mosques have been Islamized, most are not.

Among the ethnic Lebanese, Iraqis, and Syrians, the majority hold American values while retaining a love of their homeland and cultural traditions. That is one reason why the community in the Dearborn area, with over 150,000 ethnic Arabs, is not seen as a hotbed of political Islam as much as are the communities in Chicago, Los Angeles, or New York. Finally, the religious ministries of several Muslim states have authorized clerics to operate within their expatriate communities, specifically for the purpose of preventing radicalization. Such clerics can be a great resource for the struggle against Islamist influence. For example, the Bosnian community in the United States has created a formal office that oversees religious functions and controls all Bosnian-built mosques.

Traditional Muslims also do not have a religious-based political agenda. For this reason, there is no one set of opinions they adhere to; rather, they pursue individual beliefs, goals, and interests. Within the moderate Muslim community opinions will vary on social issues, the role of religion in public life, issues of social integration, and so forth. For these reasons, moderate Muslims have not collectively pursued representation in Washington. This has resulted in hundreds of poorly supported, understaffed organizations that lack a national infrastructure or a coordinating council, and which are essentially invisible to state and national government.

To turn the tide against extremists requires a marshaling of government resources to give anti-extremists the moral, political, and material support they need to prevent radicals from controlling public space, speech, and behavior. Traditional Muslims are America's allies in the fight against extremism. If they win, their societies have a chance to join the globalizing world, and America benefits; if they fail, they lose, and America loses—making our future grim indeed.

The U.S. government will often need to engage with groups and nations that do not share its values, but it does not have to partner with domestic Islamist groups that endorse militancy and radicalism abroad. It can identify and promote true moderates more representative of Islam in America, but to do so requires a concerted effort. It obliges our policymakers to invest the time to research alternative Muslim voices. It is a campaign we have won before, when we really believed there was a threat to our way of life; we are reminded once again of our determined will in the fight against communism. The struggle against radical Islamism requires that same dedication, focus, and economic investment we put into bringing down the Soviet empire.

Tackling extremist ideologies requires programs specifically designed to provide new social and cultural opportunities for Muslims both here and abroad. For example, we could facilitate the retraining of clerics, open cultural centers for youth at risk, and provide for the institutional capacity building of anti-Islamist organizations, and a range of other programs specifically designed to ameliorate the ideological paradigm Muslims find themselves in today.

When we do realize that there is an ideology unifying those who want to destroy our way of life, we have to find useful tools and approaches to counter that destructive social and intellectual construct.

There is ongoing debate about which group in Islam, or which particular ideological influences, are best suited to address the issues of terrorism and political violence. It is often argued that apolitical Salafists, who do not have the immediate goal of violent insurrection but who seek to impose *sharia* law, are a useful partner in counter-radicalization and rehabilitation. Many analysts have accepted the argument that the conservative, puritanical interpretations of Salafi Islam will not pose a problem for the West so long as the Salafists disavow terrorism and direct their efforts at "Islamizing" only their own communities. If we remember that the Salafi sect emerged as a repudiation of everything that came before it, and elevated military jihad to a status never before seen in Islam, we can see that it is not exactly a tradition of plurality and coexistence. The Salafi scholars would have to turn away from hatred and rejection of anything "other" before they could take part in a long-term ideological shift.

Most importantly, the Salafis have yet to disavow the legitimacy of military jihad. As the *New York Times Magazine* reported, the Saudis still consider military jihad to be a cornerstone of their beliefs; therefore, the Salafis' ability to reduce violence is necessarily limited.

The best ideological tool against radical Islamism is its theological opposite: traditional Islam. Its acceptance of other faiths, emphasis on an inward spiritual focus instead of outward political and social aggression, and its categorical rejection of the validity of military jihad all make it best equipped to stop extremist violence before it starts.

★   ★   ★

Long-term success in the struggle against Islamist violence requires a multifaceted approach addressing the ideological core of the problem. No matter how many schools we build or how many jobs we create, we will not overcome radical Islamist indoctrination if there are no ideological and theological alternatives for the target populations. We cannot capture hearts and minds only with voting rights or freedom of the press; it takes much more than that.

To decrease the radicals' incitement to violence, we have to stop the slide into religious fanaticism. To do that, we must invest in programs that promote an ideology that is the antithesis of extremist tenets. I am not referring just to Western notions of what this antithesis could be, but rather to traditions within the Islamic paradigm that are open, tolerant, and pluralistic. When such traditions are reinvigorated within Muslim society, this will generate its own grassroots momentum for change.

However, we must be aware that since the U.S. government has popularized the concept of "promoting democracy and freedom," there are all kinds of scholars reinventing themselves as "moderates." We must do considerable due diligence and examine the writings of scholars and clerics before supporting them. We must read what they write and what they present to their own communities, not just what they present to a Western audience. There is often a sharp contrast between the material these pseudo-moderates produce for public consumption and what they create for a Muslim audience.

Also, we must be wary of those leaders who loudly clamor for "freedom," but whose doctrine much more resembles the Communist Manifesto. Someone asking for freedom is *not* necessarily an ally. Often, especially in the Muslim world, the most radical of clerics are oppressed because they are a threat to their governments. They throw around terms such as "freedom of expression" and "human rights" when their core doctrine has nothing to do with either. We must be critical and discerning. There are leaders and clerics in the Muslim world who do share our core values of free speech, freedom of religious expression—whatever that religion may be—and acceptance of others' lifestyles or choices. However, they are often not the ones you see standing in the forefront because the extremists are not funding them. In fact, you have to be willing to seek them out.

We must also invest in counter-radicalization projects that identify Islamist extremist movements both here and abroad. These programs will make it easier for our policymakers to separate the good from the bad actors in the world arena. We cannot all expect to be experts, but we can invest in people who are. The products of their research will not only benefit policymakers, but also serve the equally important goal of being a resource for intelligence and law-enforcement agencies. Such projects include the study of recruitment and indoctrination into Islamist extremist movements, the demographics of these movements, and their activities around the world. This research will also expose the malevolent nature of their philosophy, which in turn will prevent other NGOs from inadvertently supporting their work.

The struggle for ideological primacy within Islam is a fight that only Muslims themselves can wage, but the real moderates cannot win it alone. As Americans we cherish our freedom of expression, and we need to help others who struggle every day to win those same rights that we enjoy.

We need to come together as a nation and a government to decide what exactly the threat is. Before we can devise solutions—be they military, legislative, or economic—we need a common understanding of what we mean by "radicalism" and "extremism."

If we do not do that we may find ourselves dangerously vulnerable and increasingly alienated from the majority of the Muslim community, who are quite frankly shocked that we have not yet gotten it right, and who find themselves progressively more victimized by the onslaught of radical Islamism.

CHAPTER TWO

Euro-Islamists and the Struggle for Dominance within Islam

YUNIS QANDIL

Introduction

Islam today is striving to establish a secure and dignified place for itself in the daily lives of ordinary Muslims throughout the world. Despite the increased focus on contacts between the West and Islam in recent years, the relationship is hardly new. Indeed, from its very beginnings, Islam has had extensive and wide-ranging interaction with the West, involving both intractable conflict and fruitful exchange. In recent decades, unfortunately, the tendency has been directed more toward conflict than toward mutual exchange, with tensions fueled by the increased Muslim presence in the West.

Muslim integration in the West is shaped by five critical factors:

- Although Islam's modern arrival in the West was a result of decolonization, migration, and globalization, its subsequent development has taken place according to its own independent dynamic.
- The nature and scale of Muslim immigration to the West has affected both the identity of the immigrants and the perception of those immigrants within Western cultural, social, and political structures.
- Because of globalization, the integration of Muslims in the West cannot be classified solely as a matter of domestic politics or international affairs, but as a dynamic shaped by both. However, the primacy of international events in shaping the integration debate means that the discussion of Muslim integration is disproportionately focused on security issues and developments in the Middle East.

This article was originally written in German and was translated by Emmet C. Tuohy and Zeyno Baran for this volume.

- Since the Muslim communities that have come to Europe are by no means a monolithic bloc, differences among them—ethnicity, historical legacy, or local mentalities—are highly important.
- As secularizing Western countries gradually relegated religion to a position of secondary importance over the course of the last few centuries, an opposite process was taking place in the Muslim world. Muslim migration to the West therefore presents a direct challenge to the fundamental beliefs of both the West and the Muslim world about religion's proper place in society.

While the process of integrating Muslim immigrants into Western societies is challenging, it is nevertheless vitally important. European leaders and Western Muslims must develop a new social and political framework to make integration a reality. To start, the Western political establishment must develop the capability and the willingness to differentiate between Muslims who are prepared to integrate and coexist peacefully with society, and those who represent a security risk.

Although policymakers have been desperate to find a workable integration policy—especially since the New York, Madrid, and London terrorist attacks—the preferred strategy of Western governments has not differed significantly from country to country. Essentially, it aims at fostering integration by engaging with "moderate" Muslim organizations in the belief that regular, institutionalized dialogue will bring an end to confrontation and usher in an era of peace. While attractive to Europeans in theory—especially because of the success this institutionalization model had in ending the postwar confrontationalism of the 1940s, and subsequently, in fostering real measures of European unity—it has not proven workable thus far.

In the 1950s, in meetings that led to the creation of the European Union's predecessor institutions, German and Italian politicians who declared themselves "moderate" were accepted at face value, since all sides—German and Dutch Christian Democrats, as well as Italian and French Communists—shared the same broad understanding of the nature of church-state relations and of democratic rule. What makes the current situation so challenging is not that Muslim immigrants do *not* share these unstated cultural assumptions; many—this author included—*do* share the secular democratic values behind those assumptions. The problem is that some Western Islamist groups, as part of a larger phenomenon I call "Euro-Islamism," *deliberately exploit* these assumptions in order to infiltrate the organizational structures of Western Islam.

They present themselves to European governments as "moderate" or "secular" organizations that support democracy and religious freedom, knowing full well that Westerners will understand these terms as demonstrating a true commitment to integration. Western governments must pay very close attention to any group claiming to represent Islam. If they continue to work toward integrating Euro-Islamist groups—which conceal their theocratic, anti-democratic, anti-secular beliefs behind duplicitous terminology—the danger is that the Euro-Islamists will succeed, and establish a permanent position for those who oppose social unity altogether.

The total chaos within Western Muslim communities, especially the lack of truly representative institutions, has provided Islamist groups with a window of opportunity. Since no true moderates would claim the right to speak for all Muslims, Islamists have done so instead—giving Western governments the quick and easy solution they desire. Implementing such "solutions" for integration will solidify Islamist cultural, social, and political dominance.

In the remainder of this chapter, I develop a fuller picture of the roots of Euro-Islamism by investigating various aspects of the strategy that the Islamists—the so-called moderate Muslims—have used to gain power and influence. Having once been an Islamist myself, I critically assess their seemingly innocuous, but ultimately destabilizing, visions of "integration," which I call "integrism." I discuss some Muslim organizations seen as "moderate partners" by European governments, before reviewing the ways in which they have sought—and obtained—a "privileged partnership" with the state.

I then recommend an effort to counter Islamist attempts to infiltrate Muslim representative organizations and achieve "integration" on their own terms. More broadly, I argue that these organizations' power to interpret Islam must be challenged. In the final section, I draw some conclusions and share my personal perspective as a practicing Muslim.

Stemming the Tide: "Moderate" Islam against Terrorism

Why is the West looking for partners in the Islamic world, and what are its criteria for establishing partnerships? We can point to two main patterns: one conservative and one liberal. The relatively conservative strategy seeks to respond to the challenges of the global war on terror primarily through military and security policy. To those who hold this view, the contemporary world's "security deficit" legitimizes their inclination to rely on military solutions when dealing with "rogue states." The war in Iraq is a clear example of this kind of unidimensional counterterrorism strategy. There, as elsewhere, military measures have not eliminated terrorist groups. On the contrary, reliance on forces has led to an increase in extremism, triggering new waves of radicalism among Muslims in the West and elsewhere.

The liberal approach holds that the West can negate the impact of the security deficit by incurring "deficits" in other areas as well. This would involve empowering non-military actors in the West's Muslim communities—political groups, representative organizations, and others—in the hope that the West's relinquishing of power in these areas will reduce the incentive towards terrorism. Elements of this liberal strategy—in particular, the search for "moderate" partners—have been co-opted even by conservatives, as their security-centered approach has failed to achieve all of its declared goals.

The conservative rationale is based on the assumption that this so-called moderate Islam has the ability to counter jihadist and radical groups, and to keep terrorism in check. Many Western proponents of realpolitik believe that a strategy of preventing, taming, containing, and counter-balancing the terrorist threat is precisely what is needed now, and argue that alliances should be chosen purely according to a rational calculus of which group represents the lesser evil. The rewards for both "partners" in this kind of relationship are considerable: the West would have the terror-ist threat pushed safely to the margins, while the Muslim groups would finally be granted a role in decision-making.

The liberal camp, lacking such a coherent ideology, has sought to turn over control of the entire political realm to "Muslim" organizations. These "handlers" are supposed to mitigate challenges associated with diversity, such as providing reasonable accommodation for religious belief in the context of secular society, and ensuring equal opportunities in the labor market. Over time, however, the political functions of the state are becoming subject to significant cultural influence, and existing socio-political measures aimed at promoting integration are being replaced with purely cultural initiatives. Moreover, mosques and imams are not pre-pared for this type of task; contrary to expectations, they will not present Islam in solely spiritual terms. Their positions of authority make them willing and able to exercise a degree of influence over individuals' lives far beyond the capabilities of any democratically based integration frame-work. If the path toward integration with Western societies is determined solely according to religious tenets—for example, as a series of religiously prescribed tasks—it should not be a surprise that this path ultimately leads to the integration of fanaticism (a term used here to refer to a perspective on people, society, and the world that is impervious to change).

Despite its wide application in the service of realpolitik and laissez-faire multiculturalism, this strategy is counter-productive because it has allowed anti-democratic governments and ideological movements to suc-ceed in appropriating and misusing the term "moderate." Furthermore, it prevents the Islamic world from developing its own indigenous dem-ocratic traditions. In those Arabic-speaking countries where the chal-lenges to democracy have been especially serious, the authoritarian Arab regimes benefited from both the "moderate" label accorded them by the United States, and from the West's blunders in Iraq and Afghanistan. The priorities of key political players in these countries changed, with "strange bedfellows" emerging in response to the new external chal-lenges of radical terrorism, American military power, and the increasing "Westernization" of Muslim culture. In order to deny their perceived enemies any more influence, divergent Arab political forces formed a united front behind the status quo in their countries. Now, when Syrians or Saudis are asked whether they prefer the overthrow of their countries' ruling regimes and subsequent democratization on the Iraqi model, or the continued rule of a despotic autocracy, in most cases they choose the latter.

Islamists derive great benefit from the prevailing confusion in the Middle East; they discredit those who support democracy or human rights by confronting them with images from American or Iraqi prisons, French girls' schools (where headscarves are banned), or Danish newspapers (with cartoons of Prophet Muhammad). They rail endlessly against the Western concepts of democracy and human rights, becoming "true patriots" in the eyes of the Muslim public, while their liberal and/or secularly oriented rivals are seen as lackeys of the West.

Islamists exploit the tense atmosphere among European Muslims produced by the security situation to drum up support from the Arab world, claiming that they are protectors of the "marginalized" and "discriminated against" Western Muslim population. The headscarf and cartoon affairs, for example, aroused significant media interest in Arab countries—along with widespread popular sympathy for the "moderate" representatives of "oppressed Muslims" in the West.

Islamic or Islamist: Key Characteristics of Islamist Ideology

For many people, especially in the West, it is difficult to distinguish between ordinary Muslims and extremists, largely because the average Westerner cannot distinguish Islam, the religion, from the extremist ideologies derived from it. What, exactly, is "Islamism"?

Islamism refers to any interpretation of Islam that ascribes to the religion a far greater political role than it actually claims for itself. The Islamist conception of religious belief goes so far beyond the traditional bounds of faith systems that it is better described as a *social* ideology that arrogates to itself the right to dictate cultural norms and legal codes unilaterally. For example, to Islamists, concepts such as "loyalty," "solidarity," and "civic spirit" refer to an individual's religious affiliation and to the degree to which the individual conforms with the teachings of the religion.

Islamist movements enlist the support of the masses by exploiting the fundamental human need for meaning and direction. They promise a straightforward, easily grasped solution to all of society's problems: *sharia*, or Islamic law. The dictates of the Islamic state serve as the sole guarantor of a life truly pleasing to God. *Sharia* is defined in totalitarian fashion, as a universally applicable ideology that will take effect throughout the globe once the sacred political/military task of establishing God's rule on earth is completed. Islamist political discourse is purely dogmatic, flatly rejecting any diversity within the Islamic world so as to buttress their monolithic vision of Islam.

The continual drive to expand is a dominant feature of this ideology. There can be no compromises other than temporary truces, until this "holy grail" is recaptured. Islamism believes that the world must be liberated from the Western capitalist world order. Despite Islamist opposition to Western modernity, Islamists have made selective and very successful use of modern innovations such as mass media.

Islamist Movements

The divisions within the broader Islamist movement can be defined as isolationism, integrism, and jihadism. The borders between these movements are fluid and subject to change; moreover, individual units of a given movement can differ greatly from one another.

Isolationism calls for the maintaining of distance between oneself and the rest of society, rejecting any cooperation with the "infidel" state. This type of movement generally erects physical and mental barriers to avoid being affected by the larger society's immorality until that society can be radically reformed (in the isolationist group's image). Isolationist Islamist movements demand the establishment of an Islamic order and an Islamic state, by force if necessary.

One such group is Hizb ut-Tahrir (HT), the Islamic Party of Liberation, which is active in many key European countries. Isolationism is a subversive ideology that envisions a complete revolution in existing political realities to be extended to the entire globe. This is particularly true where it presents itself as a theology of liberation, promising not just political emancipation from existing regimes, but also religious salvation for the community as a whole. The key distinguishing factor of isolationism is its insistence that the Islamic state take the form of the caliphate, or a global Islamic empire. Fundamentalist movements such as the Muslim Brotherhood (MB), by contrast, are flexible in their understanding of the state, focusing on the state's potential function—not its form.

Integrism actually embraces social and political participation, viewing it as the best means of acquiring power. The primary objective is not the replacement of the existing order, but an Islamist takeover from within. Integrist groups—especially prevalent among European Muslims—demand "Islamic education," "Islamic banking," and the integration of *sharia* into existing state law. The MB has played the largest role in expanding politically motivated Islam in the West.

Jihadism stems from an effort to synthesize isolationism and integrism. Building on the ideas of Islamism inspired by MB's leading ideologue, Sayyid Qutb, jihadism seeks to introduce a legalistic Islam into society and establish *sharia* as the highest authority. In the United Kingdom, these objectives are pursued by splinter groups of al-Muhajiroun, which itself split off from HT. Violence is jihadism's only method to bring about revolutionary social change from outside the society's structures, a characteristic it shares with isolationist Islamism.

The biggest—but least apparent—danger comes from integrist groups, which claim to be renouncing violence as part of their effort to gain socio-political influence and power, and use a strategy of "integration" to promote their fundamentalist ideology.

Integrist Islamism: The Muslim Brotherhood

Since integrist movements are flexible in their understanding of the state, and enthusiastically seek social and political participation, many Western policymakers have responded favorably to them, viewing integrists as representing broad segments of Islamic communities, and as reliable partners for addressing societal issues concerning the religion. But are they aware of just who their partner is, or what they stand for, or what they may have advocated in the past (but discarded to fit Western sensibilities)? The recent history of the Muslim Brotherhood is a particularly useful example—and should be widely known among the *Ikhwani* (Muslim Brotherhood members') "partner" governments.

The Muslim Brotherhood is in reality a rather heterogeneous network containing various tendencies and currents. Presently, the MB is the most potent and dynamic Islamic movement, with its extensive global network of local organizations that can inspire and mobilize Muslims everywhere, from Casablanca to Kuala Lumpur, and from Warsaw to Los Angeles. In the West, particularly Germany, the United Kingdom, France, and the United States, the movement's tactics are more subtle, focusing on quieter lobbying activities to ensure it retains the status of representative of Muslims as a whole.

The movement, founded by Hasan al-Banna in Egypt in 1928,[1] quickly developed a considerable following. By 1938, it had a strict hierarchy that reinforced its preexisting fundamentalist tendency (although this would later be transformed by Qutb's isolationist revolutionary Islam). For al-Banna, Islam was the solution to all conceivable problems; the Qur'an was a constitution for the *umma* (Muslim community). This militant Islam is definitively understood as "cult and political leadership, religion and state, spirituality and practice, prayer and fight, obedience and rule, Qur'an and sword; not one of the elements can be separated from the others."[2] In this principle, al-Banna laid the foundation for the Islamist understanding of Islam, which persists today in the literature of the Muslim Brotherhood.

Sayyid Qutb, who advocated a type of isolationist Islamism, revolutionized the movement's ideology from the 1950s onward. His radicalism intensified during his imprisonment and persecution by the Nasser regime, and he began to advocate total confrontation with that portion of society that considered itself Muslim. In Qutb's view, a faithful Muslim cannot practice his faith within a "godless" (*kafir*) system. In an environment "not determined by the concept of Islam," shaping a life according to the Qur'an "is almost impossible, or at least extremely difficult.... Everyone who wishes to be a Muslim must be aware that he can practice Islam only in an Islamic environment."[3]

Since the end of the 1980s, the MB has noticeably changed its course and transformed its strategy. This phase revealed that the MB was grappling intensively with Qutb's ideas, which some believed were standing in the way of the renewed strategy of political movements.

In general, the Muslim Brotherhood experienced significant global development after 1986, a period when it was supposedly taking steps to distance itself from violence, but was in fact directly involved in the Afghan jihad movement and the founding of Hamas. The Brotherhood's new approach of participating in the electoral process helped certain offshoots of the organization establish themselves as fixtures in the Middle Eastern political scene, thanks to massive support from the electorate.

Under the leadership of Yusuf al-Qaradawi,[4] the movement has, since the early 1990s, transformed the implementation of its ideology, whose essence has remained largely unchanged. Al-Qaradawi added new fundamentalist concepts to the Muslim Brotherhood's philosophy, modifying Qutb's isolationist approach and enabling the movement to keep its finger on the spiritual/religious and political/ideological pulse of the *umma*.

As part of its new attitude toward political participation, the MB now seeks to recreate society in an Islamist image. The normalization of its relations with ruling regimes, the repeal of many countries' laws banning membership in the organization, and the later integration of parts of its ideology into the collective consciousness of many Muslims (so that even those who have never heard of al-Qaradawi now hold beliefs shaped directly by the MB), have further accelerated the pace of change. The MB is triggering international and regional transformations, extending its organizational network's activities into every conceivable area of society.

The new strategy envisions a "non-violent" social revolution and taking power through subversive participation in the political process. As part of this strategy, the MB has assumed authority over key opinion-shaping institutions, and carried out several carefully orchestrated forays into civil society.

Despite the MB's efforts at transparency and openness, however, the movement remains committed to the underlying idea of divine rule (*al-hakimiyya*).

The Concept of Integrism

In the period since 9/11 the Muslim Brotherhood has appointed itself chief mouthpiece for and coordinator of "moderate Islam," utilizing concepts such as *al-wasatiyya* (the mean/moderation), *al-margeyya* (ultimate reference/authority), and *al-shahada* (bearing witness/martyrdom). These concepts are of crucial importance, since they function as basic definitions of integrist strategy; in modified form, they are found in the public rhetoric of organizations close to the MB that are active in the West. They are also present in the writings of leading figures, such as Tariq Ramadan.

Concepts such as "Islamic authenticity" and the specific details of an "Islamic ruling model" as a response to democracy and modernism have always been hotly debated in the Islamic world, as have concepts like *al-margeyya*, an Islamic approach to establishing *sharia* norms as the only significant source of legislation. Whatever is in compliance with *sharia* assumes a binding character, and whatever runs counter to *sharia* is strictly rejected.

"We are 'mainstream Islam,'" an oft-repeated mantra of MB followers (including in the West), is part of the Brotherhood's successful effort to push aside *al-wasatiyya*, the old moderate faction within the *umma*. The MB became "mainstream" only by attaining power among Muslims in Islamic countries and elsewhere, giving it the right to represent Islam in the West and define the limits of religious authority.

Despite the MB's characteristic flexibility and willingness to adapt to local conditions, all Ikhwani groups follow the same core methods. An internal MB document reveals a clear strategy: first, win over the individual; second, ensure the spiritual education of the family; third, Islamize the society; and finally, seize power.[5] According to this view, if the people and the state can be brought together, the resulting *umma* will be a perfect and ideal society, and will rule the entire world.

Euro-Islamism's Ideological Dominance in the West

Islamism is embroiled in an international struggle for political power and cultural and political dominance. The primary concern of all Islamist factions, no matter where they are in the world, is to monopolize the voice of Islam and position themselves as the "true" representative of the *umma*. Jihadist and integrist Islamists share common features, most notably (and recently) a shift in emphasis from battlefields in the Muslim world to battlefields in the West. Terrorists such as Osama bin Laden have moved the battle into the country of the "distant enemy," the superior West, to spur recruitment for their battle against the "internal and nearby enemy," the authoritarian regimes in majority-Muslim states.

Integrist groups such as the MB discovered early on that the West provided a secure setting for the development of its organizational network, and the accumulation of increasing socio-cultural and economic power. Since the 1970s, the West has offered the MB not only a secure refuge from the persecution of the despotic regimes of its countries of origin, but also a breeding ground where its ideological and operational arsenals could develop unchecked.

Despite their shared preference to bring the struggle to battlefields in the West, terrorists and integrists have vastly differing objectives, methods of implementation, and consequences for the West and the Islamic world.

For the jihadists, shifting the fight against the "hegemonic strategies" of the United States and the West to Western soil is a means to liberate the Muslim world from the autocratic regimes that govern it. Large-scale terrorist acts demonstrate jihadism's capacity to cut off the flow of support for, and legitimacy of, Western capitals that perpetuate dictatorships in the Middle East. Jihadists portray themselves as opponents of the existing regime and seek indirectly to gain power. Their aim is to bring about an Islamic political order in which Muslims are no longer inferior to the West or its minions. For this reason, the power brokers of terror mobilize and recruit individuals in the West to carry out attacks either there, or against Western forces elsewhere, for instance, in Afghanistan.

For the integrists, by contrast, successfully infiltrating their ideology into Western society and building their organizational infrastructure in the very heart of the West are doubly significant. The West is not just a means, but a worthy end in itself. Establishing their organizational infrastructure represents the means in the battle against Western hegemony, and an increase in power in the Islamic world, while at the same time allowing greater opportunities for control over Muslim minorities in the West.

Al-Qaradawi, in elaborating his concept of *fiqh al-aqalleyyat* (jurisprudence regarding Muslim minorities), had some success in arrogating to himself the unquestioned power to interpret Islam in the West, and providing adequate answers to the pressing challenges to Islamic thought and action in a world controlled by globalization and migration. For him, the millions of Muslims in the diaspora were a challenge that the MB had to address. Europe, in al-Qaradawi's vision, is the front line in the battle for dominance, as well as an instrument that can contribute to the progress of Islam. He believes Islam's highest mission is the salvation of the world (including the decadent West) by means of bearing witness (*al-shahada*) before mankind. Moreover, al-Qaradawi has not stopped at the point of abstract theorizing. He personally holds the chairmanship of the European Council for Fatwa and Research (ECFR), an umbrella organization for sheikhs and religious leaders who are members (or close associates) of the MB. The council's policy is fairly pragmatic, as its goal is to become the ultimate authority (*al-margeyya*) for Muslims in the West.

Euro-Islamists: Honey Bees or Locusts?

In Europe, the MB has made pragmatic adaptations to its strategy and methodology. Yet, with their slogan, "Islam is valid and applicable under all circumstances," MB affiliate groups in the West still define their mission according to their core ideology, rather than historical or geographical borders of Islam.

The history of the rise of Euro-Islamism in the West is best traced to the establishment of the first organizations to share the MB's ideology, strategy, and tactics. In Germany, Milli Gorus (National Vision) and the Islamische Gemeinschaft in Deutschland (Islamic Society of Germany, IGD) are very similar; they are striving toward the same goal by the same coordinated blend of political and strategic measures directed at Islamizing the West. In terms of religion, Milli Gorus is part of an ultra-Orthodox tradition; this ideology is directed by a totalitarian worldview, and its policy has always been in favor of segregated communities for Muslim citizens with a Turkish background. Along with the separate communities of other Muslim factions that sprang up in the 1970s, Milli Gorus and the IGD defined—for Germans and the German state—what it meant to be a Muslim, according to the objectives of the Muslim Brotherhood. They viewed themselves as part of an Islam in exile, conveying to Muslims the political views of the Islamists in their country of origin.

Over time, the various Muslim Brotherhood organizations, turned away from their "Islam in exile" approach and implemented the central Ikhwani leadership's changes, focusing less on the migrants' eventual return home and more on a strong and separate Muslim identity for the generations born and raised in Germany. In practical terms, the MB organizations implemented this strategy by means of a construction campaign, building new mosques, centers, and social clubs for a community that was no longer considered transitory.

After September 11, the MB increasingly dedicated itself to articulating and asserting the interests of *all* Muslims living in the West. Its efforts were rooted in fundamentalist ideology, although the MB presented itself to the Western host nations as an organization that could help solve issues regarding Islam and its interpretations. The MB established and promoted the ECFR as an authority on religious questions. The MB further reinforced its presence by its administrative roles within individual mosques and community centers throughout Germany.

All MB subgroups in Europe are tightly interwoven with one another, able to make decisions on a local, national, or European level. This network structure functions very smoothly; the national-level parts of the network (such as the IGD) work very closely with the smaller suborganizations, as well as with the global-level MB infrastructure.

The Union des Organizations Islamiques de France (Union of Islamic Organizations in France, UOIF), an umbrella organization founded in 1989, unites the different MB organizations in Europe, such as the Muslim Association of Britain (MAB), the IGD, and numerous suborganizations. These groups are part of the organizational structure of the Cairo parent organization and are therefore comprised primarily of ethnic Arabs.

In the United States, the main institutional supporter of the Muslim Brotherhood is the Council on American-Islamic Relations (CAIR), which is also linked to the MB's headquarters in Cairo. Other groups, such as the Islamic Society of North America (ISNA) in the United States, and Milli Gorus in Germany, are ideologically close to the Muslim Brotherhood but have no role in the Cairo hierarchy.

The national organizations of the MB work primarily on the strategic planning, organization, and coordination of the network. The suborganizations pursue different objectives. The broad areas of activity can be seen in the following examples:

- *Training*: This includes academic training centers in France, such as the Institut Européen des Sciences Humaines (European Institute for the Humanities) and the Institut des Etudes Islamiques de Paris (Paris Institute for Islamic Studies), as well as the Institute for Islamic Studies in Wales. In addition, there are numerous local schools.
- *Financing, aid, and fundraising organizations*: An example is the European Trust, which subsidizes UOIF projects through donations, received primarily from the Gulf States.
- *Youth organizations*: Groups such as World Assembly of Muslim Youth (WAMY) and Forum of European Muslim Youth and Student Organizations (FEMYSO) recruit and mobilize second- and third-generation youth throughout Europe. Members of national youth organizations are not necessarily members of the Brotherhood itself, but Ikhwanis' disproportionately high rate of participation in community organizations preserves a route for MB strategy and tactics to enter hearts and minds here as well.
- *Media outlets*: An example is the Al-Hiwar (Dialogue) television network, which functions as a mouthpiece for the international network and devotes a large segment of its programming to the Muslim minority.
- *Religious authorities*: This includes the ECFR, which the MB tries to use as a means of reinforcing theological and ideological conformity among Muslims. Local mosques and cultural centers concentrate on spreading the ideology of the Muslim Brothers among Muslims.
- *Think tanks*: The MB's interest in the "Islamization of science" has given it a means of disseminating its ideology via establishments that appear "scientific." The MB directly influences the U.S.-based International Institute of Islamic Thought (IIIT), and therefore has at least indirect control over the IIIT's own worldwide network. In the United Kingdom, the MB founded the Arab Orient Center for Strategic and Civilization Studies and the Institute of Islamic Political Thought, and in Germany, the Gesellschaft Muslimischer Sozial- und GeisteswissenschaftlerInnen (Society of Muslim Scholars in the Humanities and Social Sciences). These grandly named organizations help promote the MB's image as a progressive, professional organization.

The Responsibilities of the West

Apparently harmless, European Islamism offers no theological opinion regarding non-violent political action to avoid alienating the masses that are its base of support. Euro-Islamists condemn terror in general, but endorse suicide bombing as a legitimate means of self-defense and accept that the weaker party in a struggle is forced to take such measures out of desperation. In their view, the United States bears responsibility for suicide bombings against it because of the brutal arrogance of its foreign policy and its role in provoking the unequal conflict. This interpretation enjoys surprising currency not just among European Muslims, but among European non-Muslims as well—to say nothing of large parts of the developing world.

However, this explanation virtually ignores Islamism and its ideology, downplaying the real risks it poses and viewing it as just one more movement of oppressed Third World people resisting imperialist globalization. Euro-Islamism, meanwhile, rejects violence on a highly selective basis, and is probably most often associated with its legitimization of "defensive jihad" as a religious obligation for individual Muslims, which can be fulfilled by providing logistical support to jihadist activities in the conflict regions of the Islamic world.

The Islamists continue to work towards producing a model of governance whose most important criterion for citizenship is Islamic religious faith. In Europe, the MB and related groups focus their attention more on fellow Muslims, retaining their representative role by systematically excluding non-Islamist Muslims from leadership positions in the mosques and organizations they officially direct or have infiltrated. The normal pattern is for the MB and its ilk to enter a community and divide it from within by first criticizing publicly, and then simply expelling, Muslims who do not share their beliefs. Attempts to resist their dominance are usually unsuccessful, as most Muslims view the mosque as a bunker from which to shelter themselves from Western society; they are thus not easily mobilized to counter injustices *within* the mosque community, especially when the Islamist faction enjoys numerical superiority.

Western governments are now attempting to locate viable "centrist" partners, but unfortunately "centrist" refers to their position within the Islamist spectrum—not the spectrum of Muslims as a whole. While policymakers argue that they must choose the best available partners for their country, they ignore the global dynamic in which Islam, Islamism, and terrorism interact.

The Relationship between Religion and Political Power in a Secular Democracy

Shortly before reaching America's shores, Christianity—or at least the Spanish crown, which considered itself Christendom's representative—completed its "rescue" of Europe from the danger of "Arab conquest," banishing Muslims and Jews from the continent at sword point. Europe's Enlightenment had to wait until after the late Middle Ages, when militant Christianity was finally constrained to rule over the realm of the sacred.

Centuries after its "Enlightenment," Europe is once again summoning religion to the cause of political action—but this time the religion is radical Islam, seen as the only hope for rescuing Europe from the "Muslim terrorist." The approach many politicians take to integration—"exorcise the terrorist demons with the gentler spirit of radical fundamentalism"—is at most an act of incredible naïveté.

Is the unconditional empowerment of a religiously governed organizational structure in the best interests of a well-functioning democracy? Is it not better to focus on strengthening governmental structures first, rather than enabling the rapid rise in power of those who—by their own choice—remain not just outside government, but outside the constraints of the democratic system itself?

The issue of Muslim representation depends on the prevailing balance of power; as long as religious institutions concern themselves with matters of faith and promote closeness to God, they are not only desirable representatives, but necessary ones. Yet, thanks to the speed at which the ideological virus has spread, the average Muslim now accepts the possibility of eternal bliss if politics are included in the domain of religion, controlled by the imams. If this trend continues, and Islamist organizations remain as the only recognized representatives of the religious community, then religious representatives will demand political rights as well—which can logically only take the form of a "society within society."

A vigilant democratic consciousness is marked by a basic distrust and a skeptical attitude toward centralized, unchecked power, whether governmental or private. This should be brought to bear on both European governments *and* Islamist movements, for both have the same faulty approach toward religion, allowing integration problems to be overlooked in the naïve hope that "culturalization" can solve any difficulty that may arise.

Integrists are aware that the percentage of Muslim citizens grows each year, and that whichever group is recognized as the "moderate" partner will be treated with greater and greater deference each year, and granted more and more power to subvert democratic principles within its own growing sphere.

The state is seriously mistaken if it thinks social problems can be solved by establishing an "Islamic church." In fact, most "normal Muslims" are well on their way to living as "Euro-Muslims," whose real-life problems require governmental, not metaphysical, solutions: childcare facilities, schools, universities, job-training centers, workplaces, housing policies, and the like. Western politicians cannot conceal such problems behind a superficial veil of feel-good politics or substance-free public relations campaigns. Existing problems cause further problems by preventing integration.

Though mosques and other primarily religious institutions *can* adhere to basic democratic rules, it is not in their nature to do so; leaders must actively decide to emulate democratic practices. In Europe, the imam's authority in the mosque is highly centralized, meaning that the voices of a significant number of European Muslims go unheard. Therefore, the so-called umbrella organizations—which espouse extremist positions—have no right to speak for all Muslims.

Many radicalized youth have gone off-track largely because of the self-pitying preaching so prevalent in mosques. It is even more dangerous when mosques are designed to serve as cultural centers as well. Predictably, this combination exerts considerable attraction for Muslims experiencing any kind of personal difficulty, as they can take comfort from what seems familiar. Unfortunately, the widespread Islamist control of such facilities means that these vulnerable individuals can be easily brainwashed and converted to extremism. Moreover, the mosque as the center for social life, as well as religious life, creates the foundation for parallel societies.

In the long term, the strengthening of ideological Islam and the granting of official recognition to its "moderate" organizations against jihadism create more problems for us than solutions. I echo Einstein's observation that "we cannot solve problems using the same kind of thinking that we used when we created them"; many already-existing organizations were part of the problem, and thus cannot be part of the solution. What Muslims are reaping is precisely what we were fighting in our countries of origin: the instrumentalization of our religion through a totalitarian ideology. What is ironic about this is that those who speak loudest in favor of "Euro-Islam" are doing so only to gain more power and more resources which they may use to implement their ideological program. The question is how such a degenerate form of Islam could develop within liberal Western societies, which are inevitably depicted in Euro-Islamist discourse as the implacable archenemy of Islam. Their use of this type of rhetoric is hardly a secret; so why are European governments still selecting the adherents of this particular type of Islam as their privileged partners and the recognized representatives of all Muslims?

The West's Responsibility to Win over Its Muslims

After September 11, Muslims in the West suddenly stood on one side of the gaping chasm that had opened up on the highway to integration. They soon concluded that to cross the abyss they would have to sacrifice their religion, or at the very least, distance themselves from it. Many sought to facilitate integration by turning their backs on Islam altogether. The often one-sided Western portrayal of Islam gave the strong impression that every Muslim is at his core an unruly, violent criminal.

After the start of the American campaigns in Afghanistan and Iraq, Western media reporting—which was uninhibited and not exactly Islam- and Muslim-friendly—blurred Muslims' feelings of solidarity with the victims of terror, leading some to identify instead with the perpetrators.

Many people wanted to hold Muslims in general—whether resident in the West or elsewhere—responsible for terrorists' atrocities. Most Muslims watched helplessly as their religion was discredited, feeling more like victims than perpetrators, because from their perspective, their religion provided no basis for terrorism. The mood of the silent Muslim majority in the West continues to fluctuate between lethargy and indifference. Nevertheless, an open debate has finally begun on the dialectics of guilt and responsibility, along with psychological self-defense mechanisms.

The Euro-Islamists' consistent whining about the "systematic discrimination" against Muslims in the West is not wholly without foundation: individual discriminatory attitudes do exist; there are other structural issues, such as preferential arrangements between state and church, but not between state and mosque. There is also a prevailing public stigmatization of anything Islamic by the continued demonization of the religion and its cultural heritage. None of these regrettable phenomena should be minimized or tolerated.

The West must perform a balancing act on the tightrope that stretches between the need to take security measures in order to prevent terrorist attacks, and the need to promote the equal treatment of Muslims. Why are both necessary? In an environment in which Islam is associated with terrorism and violence, the faith and its cultural traditions have been devalued, and a certain type of Islamophobia is being fed.

Many Muslims also feel marginalized culturally because in the West, Islam continues to symbolize the religion of the "other"; few Western cultural assets are shared with the Islamic tradition, and those that are common to both cultures have very different connotations. Openness to Islamic religious developments was difficult for Western culture, with its strong Judeo-Christian traditions, just as Western principles evoke feelings of alienation or resentment among Muslims. Words such as "aliens" (Arabic: *gurbah*, Turkish: *gurbet*), "alienation," and "West" are all derived from the same root, "to go west," that is, to travel into the dark unknown.

Recognition and integration of Muslim religious communities in the West is a necessary and unavoidable task that must be completed sooner rather than later, and in keeping with the basic ideals of pluralism and democracy. To prepare for this task, the West must ask itself the following questions: What requirements must the prospective partners meet? How are policymakers to differentiate among the very different groups that claim to represent Muslims? What criteria must be met in order for Muslim religious communities to be treated equally? How should we respond to the Islamist movements? Moreover, since moderate groups can become radicalized—and since radical groups can become moderate— what potential is there for positive development and reform within any particular movement? Which groups have renounced violence in rhetoric, so as to set a clear and elevated norm of political behavior? And last but not least, how extensive a role should religion in general, and Islam in particular, play in public life?

Integration or Equality?

A possible way of establishing non-Islamist Muslim religious communities is first to provide support to Islamic groups which, even on a local level, operate according to democratic norms. This can be the foundation for the construction of Muslim "melting pots" on a broad, pluralistic basis. However, the process must be facilitated with a concept that was first rooted in Christian social teaching, but by now has become an essential part of the supranational European Union (EU): the subsidiarity principle.[6]

The essence of this principle is that EU political decisions should always be taken at the lowest appropriate level (municipality, then province, then member state, and only then, the European Union) so as to maintain the connection between governing institutions and the people in whose sovereign name they rule. Closely related is the principle of proportionality, according to which the reach and scope of EU laws should not be greater than is necessary to further the objectives of the founding treaties. It further states that

> as long as either an individual citizen or a smaller community is capable of fulfilling their goals with the use of their own independent resources, the larger social structure should not be allowed to intervene. Once it is apparent that these resources are insufficient however, the larger community should offer its assistance, providing as much help as necessary, while simultaneously allowing room for the individual or smaller community to contribute and take personal responsibility to the extent possible. The state must ensure that the individual citizen and smaller social structures and communities can both develop in freedom and acquire personal responsibility.[7]

It is more than symbolically appropriate for these principles to be applied to relations with Muslim congregations; in fact, it should have been done already. Currently, we see interior ministers meeting and cooperating with Muslim umbrella organizations, but city mayors have little ability to communicate with their Muslim citizens—lacking the linguistic capability and the institutional resources necessary to hold a dialogue in the first place.

With subsidiarity being properly respected, perspectives are more balanced when Muslim representatives meet their government counterparts. When village council members meet local imams, and the experience of such meetings informs the discussions at regional and national levels, a stable structure emerges. Moreover, while the territorially-based arrangement is hierarchical, it has far more legitimacy because it begins at the bottom; it is far more democratic than the current top-down models that govern many Muslim organizations. Experience bears out this assertion; most notably the "Hamburg model," in which Muslim mosques and

associations joined together to establish a small, regional umbrella organization with achievable, proportionate objectives, and transparent governing structures.

Which Islam for Europe?

There is some justification for the general fear that recognizing Islamic
culture as a full-fledged subculture of Western culture will empower the
wrong groups and increase risk. Yet this potential for risk does not absolve
us from the task of searching for possibilities beneficial to the Western
Muslim subculture and the broader Western culture.

Before Islam and Muslims can establish a positive and lasting coexistence with the modern world, we Muslims must begin demystifying
and liberating our most basic religious principles. Islam contains many
elements that can and should serve as the basis for a humanized political
culture in line with international human rights standards. We must orient ourselves toward a universalistic ethos and a consensus-based way of
avoiding conflicts over the public spaces we share with others.

We can begin this process by reconsidering our definition of the *umma*.
The Muslim *umma* has no clear political shape, nor does it have any institutionalized cultural authorities. Belonging to the *umma* is a question of
voluntary cultural association; it is inappropriate as a criterion for defining
how residents of Western democracies should engage in political action. If
we were to accept that the *umma* is a global political category (in the sense
of a common sacred space), this would necessarily imply that affiliation
with the sacred is of higher importance than citizenship in one's country
of nationality. Germany is not going to dissolve itself and be replaced by
citizens of Christendom or of the *umma*; religious groups are not direct
subjects of international law. Even the idea of Europe as a single subject
of international law is controversial—and this idea, whether in theory or
in practice, is far more established than either the transnational cultural
affiliation or separate sacred space understandings of the *umma*.

A shift in the perspectives from which we assess and respond to national
and transnational threats is therefore necessary so that local and regional
problems do not fade into the background as other transnational conflicts
garner all the attention. First, active Muslim engagement for a more just,
free, and open world order—including the demand for, and promotion
of, solutions for the *umma's* open wounds in Iraq, Chechnya, Afghanistan,
or Palestine—requires that we stop imagining the world as a scattered
system of islands among which Muslims wander as rootless vagabonds.
The advantages of democratic government, and the possibilities it offers
for influencing world events, even against Western powers, were apparent
in the large demonstrations protesting the Iraq war.

Second, there must be a faith-driven alignment with the fundamental
political values that form the basis of the Western social model. A synthesis

between Islam's ethical values and the politically binding norms in the West is necessary. Such a synthesis would demonstrate Islam's receptiveness to modern and liberal social forms. Certainly, the Islamic socioethical perspective could make a considerable contribution toward the peaceful pluralistic development of the Western value system. However, it will be able to do so only if we first acknowledge that we *are* of the West, flaws and all, rather than its passive victims. Muslims in the West must reconsider the ideas of liberal democracy and secularism and go beyond the prevailing debate over Islamic resistance.

If we understand "Euro-Islam" to mean any Islam that is willing to establish its position in society by merely rejecting the terrorist actions of some Muslims, then we lower the bar for Muslims to such an extent that at best, they are not perceived as barbarians. The simple rejection of violence does not make any of us equal and upright citizens. More is required. Ethical canons such as "do not kill a human soul" exist not only to protect individuals, but to establish a moral yardstick that pushes us away from violence. To do this, we Muslims must be clear about what it means when we say that we want to be perceived as part of European culture. Our contribution to peace in the West, and the world in general, is clear not only when we praise, in the media, Islam's capacity for peace, but also when we make our contribution to Europe visible through social engagement. This broadening of horizons toward greater peace in the world is an ethical principle that ought to be implemented in practice by everyone.

We are all still at the beginning of a long, shared journey. Much still needs to happen before Muslims will participate in society to the same extent as other Europeans who in general tend to be progressive, optimistic, and willing to seize the initiative. If our rejection of violence is limited to public declarations but does not extend to promoting peace in our own society, then our loyalty to our new countries is too fragile to be called permanent.

Toward an Islamic Theology of Universal Ethics

Theologically, Islam is considered capable of pluralism; it is based on the Old and New Testaments, and is a synthesis of the monotheistic religions.

Islam is capable of modernizing culturally because it is a synthesis between faith and rational science. Islamic culture gave birth not only to jurists, but also to Avicenna and Averroës, who mastered the dialectics of acculturation. Although this experience ended in the years before Columbus's voyage, its legacy lingered long enough to shape the basic attitudes of Europe's Enlightenment.

What are to be the defining elements of Western Islam? One of these is an Islamic contribution to the establishment of legal and political structures and regulatory norms to determine, create, and protect the well-being and interests of all, through non-violent consensus building. For me, as a European Muslim, this means that faith cannot find its place in any society without liberal democracy, because only democracy gives each of us the opportunity to worship our own God. Dictators, on the other hand, always have only one "God," but it is a false one. Fleeing from such false "deities," many Muslims have found safe refuge in Europe, and most practicing Muslims have rediscovered religion and God in the democratic conditions prevailing here. Our pledge of allegiance to democracy can be, and indeed must be, more than strategic lip service. Alas, we do not hear endorsement of these ideals anywhere in Euro-Islamist discourse.

We, as Muslims and Europeans, must reflect on ideas and strategies that will prove to be constructive and sustainable. In particular, we must put to rest the recurring battles over identity symbols (such as headscarves and ritual slaughter of animals). Our primary task is to develop and elaborate an interpretation of Islam that crystallizes the essence of our religion and promotes basic ethical values—and by this I do not mean *sharia*. What Islam and the West need is to question our historical self-assurance in an ongoing, self-critical process.

As a Muslim citizen of Europe, I would like to take full advantage of my democratic rights and obligations, including the right to practice my religion freely. However, I do not want to be perceived only as a practitioner of my religion, as a so-called creature of faith. It should be possible to lead a committed religious life, setting the course for a peaceful world, without excluding all other dimensions. As a spiritual and culture-shaping reservoir for Muslims living in the West, with an element of openness toward others, and an untrammeled right to express one's opinion, Islam can make positive contributions to society. It is contributions of this kind that can bring about an even more peaceful, more democratic, more humane, and more open Europe. By leading a committed Muslim life, we can give our new homeland, our countries of origin, and the rest of the world the prospect of a more humane life for all people, a future with Islam and with Muslims, not against or without them; we can give the world an Islam of which we are all proud. Nothing else justifies the most profoundly ethical preparedness of a truly peaceful religion, my religion.

Radicalism in the world of Islam has cast aside the independent theological rationale on which Muslims used to rely, and obtained its current position of world domination. Even if Western foreign policy changed for the benefit of Muslims, the Islamist goal of extending Islamic rule to the entire world would not change, for as long as the movement exists, it will continue its holy mission.

If Islam is to become modern and liberal, it has a long way to go on the road to internal reform. If Muslims themselves do not clear the path through free and open internal dialogue, reform will never take place. But this is not to say that the West is powerless. It helps Muslims and itself when facilitating this discussion on equal terms, avoiding unnecessary provocation, arrogance, or ignorance. Indeed, it is only in this way that the West can help set a course for a common future of peace and security.

Notes

1. Al-Banna (1906–1949) was an Egyptian schoolteacher.
2. Sayyid Qutb, *Ma'alim fi-l-Tariq* (Milestones) (Cairo: Dar al-shuruq, 1990), p. 45.
3. Ibid.
4. Yusuf al-Qaradawi, an Egyptian born in 1926, is considered the spiritual father of the Muslim Brotherhood. His political activities, publications, and weekly broadcasts on Al-Jazeera have established him as Sunni Islam's most influential contemporary religious authority.
5. Website of the Muslim Brotherhood Movement, http://www.ummah.net/ikhwan/ (accessed September 22, 2007).
6. Subsidiarity in the American context is similar to the Ninth and Tenth Amendments.
7. See www.ottensheim.oevp.at/aab.htm (accessed October 20, 2007).

CHAPTER THREE

The History of Islam in Italy

AHMAD GIANPIERO VINCENZO

Historical Beginnings

In the Middle Ages, Italy played host to an Islamic presence that left a lasting impact. For nearly five centuries, from 827 to 1300, Islam's presence in Sicily and other parts of the Mezzogiorno[1] enabled Italy to play a central role in a Mediterranean society endowed with considerable ethnic and religious diversity. The richness of Italian culture, art, and economics—all of which approached their zenith during this period—was enhanced by the contributions of the Muslim community (and in southern Italy, by Judaism as well, until the Spanish forced some 120,000 Jews northward toward Rome in 1492).

Islam did not come to Sicily as part of the religion's initial expansion into North Africa during the seventh century. On the contrary, it was only at the beginning of the ninth century—and only after a period of careful planning—that Ziyadat Allah I (817–838), the third Aghlabid Emir, landed his forces on Sicily. The Aghlabid dynasty had been charged with the administration of Africa by Caliph Harun al-Rashid (786–809), who had maintained peaceful diplomatic and cultural relations with Charlemagne and the Carolingian dynasty.[2] It was perhaps with the idea of "conquering" Sicily with knowledge, rather than with sheer force, that in June 827, the Emir decided, after consulting his advisers, to send troops to the island with Asad ibn al-Furat at their command. Al-Furat, then 68 years old, had gained vast fame as a legal scholar; in 788 and 789 he worked under the noted jurist Malik ibn Anas, and served as an editor of the *Mudawana*, one of the principal texts of the Maliki *madhab,* or school of Islamic thought. He had never before participated in any kind of military action, and the episode can be understood in terms of the doctrine of

This article was originally written in Italian and was translated by Emmet C. Tuohy for this volume.

spiritual "struggle," as expressed in the term "jihad." This concept is only partially translated by the term "holy war" as an external struggle against infidels. That external struggle, however, is only a "small war" encompassed, in principle, by the "great war," an internal struggle in which man fights the base tendencies of his own soul in the hope of earning the reward of knowledge of the divine. We can thus fully grasp the meaning of jihad as a "struggle along the path to God." The following excerpt from al-Furat's address to his troops in the *ribat*—fortified spiritual center—of Susa, in modern-day Tunisia, before their departure, sheds some light on the lived dimension of jihad as an intellectual effort—as it would be interpreted in Sicily and southern Italy:

> There is no God but God who has no equal! Only through God, oh soldiers, have I inherited this command, not from my father nor from any of my honored ancestors, though earth has not yet seen their equals; it is only by the power of the pen that I have been able to achieve that which you now see. Thus, give yourselves, body and soul, to the search for knowledge; gather as much of it as you can, but also know how to resist, and bear most tenaciously the burdens that it will place upon you. Remember, above all, that by doing this, you will ensure your reward in this life, and the next.[3]

With the success of the conquest of Sicily, a learned-elite established itself on the island—some of whom remained even after the arrival of the Normans in the tenth century. This elite fostered the growth of studies of law—that is, *fiqh*—especially the Maliki *madhab*. Although it does not appear that there was much room for the *ulum al-awail* (the "science of the ancients," that is, philosophical studies based on Hellenistic thought), poetry was held in high esteem, and both scholars and mystics relied upon it to express their most elevated and spiritual thinking. A cross-section of Sicilian society can be seen in the following description by Ibn Hawqal, the astute Fatimid emissary to the island:

> All Sicilians are convinced that their elite—the flower of their society—is to be found among their jurists, learned juridical advisers and counselors at law; they are the ones who decide among themselves what is licit and illicit; it is they who draw up contracts and hear testimony; they are the true men of letters and holy preachers.[4]

The Sicilian juridical tradition is said to have had a particularly notable impact on relations between Muslims and non-Muslims. It was apparently first formulated in the eleventh century by the Sicilian al-Mazari, who established the principle that Muslims could remain under the rule of a non-Muslim prince as long as they were allowed to continue to observe the principles of Islamic traditions.[5] During this period, Sicily was simultaneously part of Italy and of the Islamic world. Relations between the

West and East were maintained by sages and Sufis: toward the middle of the eleventh century, Musa Ibn 'Abd Allah of Kufa, a theologian, poet, and scholar, chose Sicily as his home, whereas Abu Muhammad 'Abda al-Rahman ibn Mohammed, a Sicilian who died before 996, studied and taught at al-Qayrawan (Kairouan) University in the Far East.[6]

Sufism had many followers in Islamic Sicily. In fact, according to Ibn Hawqal, in Sicily's capital, Palermo, there were many gathering places and *ribats*, or spiritual retreat centers, where people led both contemplative and active lives.[7] References to Sufism are also found in locally prominent learned poetry, as seen in this fragment by the eleventh-century Sicilian poet Ibn al-Tazi:

> The value of Sufism is not dressing up in old woolen clothes that you've patched up yourself; nor in the ability to touch the hearts of the foolish; nor in crying out loudly, leaping, writhing, and smoothing strident, nor in jumping and writhing, or in swooning as if you've gone mad. Sufism lies within a sincere and unblemished soul; in following the truth, the Qur'an, the faith; in demonstrating that you fear God, that you repent your sins, which cut you to the bone with eternal regret.[8]

The importance of Sufism in Palermo, and the way in which the Prophet's most direct and most inward spiritual teachings were followed, led Sicilian Muslims to call it "Madina" after the Prophet's city—the first time any community in the Islamic world was blessed with this honor. This is seen in the words of the poet Ibn al-Rashiq, who died in the Sicilian city of Mazara around the year 1064, and who described Palermo as the "sister of al-Madina, a name that no other city can share: go and verify it for yourself!"[9]

During the years when Islam was establishing a foothold in southern Italy, the diverse Latin, Greek, Lombard, and Norman populations—and their religious practices—coexisted peacefully. Indeed, in few other regions of Europe was the spread of so many monasteries and hermitages of different denominations—as well as the flourishing of saints and men and women of great spirituality—so evident. Even though material and political interests sometimes gained the upper hand (resulting in several episodes of intolerance and violence), those who aspired to saintliness and who placed a premium on getting close to the one God, continued to maintain close relations across religious divisions.

Throughout most of the thirteenth century, the town of Lucera, in the southern Italian region of Puglia to which all Sicilian Muslims were resettled by Holy Roman Emperor Frederick II between 1224 and 1246, was an example of peaceful Christian-Muslim coexistence and mutual respect. Throughout the period in which Christians and Muslims lived within the walls of the same city, they demonstrated an admirable spirit of mutual tolerance. We can find no hint whatsoever of religious strife, nor, even, of temporary civil unrest that could in some way be attributed to differences of faith."[10]

The Abbey of Cava, a principal center of spirituality in southern Italy, maintained friendly relations with Richard of Lucera, head of the Islamic settlement that had been founded by Frederick II. When the "Saracen colony" was destroyed by Emperor Charles I of the Holy Roman Empire in 1301, the Abbey of St. Sophia of Benevento sheltered the Muslim refugee Salem, against the king's orders.

The presence of the Islamic community was not felt solely in Sicily or southern Italy, but throughout the entire peninsula. Even in Tuscany, there was no shortage of contacts with the Muslim world due to Pisa's maritime activity and to the marked intellectual inclination of the region's dominant family in the Medieval period. A letter from Bertha, wife of Margrave Adalbert II of Tuscany—called "Bertha the Great" by Byzantine Emperor Constantine VII Porphyrogenitos—refers to a group of 150 Muslim prisoners held for 7 years in Tuscany, who acquainted the region with the Islamic world. The letter, preserved in an Arabic-language version, was addressed directly to the caliph of Baghdad; Charlemagne's great-granddaughter was seeking an alliance that was perhaps related to the state of affairs in Italy:

> I pray that God may help me to secure your friendship, as well as an agreement between us, for however many years I may remain in this world; whether or not this occurs depends on you. This agreement is something that has never been sought by anyone in my family—not by my ancestors, not by my kin—nor has anyone ever informed me about your armies, or the preeminence that you have attained; this was all told to me by the eunuch that I had sent you. . . . I have also entrusted him with a secret that he is to relate to you only once he sees you face to face; this is because I wish for this secret to remain between us, and for no one to know about it except me, you, and the eunuch. May God's greatest blessings be upon you and your people, and may God humiliate your enemies and allow them to be trampled beneath your feet. Greetings![11]

In fact, Tuscany would play a central role in the diffusion of Islamic culture in Italy from the tenth to the thirteenth century. The Court of Countess Matilda of Tuscany was renowned for its intellectual attainments and its superb library, which included a collection of works by Islamic philosophers, of whom a majority were jurists. Irnerius, the founder of the University of Bologna who is credited with the renaissance of Western juridical thought, served under Countess Matilda of Tuscany, and later argued cases before Holy Roman Emperor Henry V as *iudex* (judge). Tuscany's second city, Pisa, as well as Pavia and other northern Italian cities, all feature numerous ceramic works of Islamic manufacture that were used for decorating important city monuments, especially holy places: it is particularly significant that many of them bear inscriptions from the Qur'an, and were placed high above ground level, where they could not easily be seen. It is difficult to imagine that they were used without any understanding of their significance, as they are found too frequently in such places. For example, caskets bearing visible Islamic inscriptions were often used as reliquaries.

Unlike the Italian elite, which held Islam in high esteem, contemporary chroniclers depicted Muslims as barbarians. Their attitude stemmed from a desire to make the Islamic presence in Europe fit their preferred analogy of the ancient Roman accounts of the barbarian invasions. Thus, Muslims were labeled violent and savage; according to one chronicle, the "evil" and "most cruel" Sawdan, the emir of the Italian city of Bari, would kill over 500 Christians on an average day, using their piled-up bodies as a sort of throne-cum-dining table.[12] The identification of Muslims with barbarians is confirmed by the fact that the chroniclers, including those with direct personal knowledge of Muslims, considered them to be infidels and idolaters. To a large degree, the chroniclers have succeeded in their mission, as this kind of prejudice continued to exist in substantially the same form, over the course of many centuries, and in large part survives to this day.

Western elites were nevertheless able to maintain spiritual and intellectual relations with the Islamic world. This group was made up primarily of knights (later associated with the monastic–chivalric orders), but also of merchants and monks who had contact with Sufism and Islamic orders from which the *futuwwa*, or "Islamic spiritual knighthood," drew its strength.

This elite was forced to move with great caution so as to avoid popular resentment, but was nevertheless able to grant official recognition of freedom of religion for Muslims in Italy. Moreover, it showed a deep respect for the knowledge transmitted as part of the Islamic legacy. Ibn Jubayr reports that at the beginning of Norman rule in Sicily, during the reign of William II, Palermo was struck by an earthquake; afterwards, a group of Muslim men and women, including converts, gathered together to pray. Coincidentally, the king happened to meet them at just this time and, though they feared they would be denounced, with fatal consequences, William invited them to continue their worship.[13] This attitude was not unlike that of Frederick II when, under the watchful eyes of Western ambassadors, half his royal court got up to leave to say their daily Islamic prayers. In addition, during a consultative assembly meeting in the northern province of Friuli, Frederick paid special attention to the guests of his Muslim friends and, in the presence of princes and bishops, celebrated the *Hijra* (the Islamic New Year) with them before requesting that they accompany him south to Apulia.[14] This elite refrained from directly opposing popular positions, but left an enduring legacy in its relations with the Islamic world and in its recognition of the legitimacy of the Islamic tradition.

One notable example of this legacy is the Catholic monasteries whose feudal dependents regularly swore their oath of loyalty on the Qur'an.[15] An even better case is an episode involving St. Bernard of Clairvaux, who enjoyed relations with the Islamic world through the Knights Templar. Bernard followed events in Italy with great interest, and helped found several monasteries in Sicily.[16] The Abbot Peter the Venerable, who in 1143 completed a translation of the Qur'an as a new tool to fight the Muslims, wrote to Bernard to ask that he prepare an introduction. Not receiving any response, Peter wrote yet again, providing further details of his work in progress, but Bernard refused to reply as he would not write anything against the Qur'an.[17]

State and Religion in Italy

Italy has a long and well-established tradition of relations between the state and the Holy See. The choice of Rome as capital of the united Italy in 1871 exacerbated the tensions in this ancient and often crisis–prone relationship. Subsequently, a truly unique "Roman question" between state and Vatican emerged that would in no small way govern the politics of post-unification Italy.[18] The Lateran Accords of 1929 marked the start of the rebuilding of relations between church and state, and the relationship profoundly changed Italian life: the state in Italy was secular, but only in a relative sense.

The Lateran Accords established principles for an active relationship between the state and the Catholic Church, principles which were extended to all religious denominations under the 1948 Italian Constitution. It is worth reproducing Articles 7 and 8 of that document here in their entirety:

Article 7:
1. The State and the Catholic Church are, each within their own reign, independent and sovereign.
2. Their relationship is regulated by the Lateran Accords. Any amendment to these accords that is accepted by both parties does not require the procedure of constitutional amendments.

Article 8:
1. All religious denominations are equally free before the law.
2. Religious denominations other than Catholicism have the right to organize themselves in accordance to their own statutes, provided they do not conflict with the Italian legal system.
3. Their relationship with the state is regulated by law, based on agreements [*intese*, sing. *intesa*] to be reached with representatives of these religions.

However, there were problems with the practical implementation of the constitution. In fact, the beginning of the Lateran Treaty (the first of the Lateran Accords) restates Article 1 of the Statute of the Kingdom of Italy (dated March 4, 1848), which reaffirms that "the Catholic Apostolic Roman religion is the only State religion." The authors of the 1948 Constitution were aware of the need to revise the accords at least on this point, as otherwise the agreements with the other denominations envisioned by Article 8 would be impossible. Yet it was not until February 18, 1984 that the Lateran Accords were revised, and at that time the judicial framework regulating relations between the Italian government and religious communities, known as the *intese*, was also established. That same year, the Waldensian community established the first *intesa* with the state, which was followed by agreements with the Adventist Church and the Assembly of God in 1988 and the Jewish community in 1989.

The *intese* regulate issues such as the construction and management of houses of prayer, the appointment of clergy, marriage, religious institutions, assistance in hospitals and prisons, and the creation of cemeteries. The economic relationship between church and state is also important: the *intese* fixed the share of personal income tax allocated to religious denominations at a rate of 8 mills (i.e., .008 percent, or eight euro out of every thousand). In 2003 (the latest year for which figures are available), this share of tax revenue amounted to roughly 1 billion euro of which 87 percent went to the Catholic Church. These funds are used for constructing and maintaining houses of prayer, and supporting clergy, religious education, and humanitarian activities.

The judicial experience of relations between church and state in Italy stems principally from the state's relationship with the Catholic Church. The subsequent agreements with Protestant denominations did not pose any specific problems, as the religious structures of the Protestant churches are broadly similar to those of the Catholic Church. By contrast, the Jewish community faced greater difficulties, and more time was required to resolve them. Nonetheless, Judaism in Italy is deeply rooted, featuring a community system that subdivides the country into precise jurisdictional boundaries, and which operates according to mechanisms that have been clearly defined over the centuries. Finally, the *intese* reached thus far have each concerned a fairly limited number of adherents. As a result, their impact on society as a whole has been relatively modest. It is no coincidence that the denominations involved in these agreements have all formally waived the right to intervene in matters of public school education, accepting that the Catholic Church—which is in charge of teacher-training institutions—will carry out this function.

The prospects for Islam, however, are different—just as the social impact of Muslims in Italy is different. Islam is the second-largest religion in Italy, and its size places it in a category similar to the Catholic Church. However, even though Islam is part of the same Abrahamic tradition as Christianity, the two religions differ in several substantial ways, especially in internal organization. Nonetheless, much current thinking on religious issues, academic or institutional, is based on the supposition that every religion structures itself around a church. Because of the central role of a pastor or priest in Christianity, it is assumed that those who perform religious rites also represent the religion. In Italy, especially, this idea has long been projected onto other denominations, so that the notion of a religious minister became a point of reference even for pre–World War II legislation recognizing other denominations.[19]

Like Judaism, Islam has no priests to administer religious rites. Any Muslim can serve as imam, or prayer leader; and doing so does not automatically signify that he holds a representative position within the religious community. The members of the Islamic spiritual elite are distinguished instead by their intellectual dimension. Of course, the same person can be both an intellectual and a performer of ritual functions, but more often a narrower elite is responsible for representative functions. In France, for example, the great mosques of Paris and Lyon are guided by rectors. Thus, an Islamic organization representative of the Islamic community generally is very different from a representative of a church.

Italian Muslim Organizations

The moderation and tolerance of Italian society has generally not been reflected in its response to Islam. Islamophobia in Italy is multifaceted; the major prejudice is a religious one that views Islam as a political and social ideology lacking any spiritual dimension. The primary standard-bearers of this approach are Roman Catholic academics; two examples are Maurice Borrmans, a "White Father"[20] of Belgian origin and professor at the Pontifical Institute for Arabic and Islamic Studies (PISAI) in Rome, and Paolo Branca of the Catholic University of Milan. Their efforts are aimed at placing Islam on a different level from other religions, thus avoiding confrontation—but also interfaith dialogue—with Islam. Most recently, following the election of Pope Benedict XVI, the Pontifical Council for Inter-Religious Dialogue (which was the principal body responsible for dialogue with Islam) was downgraded to a mere section of the Secretariat of Culture. It was restored to its previous status in 2007, but only after significant protests.

The need for Italy's Muslims to have their own organizations thus became more pronounced. However, in Italy just as in other European countries, it has been difficult to identify a single national Islamic organization. Many are only local, while others dissolve soon after they are formed. Still others are born out of the particular ideologies of other countries, or of transnational Islamist movements. In any case, any organization wishing to operate in Italy must respect the Italian legal system (as prescribed by Article 8), and must be a result of the direct involvement of Italian Muslim citizens, given that citizens are the primary focus of the *intese*, which form part of domestic (not international) law.

The Islamic Union of the West (Unione Islamica in Occidente, UIO), established in Rome in 1947, was the first Islamic organization formed in Italy. Until 1965, it was practically the only such organization in the country. Its first president was Mentor Cioku Gropa, an Italian of Albanian origin who, in coordination with the embassies of various Islamic countries, created the Islamic Cultural Center of Italy (Centro Islamico Culturale d'Italia or CICI). Under the banner of the Academy of Islamic Culture, the UIO published a magazine entitled *Islam, History, and Civilization*; since 1982, it has continued to manage the only Arabic school recognized by the Italian Ministry of Public Education. Currently, the president of the UIO is an Italian of Libyan origin named Mansur Tantoush, while the general secretary is an Italian by the name of Khalid Biagioni. Since 1972, the UIO has progressively come to represent Italian Islam within the World Islamic Call Society (WICS).

In its first decade, the CICI was a charitable organization tied closely to the diplomatic community. However, due principally to the intervention of Saudi Arabia, it became involved in efforts to promote Islam in Italy and in 1973 began to take an active interest in constructing a mosque in Rome. On the recommendation of its board of directors, whose members are Muslim ambassadors to the Italian government and/or the Holy See, the CICI assumed responsibility for obtaining the cooperation of the Italian authorities. The following year, the CICI obtained recognition as an Islamic cultural entity and took possession of a plot of land donated by the City of Rome.[21]

Construction soon began on the slopes of Mount Antemnae, some two miles north of the city center. However, the project, designed by Paolo Portoghesi, took considerable time to complete and was not officially opened until 1995. The resulting Mosque of Rome, which can accommodate up to 3,000 worshipers, is the largest in Europe. Saudi Arabia covered most of the cost, officially estimated at 60 billion lire (roughly 30 million euros), although Morocco, Iraq, Libya, and private parties also made generous contributions. However, the CICI has never been able to *legitimately* claim to represent Islam in Italy, because its board of directors includes seven Muslim ambassadors to Italy, who obviously are not Italian citizens. Since 1997, the president of the board has been the Saudi Ambassador, who assumed the position after the Moroccan Ambassador. In January 2008, the CICI created a larger body, the General Assembly of Italian Muslims, which is now the most representative Islamic religious organization in Italy.

Organized Islamism was originally limited to student groups (such as the Union of Muslim Students in Italy, USMI), or to purely local organizations (such as the Islamic Cultural Center of Milan and Lombardy in Segrate, or the Cultural Islamic Institute of Viale Jenner in Milan). Starting in 1990, Islamism reached the national level by forming an umbrella organization called the "Union of Islamic Communities and Organizations in Italy" (UCOII).[22]

This umbrella organization was not the product of a spontaneous grassroots movement of Italian Muslims. As was noted in a report by

the Department of Social Affairs, "In the case of UCOII...there is evident influence of the Muslim Brotherhood (MB), a transnational organization established in 1928 during the earliest period of fundamentalist
ideology."[23]

To this day, neither the components nor the central structure of the
UCOII have been clearly defined. In the past few years it has openly
sought to extend its influence over the creation of houses of prayer in
different Italian cities using the Islamist groups' developmental model,
but there are conflicting figures about how many of these prayer centers
truly adhere to the group's precepts. UCOII's president is Mohamed Nour
Dachan, who is of Syrian origin.

As for non-Islamist organizations, the International Association of
Information about Islam (AIII) was formed in Milan; it was principally
inspired by a group of Muslim intellectuals, most of them Italian. At the
outset, the AIII focused primarily on promoting initiatives to spread awareness of Islam in Italy and Europe; it rapidly distinguished itself by its prudent and measured promotion of cultural activities. The need to guarantee
effective representation in relations with the state, and the importance of
safeguarding the religious needs of Italian Muslims, led the AIII to adopt
new bylaws in 1997 as well as a new name: the Italian Islamic Religious
Community (Communità Religiosa Islamica or CO.RE.IS.). The president was an Italian, Abd al-Wahid Pallavicini, a Muslim born in 1951. In
2000, CO.RE.IS. obtained authorization for an official mosque in Milan,
but as of mid–2009 still has not broken ground on its construction.

Other organizations that have played a significant role are associated
with countries from which large numbers of immigrants have come to
Italy, such as Morocco. The Association of Moroccan Women, directed by
Suad Sbai, has become a point of reference for many female immigrants to
Italy; Sbai has attained a place on the Interior Ministry's Advisory Board
on Italian Islam.

The understanding between the state and the Islamic community
became more problematic at the beginning of the 1990s. The *intesa* paradigm, developed according to the Catholic model, was poorly adapted
to the rapidly evolving situation of Islam in Italy. The attempts to draft
new *intese* by organizations composed mainly of Muslim immigrants had
made things worse. Culturally and legally insufficiently prepared, they
blindly copied the agreement with the Jewish community, which led to
a draft document completely devoid of Islamic religious content, thus
lacking the most important element necessary for the conclusion of an
intesa.

During this period, the UCOII produced a draft agreement whose fundamentalist overtones were so apparent that it provoked a forceful reac-
tion from a wide spectrum of the legal community, secular and Catholic
alike. To choose just one of many disquieting examples, the draft of the
UCOII agreement demanded the right to "perform and dissolve religious
marriages without any civil effects whatsoever, in accordance with the

law and with Islamic tradition" (art. 12.3). Since it was not clearly stated that such marriages would be strictly monogamous, this was widely seen as potentially legitimizing polygamy. Moreover, the draft contained no reference to the practice of Islamic prayers, thus failing to meet the very purpose of the *intese,* facilitating public worship.

In 1998, CO.RE.IS. took a different approach in the draft it developed from the work of a mixed commission made up of professors from the University of Naples Federico II and the University of Rome-La Sapienza, and of experts from CO.RE.IS. itself.[24] The broad agreement on general principles facilitated a narrower, carefully delineated framework of understanding within the *intesa* itself, which focuses on the cultural and worship activities of Muslims residing in the Republic of Italy—with special reference to the practice of the five pillars that are the fundamentals of Islam.[25]

The final text of the document refers to the religious interests of the Islamic community right from the very beginning. Regarding the first pillar of Islam, "There is no God but God, and Muhammad is the prophet of God," the final text is distinguished from the draft by the addition of the explanation that " 'Allah' is the name of God in Arabic." This does not appear in the draft text, as the intention was to avoid giving the impression that Muslims believe in a different God. Yet even the draft does not shy away from mention of Muhammad, since his status as prophet is an essential part of Islamic faith, and should be respected, just as an article of faith of any other religion would be.

Concerning the second pillar, the document insists on the right to pray even in public places, such as schools and offices:

> The republic, recognizing that Islamic ritual prayer preceded by ablution takes place five times per day...commits itself to guaranteeing the dignified exercise in private of this ritual practice in public offices, also permitting it in private businesses and workplaces. It must be kept in mind that this prayer is preceded by the ritual washing of hands, arms, face, and feet. This ritual has the obvious function of purifying the body, and must be performed in accordance with Islamic rules and practices as well as with respect for public hygiene.[26]

The third pillar, the ritual giving of alms, was envisioned as a funding source for constructing mosques and for religious instruction, and would complement existing possibilities to give freely (and through their personal income tax) to needy families and Islamic organizations. In addition, it was also hoped that public television networks would broadcast Islamic religious programs on major holidays, just as they do for the holidays of other recognized religions.

The fourth and fifth pillars, daylight fasting during the month of Ramadan and the *Hajj* pilgrimage to Mecca—which each believer must do once in his or her lifetime if possible—fall on the same date each year in the Islamic year. However, since the Islamic year is based on a lunar calendar that is shorter than the solar calendar by about ten days, they occur at varying times in the Western calendar year. The draft indicated that the precise dates of Ramadan and the *Hajj* would be communicated in advance to the authorities, to schools, and to employers, so that they could carry on with their normal activities while facilitating religious practice for Muslims to the extent possible. Similar arrangements would be made for the two great feast days, the Breaking of the Fast and the Sacrifice of Abraham, which occur at the end of the month of Ramadan and the end of the *Hajj* period, respectively.

A number of other articles were intended to facilitate open lines of communication between the state and local Islamic communities. They covered such matters as the functioning of each place of worship and the expansion of local community involvement in the management of Islamic religious practices. The *intesa* was to be considered to represent the interests of all Italian Muslims, regardless of their countries of origin or organizational affiliations. For this reason, it provided for the possibility that any Islamic institution or representative body could be legally incorporated as a non-profit organization, so long as it was truly dedicated to "cultural and devotional ends" (art. 10). In practice, then, CO.RE.IS. was not suggesting that it assume monopoly control, but rather that it play the role of coordinator, providing concrete examples and viable legal models to serve the broader Islamic community efficiently. In a similar vein, Articles 11 and 12 outlined procedures for constructing and managing places of worship and nominating imams.

The personal statute at the basis of this *intesa* with Islam was drafted with careful consideration for Italian law, notably with regard to monogamy and spousal relations. The last article emphasized the need to prevent discrimination against public schools in which teachers chosen by the Islamic community would provide religious instruction in the way that previous *intese* permitted for other denominations.

To establish a proper relationship between the state and the Islamic community, two further knots needed to be untangled, both found in Article 8 of the constitution: official recognition of at least one Islamic religious entity, and the subsequent negotiation of an *intesa* that would show the full compatibility between Islam and Italian law.

Initially, it was thought that the Islamic community had to structure itself along the lines of a "national church," through an umbrella federation of large and small organizations. However, it soon became clear that it would be impossible to create such a structure in practice, due to the profound differences among the national Islamic organizations and the even deeper divide between groups affiliated with the UCOII and all the others.

Another possibility was that the *intesa* process would be spearheaded by one organization that would take the lead on behalf of a large number of organizations. To this end, in 1997, CO.RE.IS. took the initiative of applying for recognition as an entity for religious worship; three years later, in October of 2000, it obtained a favorable opinion from the General Directorate for Religious Organizations within the Ministry of Internal Affairs, an opinion endorsed by the Council of State in March 2002. However, after reaching the presidency of the Council of Ministers that same year, the request went no further.

Similarly, in April 2000, there was an attempt to create an alliance between the Islamic Cultural Center of Italy, which manages the Mosque of Rome, and the UCOII. The idea was to form a new Islamic Council of Italy that could successfully negotiate an *intesa* with the government. The president of this new body was to be Mario Scialoja, the former Italian Ambassador and the head of Rabita, the World Muslim League, with UCOII head Mohamed Nour Dachan as his vice president. However, the request was withdrawn following Scialoja's resignation in March 2001, reportedly due to irresolvable differences between the two organizations.

A new phase began on September 11, 2001, when the truly danger-ous nature of Islamist movements and their warlike totalitarian ideology emerged with absolute clarity. A certain segment of the Italian intellectual world, exemplified by journalist and writer Oriana Fallaci, took advan-tage of the wave of emotion triggered by the attack on the Twin Towers to launch a campaign aimed at expelling Muslims from Italian life altogether. By indiscriminately accusing *all* Muslims of "terrorism," these intellectu-als not only avoided a confrontation with Islamic civilization on a spir-itual level, but also on a cultural and an intellectual level. Islam, Fallaci and others argued, is a violent and decadent ideology that has polluted and tainted the purity and liberty of Western philosophy and the Christian faith. The equation "Muslim = terrorist" has indeed spread widely since then, with the inevitable consequence of de facto discrimination against Muslims. This ideology, which is ultimately grounded in racism, has been embraced by a number of leading political figures, as well as the Lega Nord (Northern League) party, which until that time had been far closer to Celtic neo-paganism than to Roman Christianity. The subsequent political activ-ities of the Lega Nord have had considerable impact on public life in Italy, especially in limiting freedom of religion and preventing any possibility of an *intesa* between the state and the Islamic community for years to come.

The crisis of September 2001 came at a rather complex moment in Italy's political life. In December of that year, at the Lega Nord's instiga-tion, the Chamber of Deputies approved a motion to reject the Region of Campania's project to build a mosque in Naples, which was part of a larger neighborhood-redevelopment program in Ponticelli. The committee pro-moting the plan was composed of this author, representatives of national and local Muslim organizations, and the consuls of Tunisia and Algeria. It would have been the first such project to be financed and controlled directly by the state, and would have served as a useful model for curtailing the influence of Islamists and their foreign financiers over places of worship.

Only on September 10, 2005 was the committee finally able to organize the Advisory Board for Islam in Italy under Interior Ministry auspices. The board comprises sixteen Muslim advisers, whose shared purpose—while not overtly expressed—is to prepare and negotiate the *intesa* as provided by the constitution. Four national organizations are represented: the UIO, the World Muslim League, CO.RE.IS., and the Association of Moroccan Women. Others, including imams from various places of worship, participated as individuals. Since this initial meeting, the board has reconvened irregularly and has focused more on the occasional scandal caused by the UCOII representative, one of the sixteen advisers, than on the problems of Italian Islam.

As the backlash of the post–9/11 period began to subside, the multicultural character of Italian society—and the spirit of knowledge and engagement that has animated its leading intellectuals—seemed to be reemerging. In 2008, then–Interior Minister Giuliano Amato sent a Ramadan message of goodwill to the Muslim community reaffirming the need for a "spirit of dialogue and cohesion." Moreover, he encouraged the creation of a federation of moderate Islamic organizations that would work to exclude the Islamists, thereby allowing the emergence of a single partner with which the government could conclude the *intesa* and overcome the stumbling block of the lack of a single authority within the Islamic community.

Since then there have been some positive developments, though we are still at the beginning of a long and difficult process. The lack of a single representative authority in Islam (analogous to the Vatican for Roman Catholicism) makes reaching *intesa* with Italian Islam particularly challenging. Moreover, those who claim to represent Islam in Italy are often connected to the international Islamist network, just as in other European countries. In pursuit of a truly Italian Islam, which fully respects Italian law and social norms, non-Islamist Muslims like myself in Italy have formed the Intellettuali Musulmani Italiani. (See below our founding declaration.) Our hope is to elicit a more active role for the Italian Muslim community in demonstrating Muslims' respect for other religious traditions and for the secular character and universal values of the state.

★ ★ ★

The following is an excerpt from the founding declaration of Intellettuali Musulmani Italiani, a group of Italian Muslims open to dialogue and cooperation with people from other cultural and religious backgrounds:

> The association Intellettuali Musulmani Italiani intends to present moderate and liberal Islamic thought on politics and culture with

the declared goal of stopping the spread of fundamentalist and radical ideologies, and promoting the integration of all members of the Islamic community and all other ethnic, religious, and cultural minorities. Until now, the moderate component of the Islamic world has not been well represented in the public sphere, yet it has much to contribute to the balanced development of our national life.

The association supports studies, legislation, and political actions that promote the security and integration of the various components of Italian society, with particular attention to religious and cultural minorities. The association intends to represent the cultural interests of all members of the Islamic community, both citizens of Italy and non-citizens, and of all those who recognize that the values of liberty, security, and personal development are to be found in all the great religious traditions.

Open to intellectuals of all extractions, both lay and religious, and to members of all nationalities, the association Intellettuali Musulmani Italiani plans to make its voice heard internationally. By promoting foreign policies that aid the expansion of cultural and economic exchanges with all the people of the Mediterranean Basin, it will help to ensure that Italy's role in the region will, over time, become more active and responsible.

Notes

1. Editor's note: Mezzogiorno (literally, "land of noon") is a term commonly used to distinguish the predominantly agrarian regions south of Rome from the more industrialized areas to the north.
2. Giosuè Musca, *Carlo Magno e Harûn al Rashid* (Charlemagne and Harun al-Rashid) (Bari: Dedalo libri, 1996).
3. Michele Amari, *Storia dei Musulmani di Sicilia* (History of the Muslims of Sicily) (Catania: Romeo Prampolini Editore, 1935), 1:392.
4. For more on Ibn Hawqal (author of the *Surat al-Ard*) and his description of Palermo, see F. Gabrieli, *L'Islam nella Storia* (Islam in History) (Bari: Dedalo, 1966).
5. Bernard Lewis, *Il linguaggio politico dell'Islam* (The Political Language of Islam), trans. Biancamaria Scarcia Amoretti (Rome: Laterza, 1991), p. 122. This concept, which is tied to the principle of necessity, *darûradarura*, which is invoked when Muslims find themselves in special circumstances, assumed a great deal of importance after 1258, the year of the fall of Baghdad and the end of the Abbasid Caliphate. This marked the end of central authority in the Islamic world, and the beginning of a period in which increasing portions of the *dar al-Islam* came under the control of non-Muslim rulers.
6. Amari, *Storia dei Musulmani di Sicilia*, 2:557.
7. Francesco Gabrieli, "Ibn Hawqal e gli arabi di Sicilia" (Ibn Hawqal and the Arabs of Sicily), *Rivista degli Studi Orientali* 36, no. 8 (1961): 245–253.
8. Amari, *Storia dei Musulmani di Sicilia*, 2:557.
9. Umberto Rizzitano, *Storia e cultura della Sicilia saracena* (History and Culture of Saracen Sicily) (Palermo: S. Flaccovio, 1975), p. 152. The use of *al-madini* for the people of Palermo is truly exceptional and unique. Many scholars, such as Michele Amari, had argued that other examples existed before the famous Orientalist Carlo Alfonso Nallino settled the issue conclusively.
10. Pietro Egidi, *La colonia saracena di Lucera e la sua distruzione* (The Saracen Community of Lucera and Its Destruction) (Pierro, Naples, 1911), p. 139.

11. Giorgio Levi della Vida, *La corrispondenza di Berta di Toscana col califfo Muktafi* (The Correspondence of Bertha of Tuscany with the Caliph Muktafi) (Naples: Edizioni scientifiche italiane, 1954), p. 27.

12. Editor's translation: "Not a single day would pass without that tyrant killing at least five hundred men and then, like a rabid dog, sitting and eating on top of their corpses." G. H. Pertz (ed.), *Monumenta Germaniae Historica, Scriptores, Cronica Sancti Benedicti cassinensis* (Monuments of German History, Writings of the Chronicle of Saint Benedict of Monte Cassino) (Hannover: Gallica, 1839, 1925), p. 476.

13. Amari, *Storia dei Musulmani di Sicilia*, 3:542.

14. Ernst Kantorowicz, *Federico II imperatore* (Emperor Frederick II) (Milan: Garzanti, 2000), p. 180.

15. Daniel Norman, *Gli Arabi e l'Europa nel Medio Evo* (The Arabs and Medieval Europe) (Bologna: Il Mulino, 1982), p. 237.

16. Ibid., p. 234.

17. Dom Jean Leclercq, *Pietro il Venerabile* (Peter the Venerable) (Milan: Saint-Wandrille, 1946), p. 184.

18. Mario Tedeschi, *Manuale di diritto ecclesiastico* (Handbook of Church Law) (Turin: Giappichelli, 2007), p. 15.

19. Law No. 1159, June 24, 1929, and Royal Decree No. 289, February 28, 1930.

20. Priests of the Missionaries of Africa, a Catholic missionary society founded in 1868 to proselytize the Arabs of the Maghreb and Sahara Desert, are known as "White Fathers" due to their traditional white cassocks (which resemble traditional Arab dress). The society founded the Pontifical Institute for Arab and Islamic Studies (or PISAI in its Italian acronym) in 1926, originally in order to train future missionaries for the region.

21. DPR (Decree of the President of the Republic) No. 212, December 21, 1974.

22. On the birth of fundamentalism, see the author's *Islam, l'altra civiltà* (Islam, the Other Civilization) (Milan: Mondadori, 2003), pp. 184–192.

23. Khaled Fouad Allam, *L'Islam contemporaneo in Europa e in Italia* (Contemporary Islam in Europe and in Italy), part of the Second Report on Immigration in Italy, Commission for the Political Integration of Immigrants, Department of Social Affairs (Rome: December 13, 2000), p. 346.

24. The author served as coordinator of the commission's work.

25. CO.RE.IS., *Intesa tra la Repubblica Italiana e la Comunità Islamica in Italia* (*Intesa* [see earlier] between the Italian Republic and the Islamic Community in Italy), p. 60.

26. Ibid.

CHAPTER FOUR

Democracy and Islam in the Maghreb and Implications for Europe

FOUAD LAROUI

Democracy's reputation has taken a severe beating in recent years in many areas around the globe—especially in Arab and Islamic quarters. Although in *theory* virtually every country on earth has in the past century proudly trumpeted support for the principle of popular sovereignty, in *practice,* there has been no shortage of governmental and non-governmental opposition to democracy. Whether in Eastern Europe, Africa, or elsewhere, venal dictatorships and centralized one-party states have all referred to themselves as the "Democratic Republic of" their respective countries. Even Enver Hoxha—the Albanian communist who was so hard-line that he returned from visiting Kim Il Sung's North Korea convinced that the country was "dangerously implanted" with bourgeois revisionism—organized regular elections in which the people could, in theory, vote him out of power. To take one election during the last years of his reign as an example, some seven people did vote against him—but they were outweighed by the 2 million who approved of the "Paradise on Earth" that the dictator was establishing. To the north of this Eden lay the German "Democratic" Republic, for whose regime the presence of the sacred word in the state's name was sufficient proof of its virtue (certainly, compared to the mere German "Federal" Republic to the West). As the saying goes, hypocrisy is simply the homage that vice pays to virtue!

Now, however, it is evident that times have changed. On any visit to Algeria or Saudi Arabia, one can meet plenty of people who squarely reject democracy, whether in practice or simply in name. In fact, there is no need to travel at all: turn on the television and watch Al-Jazeera, or any of the 250 satellite channels available to the Arab world, and before long you will see these kinds of statements. I must add, however, that I believe Al-Jazeera is a quality network that is having success at promoting free speech in the Arab world. The problem is not with Al-Jazeera, but with some of the self-proclaimed "true Muslims" who regularly appear on its programs in order to air their points of view—thus taking advantage of the same freedom of speech that they themselves would abolish immediately were they to seize power!

The Strange Case of the Front Islamique de Salut (FIS)—and What It Teaches Us

In Algeria, attitudes toward democracy are clouded by the nearly schizophrenic relationship many people still have with France. Seemingly without any awareness of the irony, they proclaim their hatred of France with so much passion that it seems like unrequited love, and they celebrate independence from France with not one but two national holidays; yet every year more and more appear at the French Embassy to apply for visas. Algerians understand "democracy" only as "something that came ashore with French troops when they invaded in 1830." There is no use explaining that nineteenth-century French democracy was not exactly a paragon, even by the standards of its day; nor that even the relatively limited rights enjoyed by French citizens in 1830 were of value—since, after all, they were never extended to the indigenous population of Algeria.

For the two-thirds of the Algerian population that voted for the Front Islamique de Salut (FIS, or "Islamic Salvation Front") in 1991–1992, democracy was indeed something foreign—and something French. The FIS had clearly identified the enemy as the Hizb Fransa, the Party of France. Though there was no such party on the ballot, FIS claimed to know exactly who its members were. First, all those in power were members of Hizb Fransa, as were all those who spoke French, read French-language newspapers, or watched French channels. Of course, many such "members" were outraged, as they had fought against France in the War of Independence in 1954–1962 and lost family and friends. Their indignation at these accusations of treason was ignored, as it was when they protested the unsubtle religious implications of the Front's rhetoric. In the Qur'an, the faithful are called *"Hizb Allah,"* the party of God; thus, both the FIS and its opponents understood the charge of belonging to another party as a charge of apostasy, of being an enemy of God.

Against this background the FIS was able to exploit the government's declared commitment to democracy, arguing that democracy was something only the Hizb Fransa would be concerned about. The Berlin Wall had fallen, and the Cold War was over. Throughout the globe, a virtual spring cleaning was taking place as regimes began dismantling the hollow facades that had served them during the previous half-century in order to replace them with more substantial democratic structures. There were no more excuses; the right-wing authoritarian regimes no longer had a communist bogeyman, and the Marxist-Leninist claim that a small "advance guard" *was* "the people" no longer had any authority.

Democracy, then, was the order of the day; although the term *dimoqrat-tiya* was borrowed directly by the Arabic-speaking world, it has retained a distinctively alien flavor in Arabic. All "true" Arabic words—that is, linguistically Semitic—derive from a three-consonant root and are immediately recognizable. But how many consonants are there in this strange word *dimoqrattiya*? Four, five, no, six! Its *sound* is unmistakably foreign. To Western readers, this may seem to be an arcane, exotic, or contrived point: since when does the number of consonants in a word explain such critical events as a revolution, a campaign of repression, or a civil war—all of which occurred in Algeria?

Yet it is undeniable that discussion about "the word" took place at the beginning of the series of events that led to civil war. Since *dimoqratiyya* does not sound Arabic, it was easy for the FIS to label it a foreign import and to charge those who promoted it with being foreign sympathizers and traitors, conveniently bundled together into the concept Hizb Fransa.

To further understand how this was possible, recall that for devout Muslims—including even those of the second and third generations in Europe—there is nothing worse than *bid'a*, or "innovation." By the time they reach adulthood, they will have heard the phrase "all innovations lead to hell" (*kull bid'a fi-nnar*) a thousand times; the association becomes automatic in their minds. It is true that by "devout" I mean "Orthodox" here; unfortunately there has been little thinking outside this orthodoxy for at least eight centuries—ever since Ibn Rushd, the last true Muslim philosopher, died heartbroken and bitter in the twelfth century. In that period, the Abbasid Caliphate established the rule that "the doors of *ijtihad*"—independent interpretation of scripture—"are closed." The little refrain we learned as children—that all innovations lead to hell—dates from this period. One decision to close a door, and no one would be allowed to innovate! Knowing this, it should no longer be a mystery why the once-glorious Islamic civilization wilted and then virtually died; the explanation is as loud and clear as the thudding sound of a giant door slamming shut.

This psychological background made it simple for the FIS to give democracy a bad name. They shouted at rally after rally, "Don't you see, it's not even an Arabic word! It is a *bid'a*! And what happens to a *bid'a*?" That was enough; the mobs knew the answer all too well.

However, the FIS made a huge mistake: it was too candid about its intentions. Since it hated democracy, item number one on its agenda was to abolish it after seizing power. The fact that it was using elections—that is, democracy—as a means of taking control did not in any way trouble the FIS. If turkeys want to vote for Christmas, as it were, why would we stop them? On a more sinister note, even Hitler was duly elected chancellor according to strict democratic procedures, following a reasonably free and fair election.

The overconfident leaders of the FIS, by contrast, did not even attempt to be seen as playing by the rules; they thus overlooked the fact that the army, still enjoying the legitimacy it earned during the bloody eight-year war against France, had no intention of turning over power to a party keen on destroying the system the army had created. It was not a stretch for the army to imagine a scenario in which the FIS would decide to dismantle it; every single one of the generals spoke French and, in fact, had begun their careers in French uniforms. Indeed, what institution better represented the hated Hizb Fransa than the army? A shiver went down the collective spines of the generals, who canceled the expected second round of the elections—which the FIS was predicted to win easily—and declared a state of emergency. Thus came to an end the only genuine attempt at democracy in Algeria.

Morocco: Between the Justice and Development Party (PJD) and the *Qawma*

Next door, in my own country of Morocco, Islamists have been steadily gaining political strength, becoming one of the key stars in Morocco's political constellation. The lessons of the FIS debacle in Algeria have not been lost on them: one could not imagine gentler and more modest Islamists than those of the Moroccan species—at least for the moment. They go by the name of "*Hizb al-adala wa at-tanmiyya*," the Justice and Development Party (PJD in its French acronym). This name offends no one—after all, who opposes justice or development? If you ask party members why their group shares a name with the party now governing Turkey—albeit under the watchful eyes of the military—they point out that they chose the name first, and it was the Turks who copied it later. If you ask them whether democracy is a *bid'a*, an innovation, they quickly reject the idea: democracy is, in fact, an Islamic value, they say. After all, does the Prophet not recommend that Muslims establish a *shura* council in order to govern a city? *Shura* means something like "consultation." One must "consult" the people on every question—how democratic, after all! And when pressed to explain how they will strike a balance between the tenets of Islam and the principles of democracy—such as freedom of speech, freedom of conscience, absence of religious discrimination—they repeat ad nauseam that they do not see any contradiction between the two. Even when confronted with unavoidable contradictions, notably regarding equal rights for women or homosexuals, they repeat their vague credo that "there are no problems."

Not everyone is convinced. Many people, in fact, think that the PJD is practicing what is known as *taqiyyah*, which could be loosely translated as "sacred hypocrisy" and means that it is permitted to lie about one's faith or intentions when under duress, or when circumstances require it. Ironically, *taqiyyah* has come to be associated with Shia Islam and is used routinely by Sunnis as an insult (Hypocrites! Liars!). Morocco is entirely Sunni, so it is quite puzzling that the PJD is practicing *taqiyyah*—if that is indeed what is going on. (It would be interesting—but beyond the scope of this chapter—to explore how much *taqiyyah* is practiced in Europe by those well-dressed and soft-spoken Islamists, pampered by the governments of countries such as Britain and the Netherlands as "good Muslim" partners, in contrast to the "bad guys" of al-Qaeda.)

In Morocco, we have yet another example of an uneasy, if not strained, relationship between Islam and democracy. Certainly, in light of the disastrous experience with the FIS, the more cautious PJD has taken to heart the idea that "if you can't beat 'em, join 'em." And thus it claims to be as democratic as any other party, if not more so. Its evidence for democracy, the divine concept of *shura*, carries more weight than something devised by "sinners" named Rousseau or Mill. Should we believe the PJD? As a French politician once said, "Promises only bind those who listen to them...."

In its defense, the PJD *can* at least point to a group nastier than itself: the illegal (but tolerated) Islamist group called "al-Adl wa al-ihsan," meaning roughly "Justice and Good Deeds." The name itself has no significance. Al-Adl, as it is commonly known, is, in fact, a cult led by a Sheikh Yassine—no relation to the Hamas leader, also Sheikh Yassin, killed by Israel in 2004. (Actually, many followers of al-Adl used to believe that the two sheikhs were the same man. This truly amazing Moroccan ex-schoolteacher could be in two places at the same time! His ubiquity was proof of his quasi-prophetic status; the sect's leaders never denied such rumors, which were certainly lapped up by the rank-and-file. I point to this and other absurdities to indicate just what kind of struggle democrats face in a country such as Morocco.)

Al-Adl has an unambiguously clear opinion of democracy: it hates it. (This is not an exaggeration or a hostile characterization; in fact, it *has to* hate it, because democracy is a *bid'a* and God has ordered the group to hate such things.) And so we return to a similar situation. Democracy is a despicable innovation propounded by the Frenchified elite of Morocco—so explains Nadia Yassine, the fanatical daughter of the sheikh, in the perfect French she acquired in the French schools to which her father sent her long before he discovered his divine mission on earth. In contrast to the FIS of the past, al-Adl takes this belief to its logical consequences; since it does not believe in democracy, it will not participate in elections. Why would people want to join a party if it does not plan to seek power? The answer is that it *does* plan to attain power, just not through elections. It instead plans a *qawma*; that is, an insurrection, which is supposed to take place soon. Since the PJD also plans to accede to power soon, albeit by democratic means, it is understandably uneasy about al-Adl's prophesies. Yet such unease is also beneficial to the PJD, which gains thereby an aura of respectability. Its unspoken question to Moroccans seems to be as follows: since Islamists are going to govern you in the years to come, would you not prefer the PJD, which plays the democratic game, to that madman Yassine and his *qawma*? I must say that many Moroccans seem to answer with a resounding "yes," whereas many others frown at having to choose, as they say, between cholera and the plague.

Implications for Europe

Almost all of the 250 satellite TV channels in the Arab world can be watched in Europe, which causes an interesting dilemma: should we, in the name of democracy, allow anti-democratic voices to be heard? This is especially relevant in the country where I live today; integration in the Netherlands has become harder now that you can easily immerse yourself, twenty-four hours a day, in an entirely non-Dutch world, where Arabic is the language, and a bearded, anti-democratic TV imam is the authority. Should that imam be tolerated? This is a well-known problem: more than two centuries ago, Saint-Just and Camille Desmoulins were already shouting, "Pas de démocratie pour les ennemis de la démocratie!" (No democracy for the enemies of democracy!). Regarding the FIS, the PJD, or al-Adl, all we can do at the moment is pay close attention to the situation. After all, the *qawma* might not take place in the near future; in the 2007 election, for example, secular political parties won a majority.

But here in Europe, where there are millions of hearts and minds to be won, this is an existential question. The second and third generations of Muslims are Europeans, and they are here to stay. No discussion about the need to protect and promote democracy can ignore the fact that these men and women have been exposed to the ideas outlined earlier. In this light, a careful distinction must be made between two possible attitudes regarding Islam and democracy.

The first concerns the question of *bid'a*. It is pointless to engage in a debate on whether democracy is an innovation. Instead, we must reject the whole notion of denouncing "innovations" to begin with. This notion has nothing to do with Islam as a faith and is certainly not one of the religion's tenets. Even the most orthodox Muslims have to concede that there is only one equivalent of the Roman Catholic "mortal sin" in their religion, which is polytheism (*as-shirk*); therefore, innovation cannot be a mortal sin. They must further concede that there are exactly five canonical obligations, no more and no less: (1) the *shahada* (profession of faith), (2) daily prayer, (3) fasting during the month of Ramadan, (4) the giving of alms (*zakat*), and (5) the pilgrimage (*Hajj*) to Mecca, for those who can afford it. Therefore, rejecting every *bid'a* cannot be a canonical obligation. One can be a good Muslim and embrace any innovation that does not contradict the five canonical obligations. Simply stating that democracy is a *bid'a* does not imply anything about its value or pertinence.

Much less clear is the second attitude, that the *umma* (Islamic community) is supreme over all other groups, distinctions, or differences in opinion. For the most extreme proponents of this idea, the *umma* is still waiting for its caliph, or supreme ruler. Since the catastrophic day in 1924 when Turkey's founder Ataturk abolished the caliphate and sent the last caliph into exile in Switzerland, some Muslims have hoped for a kind of restoration. In Morocco, I was surprised to encounter recently some individuals who refuse to pray in the mosque on Fridays because it "makes no sense" to them without a caliph in whose name to say the collective prayer. I refrained from asking them whether the new caliph should be a Turk, an Arab, or an Iranian: the resulting discussion would have been never-ending.

I also did not share with them the conclusive answer given by the Muslim judge Ali Abderraziq, who showed in 1925 that it did not make much sense to have a caliph. One can be a perfectly good Muslim without having a person who is the incarnation of a kind of spiritual power. And a caliph made even less sense for secular power according to the esteemed judge. Shortly after meeting those unusual individuals, I saw Abderraziq's booklet, *Islam wa usul al-hukm* (Islam and the Origin of Government), on sale in Marrakesh for a very reasonable price. This shows that there is no shortage of serious reflections on Muslim culture and religion, whether from the early twentieth century or afterward. What is missing is a serious effort to promote and spread these works. There are plenty of petrodollars set aside to promote the views of those who mechanically repeat orthodox teachings. Perhaps some European institution should devote funds to translating and distributing books such as Abderraziq's? Maybe it should be given free of charge to every young person, in the same way that extremist propaganda is distributed gratis?

However, what about those young Muslims who are not waiting for the new caliphate but who are, nonetheless, very much seduced by the idea of the *umma*? The problem is simple to grasp when stated clearly: the notion of a community that transcends all geographic boundaries, all social classes, all personal differences, and the like is at odds with the idea of democracy. If a Muslim in the Netherlands feels that he is closer to a Pakistani 5,000 miles away than to a next-door neighbor who happens to be Christian, agnostic, or Jewish, then something is wrong. Politics most of all refers to the running of the *polis*, the "city" where people live—not some imaginary polity made of people separated by thousands of miles. The geographic position of the Netherlands means that it is constantly threatened by flooding, whether from the North Sea or from its rivers. Running the country means ensuring that all inhabitants care enough to cooperate in addressing such challenges. The degree of "cohesion" of a European society (or of any other) is largely determined by such practical issues. Dutch Moroccans or Dutch Turks, many of whom have dual citizenship, cannot delete the part of themselves that makes them responsible for fighting the clear and present danger of, say, flood. They can feel nostalgic toward the country where their parents were born, they can be devout Muslims if they want to, but they must fight against the water with their fellow Dutchmen.

If you do not think you are in the same boat, then something is wrong. This is exactly what is happening with some second- and third-generation Muslims in Europe. It is a worrying development and is far from being strictly theoretical. Think of the two Dutch teenagers of Moroccan origin who died in Pakistan while trying to find a way to join the Taliban. Think of the young Frenchmen who died in Chechnya fighting the Russians. Think of the young British men who blew themselves up in the London tube, killing other Britons with whom they felt no solidarity or sympathy since they were not part of the *umma*.

In the Netherlands, this does not appear to be seen as a problem. The Dutch are used to the *verzuiling* system of denominational "pillariza-tion," which divided much of social life along religious lines. There is one good reason why it should not work now as it did in the past: the understanding of the *umma* now propagated in Europe, even by those whom the foreign minister is glad to host in The Hague over coffee, is an *aggressive* one. They say that the *umma* is involved in a fight to the finish. Either they will destroy us, or we will destroy them. The clash of civilizations was not invented by Samuel Huntington or Bernard Lewis (who did use the phrase first), but by the founders of the Muslim Brotherhood many decades before. As long as such ideas are allowed to prevail, pillarization will not bring pacification. On the contrary, forcing people into a Muslim pillar will in some cases breed resent-ment. This is what a young man could say: "I was born in this country, I was raised in it, I have a Dutch passport, and yet you see me primarily as a Muslim? Okay, I will be that, and even worse: I will be an alien. I will have nothing to do with your society." So much for democracy. Those who think that this is fictional should read what Mohammed Bouyeri—the young man who killed Theo van Gogh—and people like him have said or written.

I remember how shocked and angry I was when, some years ago, I received a letter from the head of the Amsterdam Police Department wishing me a happy Ramadan. The intention was good, but then again *bid'a* is not the only thing that leads to hell. What shocked me most was that the police seemed to have a list of all "Muslims" living in Amsterdam. That raised an interesting parallel: did the police have a list of all Jews liv-ing in Amsterdam during the war? Of course, they did—something the Germans found very useful. When I inquired, I was told that such a list did not exist—the police had, instead, used the "highly sophisticated" method of sending the cards to those with "Muslim-sounding" names. Thus, a fashion boutique, owned by a very blue-eyed Dutch person, received a card congratulating the store on the occasion of Ramadan. The boutique's name: Baobab. Definitely "Muslim." This is not merely all in good fun, as it proves my point: people do not seem to realize how dan-gerous it is for a democracy to allow groups to form that then begin to estrange themselves from the nation.

What to Do?

What can be done? It seems to me that we must be unrelenting in explaining, again and again, that the whole progress of civilization was based on the emancipation of the *individual*. And we must be equally unrelenting in defending the rights of the individual, specifically those of individual women and individual members of all minority groups. As for groups, we should treat them along the lines of the famous speech of Clermont-Tonnerre to the French Constituent Assembly in December 1789, when he stated what emancipation really meant: "We must refuse to give anything to the Jews as a nation, and to give everything to the Jews as individuals!"

What would the proponents of the FIS have to say in response? No doubt they would criticize this author as another Frenchified person trying to introduce an alien concept into our glorious Islam. This could impress some people who do not know their history, but those who are familiar with the past know that it is not so alien. One could argue that the whole movement of emancipation of the individual began on Islamic soil; first in the Baghdad of the Abbasids, and later in Muslim Andalusia. To state but one fact with a question, how many Muslims in Morocco have ever heard of the *Ikhwan as-safa* (the Brothers of Purity), the first encyclopedists, who tried to record on paper the entirety of secular knowledge of their time? Answer: possibly zero. I asked the question repeatedly during a recent trip to Morocco. Nobody seemed to know anything about the Ikhwan as-safa. Does it matter? It does. The French Encyclopedists, led by Diderot and d'Alembert, represented an essential moment in the emancipation of the individual, which eventually led to democracy in its present form. Would democracy and the primacy of the individual not be more acceptable to Muslims—more natural—if they knew that these are not alien innovations? Here again, we see how destructive ignorance can be.

Yet ignorance comes from both sides, alas. In all my years of studying in various French schools, lycées, and universities, I never heard any mention of the Ikhwan as-safa. I never heard anything said about Ibn Rushd (Averroës) or al-Farabi, either, though I did learn a lot about Voltaire and the French Encyclopedists, a learning that instilled in me a profound attachment to freedom and democracy. But for the new generations in Europe, subjected to the propaganda of anti-democratic fundamentalists at home and in the mosque, Voltaire may not be enough. We must tell them—and show them—that the desire for freedom and democracy ran in the veins of their own ancestors.

PART II

Reaffirming and Protecting Islam

CHAPTER FIVE

Rebel with a Cause: A Personal Journey from Sufism to Islamism and Beyond

COSH OMAR

Turks do not use the word *imam* very often. Instead, they use *hoca*, which means teacher. My father was a *hoca*, albeit a part-time one. Trained as an electronic engineer and a computer programmer, at a young age he became a *murid*, a person who is formally "committed" to a Sufi teacher. Sufism is an Islamic spiritual movement that emerged as a backlash against the increasingly institutionalized nature of Islam in the eighth and ninth centuries. Sufis themselves trace their teachings back to the Prophet, although many Muslims are reluctant to consider Sufism as part of Islam. Seeing Sufi practices as "deviations" from the faith, many even brand Sufis as heretics. Nonetheless, Sufism can be found on several continents, and is practiced through various orders, or *tariqat*. My father belonged to the Naqshbandi Sufi order, and his teacher was the leader of this order, Shaykh Nazim.

A fellow Turkish Cypriot, Shaykh Nazim began to guide my father spiritually while he was a student at technical college in Lefke. They had much in common. Shaykh Nazim himself had excelled in his studies in chemical engineering at the University of Istanbul. Muslims believe that Islam is a religion that conforms with scientific facts, and so my father and his Shaykh had a lot of shared interests.

When my parents immigrated to London in the late 1960s, both my mother and my father began performing the Sufi practice of *mevlit* for the Turkish Cypriot community. From that time on, my father was known as "the Hoca" to his people. First appearing in the twelfth century as a means of celebrating the Prophet Muhammad's birthday, the *mevlit* had changed over the ensuing years and, among London's Turkish Cypriots, was practiced most often for a death or for the birth of a daughter. Except for my parents, the Turkish Cypriots were not a community that adhered to all the dictates of Islam. The birth of a son was always celebrated (when the male child was old enough) by a circumcision party, and this was always an alcohol-soaked affair. At the *mevlits*, however, the entire community would be emotionally moved by Islam, even if only for an hour or two.

Sitting by my parents in some strangers' home almost every evening of my childhood, while my parents sang the celebrated text of Suleyman Celebi from the fourteenth and fifteenth centuries, I would always see a familiar face among all the photographs—that of a person who had died almost half a century before I was born. This face, which could be seen in our home and in all other Turkish Cypriot homes, was as well known to me as my own father's. To some extent this person *was* my father: Ataturk, which literally means "father of all Turks." My father taught Islamic studies in part-time Turkish schools for children, and my mother, for the first ten years of my life, headed the Turkish Women's Philanthropic Association. Everywhere you looked, there was always Ataturk, looking down at you, an attractive and glamorous figure reminding you who and what you were: a Turk. It would be years before I would discover just how wide the rift actually was between the nationalist ideology of the man in the image and the Sufi Islam of my parents.

For a time, I was content with observing my community's nationalism and my parents' religious beliefs, going with my father to mostly empty Turkish mosques and observing my friends' families drinking alcohol and eating pork. But as time went by, my ability to identify with my community diminished. When I visited another Turkish Cypriot home, I never experienced the same atmosphere as in ours. Where were all the books on spirituality? Where were the prayer mats? Why did they never recite the Holy Qur'an? Ataturk was always staring down at me, just as he did in my own home, but everything else was so different.

On top of all this, the heads of the homes I would visit were most often in the second-hand goods or food-service industries. My parents, by contrast, were both highly educated; my father was an electronic engineer and had a computer business. My older brother attended private school, and spent most of his time locked in his room oil-painting, or reading endless books that led him to study political philosophy. Spirituality? Recital of the Holy Qur'an? Electronic engineering? Oil painting and political philosophy? The best thrill I got at Turkish Cypriot homes, when feeling a little rebellious, was a pork sausage roll.

By this I do not mean that my family was superior to the other Turkish Cypriots, just different. Because of who my mother and father were, we were invited to endless functions. Unless you have been to a Cypriot wedding, you cannot possibly know what a collective frenzy it can be; but because my father was "the Hoca," no alcohol could be placed on our table. I so desperately wanted to be like the rest of my community, to belong, but the stronger my desire to be like the others, the more evident was the disparity. Of course, there was always the other half of London's Cypriot community, the Greek Cypriots.

★   ★   ★

Until the age of ten I lived in Tottenham, north London. To the south of where we lived was a large Greek Cypriot and Afro-Caribbean community, but in our block and the surrounding areas we and one other Turkish Cypriot family were the only foreigners.

All my friends were English. Of course, as they kept pointing out, since I was born in England, I, too, was English, but deep down I knew I was different. The moment I walked into their homes I knew this, from the way things looked, the way things smelled, and the way things tasted. No matter how often my English friends' parents told me that I was English, my parents told me that I was Turkish, as did the glare of Ataturk. But others were also letting me know I was different, "not English." The 1970s were the heyday of the National Front, an extreme-right political party that won support mostly from the disillusioned working class, which felt aggrieved at the stream of immigrant competition in the labor market. The National Front always made its presence felt at football matches. Every other week, when our local team played at home, I would see English flags parade past our front door to the sound of racist chanting.

When I was ten, my family moved to Palmers Green. There were Cypriots everywhere, including Greek Cypriots. These people that I had been watching from afar, at weddings and in the streets, were all around me. It was a real shock at first, but it was fantastic. As I heard my parents alternating between speaking Greek and Turkish in the street, it was as if the black-and-white photographs from their early years in Cyprus had come to life.

Then came my first day at my new school. Even that was different; a large, imposing Edwardian building, unlike the small modern school I had attended before. My new teacher asked all students with an empty seat beside them to put up their hands. As I scanned the classroom, I suddenly fixated on a certain boy in the front of the class, his hand up, and I prayed to God I would not have to sit next to him. With a mature, learned smile, my new teacher looked hard into my eyes before making her decision.

The walk to my new seat seemed like the longest walk of my young life. That boy scared me and, as I approached, his eyes never left my alarmed face. Once I sat down, he turned and introduced himself as Chris. Immediately, I felt guilty. His whole demeanor told me that it was all right to be frightened, and that this was not the first time that someone had been startled by his appearance. His face and hands were deeply scarred from a house fire he had been in as an infant. He looked like he was wearing a mask. His fingers were mostly distorted and warped. Yet that day was the beginning of a very long friendship; Chris was my best friend for the rest of our time at that elementary school, and remained so all the way through high school.

Chris was a Greek Cypriot, but my family embraced him as one of their own, and his family took me into their hearts without prejudice. We were always in one another's homes; we did homework together, played together, and attended the respective family's functions together. In fact, I would say that most of my adolescent experiences of family love took place in Chris's home. At Greek Easter his mother would send a plate full of freshly baked *flaounes* to our home, and at Eid my mother would always return the plate—this time full of *baklava* or some other Turkish treats.

Looking back now, I realize how lucky I was to spend my developing years in both a Greek and a Turkish Cypriot home. I absorbed the culture of both communities, and I also saw, with time, how much they had influenced one another. With their long, shared history they had so much in common culturally, and with the hunger of an inquisitive youth, I digested all of it.

★   ★   ★

Unfortunately, the love I experienced in Chris's home failed to prepare me for what was to come. This was the early 1980s, and the Cyprus conflict of 1974 (together with all that had given rise to it) was still very present for Cypriots. Although Greek and Turkish Cypriots inhabited the same areas of London and, indeed, socialized in the same way as before the troubles began, tensions nevertheless flared any time politics or nationalism raised their ugly heads. I had several experiences that were extremely hurtful to me and, of course, in a culture where strutting one's machismo was commonplace, blows were sometimes exchanged. Each time I went home saddened and confused. The kids I had just grappled with were of the same habits and heritage as Chris and his family, and, in fact, of the same habits and heritage as my own. Sitting at home, licking my wounds, I always felt so alone.

Or was I? There was always Ataturk, staring down at me, telling me who and what I was. But there was another group of immigrants I felt in tune with, the earliest migrants of them all, not just here, but anywhere; the original "outsiders" who were forced to move and set up homes in foreign lands long before any of the rest of us had emigrated anywhere: the Jewish community.

Although my older brother had a number of Jewish friends from his private school, my own experience with the Jewish community was somewhat limited. I do not remember any Jewish boy or girl at my comprehensive school (ordinary state school). Once a flourishing and significant group in Tottenham, the Jewish community had all but moved on to other areas by the time my family bought a home in this north London district.

In the late 1970s, the most significant passing of the cultural baton took place. The Shacklewell Lane Synagogue in the Dalston area of London's East End, which had served the Jewish community since it was built in the mid-nineteenth century, was bought by the Turkish Cypriots and converted into a mosque. Most days my father, a member of the committee, brought his young son along to help with the work of transforming the synagogue interior into a mosque interior. The exterior was already very much in the Andalusian style, which to me always poignantly hearkened back to the days when Jew and Muslim were so successful together in that part of the world. I remember clearly helping to rip out the old wooden pews to make a flat surface for the prayer carpet. I also remember removing the ark. But way above the reader's platform was a large, stained-glass ceiling dome with the Star of David, which to this day remains. And through the years, when my father would drag me reluctantly to that Shacklewell Lane Mosque, mostly for Friday or Eid prayers, I would often look up at that Star of David, knowing it was not of my faith, yet feeling that it symbolized a community with which I strongly identified. How did I have this close rapport with these people with whom I had so little personal contact?

From the time I was very young, all I wanted to do was watch television. I had no siblings or cousins close to my own age, so television became my constant companion. I was deeply obsessed with films, musicals, sitcoms, and all forms of entertainment, and completely captivated with the act of staging a performance. Within the world of entertainment, I recognized myself only in Jewish characters. They were people who were not part of the indigenous Christian population; they looked and sounded like me. I loved them all, from the Marx Brothers to Barbra Streisand. When I watched Tevye in *Fiddler on the Roof* sing "The Sabbath Song," with his family gathered around the table, I screamed for whoever could hear to gather around my television. He looked and sounded just like my father the imam, beard, skullcap, and all. I had never seen any other Turkish Cypriot father who looked and sounded like that, and certainly no English characters, on or off the TV. Yet there was Tevye the milkman, trying to maintain his religious traditions for his family, while the world around him was changing rapidly. I was thunderstruck when I heard Tevye declare, "And because of our traditions, every one of us knows who he is and what God expects him to do." My father the imam, the Hoca, through and through!

★   ★   ★

When I reached the age of eight, my parents decided that I needed a private tutor. The contrast between their sensible elder son and my intensely energetic self led them to conclude I was destined to be a "nobody." After a few embarrassing occasions when they were summoned to my school and informed that my lack of concentration was disruptive, my parents placed my future into the hands of Ms. King.

This was the mid-1970s, and my newly appointed private tutor was a very attractive young English "hippy chick." Every Monday and Thursday evening my mother would take me to Ms. King's home in Crouch End, an area that had many renowned residents from the arts. I lived for those lessons, and my mother could never drive fast enough. My heart would start racing when I saw the red brick clock tower that told me we were almost at her home. Standing on the porch, I could smell the burning sandalwood joss sticks from inside, teasing me until, after what seemed like an eternity, she opened the front door. When she closed the door, we were in a world where it was only the two of us. Yet as captivating as was the experience of being alone with Ms. King, it was what I could see from her window that slowly grabbed my attention.

Opposite Ms. King's home was the Mountview Theatre School. Before long, my tutor told my mother of my lack of attentiveness, but I could not help it. Twice a week, through illuminated windows, I would see all kinds of goings-on, and while I had a clear view of the physical activities, I could never quite make out what these other beings were actually doing. I knew, though, that I wanted to find out. As time went by, and my thoughts drifted more and more out of Ms. King's window, my "hippie chick" became aware of my quest.

One Thursday evening at pick-up time, she told my mother where my mind had been, and advised her to visit the building across the street. Grabbing my mother by the hand, I dragged her across the street, leaving a series of Turkish profanities in our trail. Standing outside the Mountview Theatre School, I begged her to go in. "Why?" she asked. Knowing that it was a matter of seconds before my mother shoved me into our car and headed back to Tottenham, leaving the creative world of Crouch End behind, I quickly listed all the reasons why going in was essential.

I wanted her to appreciate that every time I saw a film on television, I reenacted it for her, even going to the trouble of making costumes and props at home so I could present a low-budget version of the spectacle I had just so studiously inspected. This was the place where I would perfect those things. Reluctantly, my mother accompanied me into the school. What I remember of that rather perfunctory visit was standing by the door of a class of actors who were performing a mime of climbing ladders. With one venomous look, my mother communicated to me that she would never pay good money for me to do the same foolish nonsense as I did at home. But I also remember that on our way out, she paused to observe a voice coach demonstrating to his student how to project his voice. This time, with a self-assured smile, my mother let it be known that she had no need for a voice coach, that she had been projecting her voice perfectly through all the years of performing the *mevlits* with the Hoca.

As my mother drove me home that night it dawned on me that theater school was a concept remote from the world I lived in, and that the closest I would ever get to performing was the charity productions for my mother's philanthropic association. At home the Hoca concurred with his wife, adding that he would never allow any son of his to enter such an unethical profession as acting—one so full of "them." I am not sure I knew which "them" he was referring to at that point, but apparently there were many of "them" in the world of entertainment. Drama was not considered an important part of education in rough schools such as mine, so I hid my ambitions from my school friends and never mentioned them to any teacher. I continued being one of the "tough kids," and expressed myself through other means.

Like many in the Britain of the 1970s and 1980s, I satisfied my interests through various subcultures. At a very young age I showed a great interest in rock 'n' roll, and I loved all things related to the 1950s, especially Elvis. Through the remainder of my school years, I took an active interest in the music trends of the period, but I never took an equal interest in my schoolwork. When not entertaining my classmates, I spent most of my secondary school years sitting at the back of the class, staring out the window, daydreaming about being an actor, and writing scripts in my head.

During my third year I actually informed my teacher that I would like to pursue a career as a geologist. After a long pause, with a bewildered expression, he advised me to make better use of the years it would take to acquire the qualifications. "Let's face it," he said, "why work so hard when your parents will buy you a kebab shop?"

★　★　★

When I went out into the big wide world, I embarked on a number of careers. My first ever job was as junior hairdresser, but soon, realizing that the hours were long and my earnings low, I moved on to the world of fashion retail. Of course, both these professions were full of "them," but this went unnoticed by the Hoca. I had a couple of excursions back into education but this was purely to attend colleges where most of my Cypriot friends were, and both times this ended with expulsion. The truth is I was killing time. Although berated on a daily basis by the Hoca, who said that I was now an adult and had to make something of myself, in my head I was still staring ambitiously out Ms. King's window, desperately wanting to partake in the goings-on in the building opposite. At that time it was rare for a drama school to accept applicants under the age of twenty; so with a few years to occupy, and to escape the Hoca's sermons, I decided to travel.

While working in the West End of London, I befriended a young man who told me of his jobs as a camp counselor in America. When the camp closed for the summer, he traveled and explored. As weeks went by, and I listened to his accounts of seeing the United States, I knew that I, too, had to go. Having applied to the necessary organizations and suffering the emotional farewells, to my complete disbelief, I found myself on a jumbo jet crossing the Atlantic. I had been to the States once before, at the age of ten, but that was to stay with family near Chicago. Now, left to my own devices, I fully intended to see a lot more of the huge country that I had been so assiduously examining all my life through my old companion, the television. When the pilot announced that we should all look out the windows to the right, then tilted the aircraft to reveal New York on a glorious sunny day, I not only forgot my complete fear of flying, but was awestruck by the breathtaking view. I was in America.

My time in the summer camps was unfortunately cut short, through no fault but my own, because of distractions that were too tempting for a young man on the other side of the world who had been set free from the Hoca's leash. Nevertheless, the two camps where I was employed were Jewish; and I was now in a position, however briefly, to experience first-hand the community with which I had always felt such an affinity. Before every Friday dinner, I would watch as candles were lit and the blessing was recited over the *challah* loaf, reminding me, of course, that on the other side of the earth, the Hoca was also observing our Sabbath at Friday prayers. Still, as the saying goes, boys will be boys; after I was ejected from these American Shangri-Las, I was free to roam that mammoth country.

I headed to New York's Greenwich Village, mostly to enjoy its bohemian reputation, and I soaked up New York through every pore in my thirsty young body. Everything I had ever been interested in was there: theater, museums, architecture, fashion, music, and, at the heart of it all, various subcultures and communities. After the Big Apple, I continued my exploration of the East Coast before going off to see the American South.

My first stop, of course, was Tennessee. I have always loved country music and the cowboy persona. I absorbed all that Nashville had to offer with rushed enthusiasm, but a steam train inside of me was impatient to get to my next destination, Memphis. Passing through the wrought-iron music gates at Graceland had to be the single most emotional experience of my eighteen years. Elvis was an incredibly beautiful man with an extraordinary talent that not only made him a spokesman for his generation, but also a symbol for the postwar era.

From Memphis I moved on to Texas, traveling from Houston to Dallas, and then to Lubbock, to see the city that gave us the great Buddy Holly. From there I went to San Antonio to remember the Alamo. From there, I took a long Greyhound bus ride eastward to New Orleans. I wanted to see the French Quarter, which had cast a magical spell on me from a young age, through such characters as Huckleberry Finn, Tennessee Williams's Stanley Kowalski, and, of course, Elvis in *King Creole*.

Away from the picturesque tourist traps, I saw a different New Orleans. My accommodation was in a poor and neglected part of town and, after befriending a number of guys from the black neighborhood nearby, I realized that a lot of attitudes toward their community had remained the same. Eventually, it was time to move on and, in fact, to go home. My last memories of New Orleans, indeed of America, were helping my new African-American friends to board up their windows in preparation for Hurricane Gilbert.

★   ★   ★

Once back in England, I sent away for brochures from a number of accredited drama schools, and inquired about private drama tutors who could coach me with monologues for auditions. One day I met an actor who gave me a card with a woman's name and telephone number. "Call her and tell her I sent you," said the actor, and so I did. After a long conversation, I asked my prospective coach where she lived, and she said, "Crouch End." I was at a loss for words. The lady coached me for quite a few months, and I would often arrive early in Crouch End to have a cappuccino in a local coffeehouse, or to browse one of the many arts and crafts shops. It was around this time that I started visiting the London Central Mosque in Regent's Park. This building, designed by Frederick Gibberd, a key figure in British modern architecture, had fascinated me ever since it opened in the 1970s. But it was more than beauty that was causing me to take a trip to this cultural center.

One day in Crouch End I purchased the Cat Stevens album, *Tea for the Tillerman*. I remember at the age of ten being introduced by my father to "Yusuf Islam" at a gathering with Shaykh Nazim. At the time, the media were wild with the story of Cat Stevens's conversion to Islam, and I knew exactly who he was. Now, listening to his albums, I could hear his spiritual journey from trendy "mod," through heartfelt peace activist, to award-winning Muslim humanitarian. Every Saturday, Yusuf Islam would be part of a circle of Muslims who gathered at the Central Mosque to read the Holy Qur'an and discuss its meaning. Here was a man who was not only brought up in the same Christianity as the Greek Cypriot boys I had grappled with, but who embraced the ethos of my father, the Hoca—a way of life that my own community had all but rejected. Every Saturday I would listen to his gifted voice reciting the Holy Qur'an—and afterward I would fling a thousand questions at the poor man in private conversations.

At this point someone else entered my life. At a friend's party I was introduced to a girl of Indian descent, and we started seeing a lot of one another. Reading poetry and listening to Cat Stevens songs became a regular part of our courtship, which then led to reading the Holy Qur'an. With time she started coming with me to the Central Mosque, and we began to embrace Islam more and more. There was only one problem: this young lady was a Hindu. Although we did not want to hurt her family, as time went by her conviction grew stronger, and one day, surrounded by newly acquired friends from the Central Mosque, she made the *shahada*, proclaiming her faith that "there is no God but Allah, and Muhammad is

His Messenger," thus becoming a Muslim. We continued courting each other and studying together the teachings of Islam.

*   *   *

One Saturday in the Central Mosque courtyard, I was approached by a young man of Pakistani origin. I remembered his face from years back, when I had seen him in various hangouts, and here he was, beard and all, at the mosque. He told me of a number of seminars to be held at Wood Green Library the following week, and said that he was sure I would find them very interesting. Since Wood Green was a five-minute drive from my home, I agreed to see him there. The following week, I showed up at Wood Green Library and found a stall outside with various written works, along with audio cassettes and videos, on display. Islamic flags surrounded the stall, and a number of young men were handing out leaflets to passersby, while another passionately denounced the evils of Western society through a megaphone. Rather intrigued, I picked up a book entitled, *The Islamic State*, under which was written, "Hizb ut-Tahrir." At this point I felt a hand on my shoulder. "You can take that home to read, if you like, and then you can tell me what you think." It was the young man who had invited me along. "We'd better go in now. The seminar is about to begin." With his hand still on my shoulder, I was led in.

On that day, I heard Omar Bakri Muhammad—or OBM, as he was affectionately known to his followers—give a speech. This Syrian-born cleric was the most charismatic rhetorician I had ever come across; before then, I had never seen anyone who could enliven a throng of young listeners with sheer wit and vivacity the way OBM could. This was all new to me: never had I seen such a concentration of Muslim youth, people who were passionate about their identity. Unlike the Qur'an readings at the Central Mosque, where a small number of middle-aged men were scattered around the prayer area, here the conference room was brimming with male and female youngsters seated separately, men taking up half the room, and women, mostly in *hijabs*, filling the other half. When driven to an emotional crescendo by OBM, both halves proclaimed with equal zeal, "*Allahu akbar!*" (God is great) to the cue of "*takbir!*"

That day, I met Muslims from different cultural backgrounds, some of whom were raised as Muslims and others who converted from other faiths—including a number of Greek Cypriots. Yet the Islam portrayed that day was unlike the Islam that I had observed before. There was no concern with the spiritual path to mystical union with God. Although once a Sufi himself, OBM was now the "spiritual leader" of Hizb ut-Tahrir (HT), a pan-Islamist political party whose main goal was to unite Muslims in a *khilafah* (caliphate), an Islamic state ruled by *sharia* (Islamic law), under the rule of an elected leader, or caliph. The political rhetoric was very appealing to young Muslims who felt no connection to their parents' spiritual interpretations of Islam, and yet felt like political and social aliens in their own country. HT empowered them not only with a coherent identity, but with cogent arguments they could use when engaging both politically and socially with the broader society. Looking around the conference room of the library that day, I saw more familiar faces that I had known from long ago. This inflated sense of self truly was infectious, and I had only just caught the bug.

The drama coaching finally paid off, and I gained a place at an accredited drama school. Gone were my days of being an inattentive student. The academy I attended was, in the end, one of the few institutions that did not expel me. Of course, the fact that the Hoca remortgaged his house to pay for the first two years of fees had something to do with that. I was beginning to be the despair of this pillar of the Turkish Cypriot community, so his fears of my turning into one of "them" were put aside in the desperate hope of some favorable outcome. However, my appetite for knowledge was not just fed by a sense of guilt-ridden responsibility, or my long-held captivation with the act of staging a performance—I was also hungry to know more about politicized Islam. So, as I studied Shakespeare's iambic pentameter, I also researched Qur'anic verse, which Muslims believe to be perfect in its form, and therefore the proof of Muhammad's prophethood. As I read Anton Chekhov's *The Cherry Orchard*, a play so inextricably entwined with the failed 1905 Russian Revolution and the anti-government hostility that produced it, I also scrutinized literature on Muhammad's revolt against the wicked ruling elite of the Quraysh tribe in Mecca. As I learned more about Bertolt Brecht, his lifelong commitment to Marxism, and how he turned theater into a forum of political ideas and debate, I also familiarized myself with the political, economic, and social systems of past caliphates. My drama school was in south London; so it was easy to leave student social life on the other side of our city as I traveled home, my rucksack full of works by theatrical masters and by Hizb ut-Tahrir. At first I went to a few parties, but I found them terribly pretentious, and, more unforgivably, un-stimulating.

With time, my political views moved further and further toward those of HT. Its goal of "Islamic sovereignty" is, after all, not without precedent. Its literature is replete with references to an Islamic state that existed for thirteen centuries, dominating a large portion of the earth and creating a society where Muslims and non-Muslims lived in harmony. A key factor in this Islamic power was the stability and peace brought about under the centuries-long rule of the Ottoman Empire. But in the early twentieth century, the weakened Empire suffered a disastrous defeat in World War I against the Triple Entente (Britain, France, and Russia); Turkey was attacked on all fronts.

A young military commander, Mustafa Kemal, came to the rescue, directing what would be called the Turkish War of Independence against the Triple Entente's plan to partition the Ottoman Empire. After creating a provisional secular government in Ankara, Kemal defeated all Entente forces. After his successful military campaigns, however, Kemal refused to take orders from the sultan, and resigned from the Ottoman Army. Not long after this, in 1923, he established the Republic of Turkey, officially putting an end to the Ottoman Empire and to the institution of the caliphate that HT is now seeking to restore. Kemal sought to create a modern, democratic, secular nation-state through major reforms in politics, economics, and culture. The Turks affectionately awarded him the honorific title of "Ataturk," father of the Turks. Nothing like this had ever happened in all of Islamic history; and to Islamists like those in Hizb ut-Tahrir, this man is forever to be known as evil incarnate.

Sitting at home under Ataturk's portrait, still feeling that gaze from those piercing blue eyes, I read Hizb ut-Tahrir's literature about the implementation of the Kemalist ideology in modern Turkey: how Ataturk had replaced the Islamic calendar with the Gregorian system, substituted Latin script for Arabic script in the Turkish language, closed all *madrasas*, and had all imams appointed and regulated by the Ministry of National Education. Ataturk, seeing modernity as everything non-religious, even banned the fez and the headscarf. But the Sufis were hit hardest. Regarding them as decadent, reactionary obstacles to Turkey's modernization, Ataturk first ordered the abolition of all mystical orders before then banning their ritual practices in 1925. This, of course, included *mevlits*, the same services at which I would sit, staring at Ataturk's image and listening to the voice of my dad, the Hoca. In Islamist literature, I would read that Ataturk controlled and manipulated Islam in Turkey by "Turkifying" it, that is, by teaching Islam through the framework of Turkish nationalism.

Although other, non-Islamist nationalists had tried to copy Ataturk's example in other Muslim countries, none had accomplished nearly as much. Though never prone to strong patriotic emotions, it was still hard for me to let go of the man who was, frankly, my third parent. Furthermore, to add to the emotional complexities, I was told that Ataturk was a Jew and a Zionist. Born in the heavily Jewish, Ottoman-ruled city of Salonika (now Thessaloniki, Greece), Ataturk later played a decisive role in giving escaping Jews a safe passage out of Nazi-occupied Europe. Some of these Jews were academics who went on to be instrumental in the cultural and educational growth of the new Turkish Republic. Of course, not only had Ataturk committed the most evil deed by putting an end to the caliphate, he had also created a secular state that would enjoy full diplomatic, cultural, and commercial relations with HT's other modern Satan: Israel.

This truly was a difficult obstacle for me. I had always had such a strong affinity with the Jewish community, and although I never experienced overt anti-Semitism within HT (as we were told to respect Jews as "people of the book") I knew that by adopting the party's stance on the issue of Israel, I would be building a barrier between the Jews and myself. No matter how many of my show-biz heroes had fought for this new Jewish state, the more I investigated the plight of the Palestinian people, the more I was radicalized. However, there was another conflict that was a more decisive factor in my radicalization: Bosnia.

★   ★   ★

By my second year at drama school, the television images of the atrocities inflicted on Muslims in Bosnia became more and more pervasive. On a daily basis, I would see horrific reports on the Serbs' ethnic cleansing campaign against the Muslims in that country. Those scenes of emaciated bodies in concentration camps reminded me of old newsreels of the Holocaust. They were taking place here and now, at the end of the twentieth century in Europe—only this time, it was a genocide against Muslims. Every Friday I made a telephone call to ask where Omar Bakri Muhammad would be giving the *khutba*, a sermon delivered before every Friday prayer.

One Friday, I was traumatized by what I saw at a mosque. At the back were some refugee Bosnian Muslims. The image I will never forget is of a short, old Bangladeshi man clasping a tall, blond, and very gaunt-looking young Bosnian. They could not have looked more different, yet their emotions were being conveyed through their strong embrace and the tears they were both shedding. In his *khutba,* Omar Bakri Muhammad asked the large congregation to take a long hard look at the back of the mosque, as he reminded us all of the horrifying reports coming through that day of the Serbian policy of raping Muslim women. "The Muslim *umma* (nation) is one body," OBM proclaimed, "and like any other body, if you attack one part of it, the whole body aches!" Of course, the scab had been picked off the old wound, revealing the enmity between the Orthodox Church and the Islamic world. Living in the heart of the Cypriot community, I did hear a few Greek Cypriots voice unconditional support for their Serbian co-religionists. Deeply affected by such ultra-nationalistic sentiment, I myself began supporting the Islamic state, thinking it was the only true sanctuary for the "Muslim nation."

By this point my Muslim convert girlfriend had become my wife and was living with me at my parents' home. Now in full *hijab* and *jilbab* when in public, she, too, was affiliated with Hizb ut-Tahrir. We both attended "closed circles" where we not only learned more about the Islamic state, but also learned how to replace our old selves with an "Islamic character." This created complications at home, since the house was always crowded with guests from the Turkish Cypriot community, and my wife and I would cocoon ourselves in our bedroom after expatiating on the wrongs of free mixing between the sexes. The profane visitors would just stare in perplexity, as did Ataturk on the wall, and ask the Hoca, "Is this really

Islam?" "No!" the Hoca would politely scream, as he ran up our stairs to give my wife and me a dressing-down. But our parents' anxieties about our radicalization fell on deaf ears.

★　★　★

HT's campus organizations became some of the strongest in the country, especially those at the renowned universities that attracted the most promising students. Organizing debates between their own speakers and other parties (of various political and religious persuasions), HT empowered the young Muslim attendees with arguments against the other viewpoints presented. Of course, whenever it was OBM taking the stand, the venue would be packed with expectant followers, and he always delivered by whipping the young crowds into a state of political frenzy. Over time I watched the numbers at these events grow, until there were hordes of attendees standing outside overcrowded halls, listening to the debate on speakers. Numerous female students started out in trendy Western attire, then switched to more modest apparel, and then finally dressed in full *hijab* and *jilbab*. You could see them getting rid of their old selves, and replacing them with "Islamic character." It was always from that side of the segregated hall, from a sea of *hijabs*, that you would experience the most missionary zeal, or hear the most cogent and incisive comments.

The rhetoric was always fiercely against the major powers, specifically the "Anglo-American conspiracy to control Muslim lands." Ataturk and other twentieth-century leaders of Muslim countries were defamed as tyrants who sold their allegiance to their "Western masters," whose aim was to carve up parts of the dissolving caliphate for themselves. Britain, which in its day had acted as kingmaker and played a major part in drawing up treaties between the squabbling new Muslim "buffer" states, while securing military bases for itself, was eventually relegated to its current status as impotent lapdog of the real foe, America.

It was genuinely impressive to see how many of HT's young activists could with ease quote the mid-nineteenth-century British prime minister, Lord Palmerston, who had declared, "We have no eternal allies, and we have no perpetual enemies. Our interests are eternal and perpetual, and those interests it is our duty to follow." America's primary national interest, we were told, was to control the oil supply of the Muslims, and by doing so, eliminate any future aggrandizement on the part of an Islamic state.

This really was a bitter struggle for me. America was my first love. I had spent many a lonely hour throughout my boyhood surveying all she had to offer through my television screen. Completely smitten by her charm, I fell in love with her hook, line, and sinker. I later found out that I was not the only one. Many of my newly acquired HT friends had also had a strong connection with America and had fallen for her charms. We were hurt, and felt used, betrayed, and angry.

★   ★   ★

Although absorbed in cultivating my new "Islamic character," my attention to my drama studies did not wane; on the contrary, my now-questioning mind pressed me to dig more deeply into the significance of all the great literary works and their authors. With time, I started gaining respect not only for my work as an actor, but also for my political and theological ambition. Of course, there were the irritating demonstrations that my fellow budding actors had to endure. Practicing my religious obligation of praying five times a day, I would often slip off from a rehearsal, prayer mat in hand, and apologize for disrupting the proceedings. As for Friday prayers, half of everyone's day would be spent anticipating how long it would take me to get back from the nearest mosque. As I write this, I cannot help but think of our third-year public performance of Reginald Rose's *12 Angry Men*, which would have been more appropriately entitled, *11 Irate Actors and One Spiritually Content Radical*. In the face of the besmirching of Ataturk and of the free mixing of the sexes in our house, the Hoca was rather delighted, if not shocked, to see his youngest son practicing Islam and being a conscientious student. His astonishment was only heightened when my hard work and potential secured me a scholarship to pay for my third year at drama school—the first to be given to anyone in five years. Now I was not only a source of pride to the Hoca; I was also saving him money.

★   ★   ★

Despite a growing concern amongst some in the Muslim community, HT was beginning to garner a reputation for sparking a commitment to Islamic ideals among young people. This was the early 1990s and words such as *jihad* and *mujahedeen* did not conjure up images of a well-armed, malevolent foe. In fact, the widespread sentiment on such Kalashnikov-wielding, turban-clad warriors at the time was one of amazement, as the American-funded *mujahedeen* waged a successful jihad against the Russian occupation of Afghanistan. I even remember giving the Islamic greeting *"Salaam aleikum"* to a number of young men at various mosques who had come back from Afghanistan and who were about to head off to fight in Bosnia as part of a *mujahedeen* task force.

However, preparing the youth for guerrilla warfare was not HT's policy. Though OBM praised such young men for carrying out "Allah's work," Hizb ut-Tahrir was a political party, and its job was to win people's hearts and minds toward attaining its overall objective, the Islamic caliphate. I can recall a number of times when OBM roused a crowd of young followers into political hysteria, with one or two eager acolytes even screaming condemnation of loathed Western and Muslim leaders and vowing lethal retribution. But HT's battle was not fought with terrorism, as it was striving instead for emotional and intellectual control. This is why it was important for HT to infiltrate university campuses and establish a stronghold amongst white-collar workers, all of whom would be welcome benefactors of the cause.

However, I was not training for the legal, medical, or scientific careers of other HT members. Rather, the bohemian circles I was entering, with their informal and unconventional social habits, were a complete contrast to the "Islamic character." As HT continued to foster this new persona of mine, I was continually told that acting was a sin. I was informed that standing on stage and passing oneself off as a character falls under the transgression of lying. I was asked to rethink my future. Rethink!? What my HT superiors did not know was that it was not my future that they were so insensitively dismissing, but my past! As far back as my memory will allow me to venture, I have been completely captivated and stimulated by the act of performance. What about the *mevlits* and the whirling dervishes? "Sufi nonsense," I was informed. Had they not heard of how Bertolt Brecht turned the theater into a forum of political ideas and debate? But putting a Marxist forward as a precedent was not the brightest move. HT found the theories of Karl Marx "rationally repugnant," and as for theater being a forum of political ideas and debate, forget it!

Why had the group invested so much time and attention in me? Its intent was soon made clear. One day I was invited to the house of a high-ranking party member. I explained my conundrum, and my significance to the party was spelled out. Hizb ut-Tahrir had successfully penetrated most sections of the Muslim community in Britain, but the one group that they could not maneuver into was the Turkish Cypriots. No matter how much HT tried, the Turkish Cypriots' attachment to secular life had so far made it unsuccessful. But there was one man who had managed to create a tiny spark of attraction between the worldly Turkish Cypriots and Islam, albeit a Sufi Islam—the Hoca.

I was reminded that for over two decades, my father had served his community by performing all their ritual needs. Now that the preliminary work had been done, the time had come for his son to take over from his father, and gradually disseminate the knowledge of Hizb ut-Tahrir's "authentic" Islam. Yes, I was to be the savior of the Turkish Cypriots, the guiding light to this lost race, whose infatuation with Western culture had led it into a maze of cultural uncertainty. Under a scowling image of the man himself, I was to be the one who told my fellow Turkish Cypriots just how wrong Ataturk had been, and that it was under the caliphate that they would thrive. But what about acting? Forget it!

Frankly, this was not the first sign of my dissatisfaction with the party. Although I shared its concern about global injustices, I had started questioning its solutions and whether I could actually live in HT's proposed

Islamic state. As my enthusiasm evaporated into a bored state of disillusion-ment, I started enjoying being slightly disruptive. When a "closed circle" was halfway through an in-depth study of the caliphate's socio-economic system, I would suddenly bring up the question of whether God actu-ally exists. After all, my new "Islamic character" was taught to believe that the more you question God, the more you will be convinced of His righteousness. As expected, the other HT students would fire back with all the proofs of God's existence. I would then point out that if God was all-powerful, and He created me powerless against my limitations, then surely it was unfair for him to pass judgment on me. That was persecution. In the silence that followed, I would be escorted outside by the instruc-tor to be chastised on losing the focus of the group. "But I thought it was permitted to question God?" I said. "No!" the instructor retorted. "Not in the closed circles. Once you are convinced, there is no need to question Him over and over again!" Eventually, my time at the circles was spent staring into space and dreaming of what was to become of me after my impending graduation from drama school. In short, my days with HT were over.

★ ★ ★

There is nothing like the casting of actors to illustrate social attitudes. Throughout my time at drama school, I knew that my future as an actor lay in roles as Italian waiters or, fearing my old teacher's prophecy, kebab shop owners. Determined to make a career that involved more than asking actors with more substantial roles what their characters would like to order for dinner, I knew that I had to write plays of my own.

For a long time I had fostered a desire to document the life and cul-ture of the Cypriot community. Growing up in the heart of this eth-nic minority I experienced a culturally rich way of life that was almost unknown to the larger population, and no one had worked to capture it. To be fair, a few had tried in vain, but those projects concentrated only on the Greek Cypriots and, therefore, in my opinion, failed to grasp the main attraction of our community, which is the relationship between the Greeks and Turks. It is only through such tensions that the human condition can be truly explored. A piece had to be written that was not full of immigrant clichés, one that did not take a generic American immigrant story and merely change the names. This story had to be authentic to us, a British minority. But I knew that the piece would need more. The story of the Cypriots alone was not enough to attract an audience, or to stimulate my writing, and it was for this reason that I had put the project on the back burner. Now, as I slowly divorced myself from HT and reached the end of my days at drama school, I knew I finally had my story.

As soon as I graduated, I sat down to write. The narrative followed the friendship of two young Cypriots, one Greek, one Turkish. Both men try to overcome the nationalistic prejudices that surround them. But as our Turkish Cypriot protagonist feels more and more disconnected from the Turkish identity his father tries to teach him, yet feels no connection to being British, he questions who and what he really is. He befriends a group of young Muslims who slowly teach him about the demise of the "Islamic empire" and the fight for the future caliphate. We watch as he is gradually empowered with a new sense of self. Although set in the Cypriot community, the Cypriots symbolized the old rivalry between East and West: Christendom versus the Islamic world. Once I started writing, I could not stop. I was confident that I was not only recording a community that with each new generation would lose its ethnic potency, but I was also introducing the growing threat of politicized Islam.

Unfortunately, the conviction with which I wrote my play was not mirrored in the response to it. Even other Cypriot artists told me to stay clear of the subject matter, saying that no one would be interested. This was back in the days when many Cypriot and other ethnic actors of Middle Eastern origins were changing their names to pass themselves off as indigenous, only to secure some type of future in their already precarious careers. But I knew this was the wrong way to go. Deep down I was convinced that our future as artists lay in our cultural past, and that soon many actors would be changing their names to sound more Middle Eastern. Sadly, the reply from the industry that I had just entered was no more enthusiastic than that of my artistic peers.

Entitled *Fruitcake*, because of an old quote—"Cyprus was an ethnographical fruitcake in which the Greek and Turkish currants were mixed up in every town and village, and almost in every street"—the only interest my play produced was about the person who had written this mumbo-jumbo, and it was for this reason that one literary manager actually called me in for a meeting. Intoxicated with nerves and the sheer prospect of some form of validation, I turned up to the meeting in my best attire. Having been led into an office by a snickering assistant, I sat opposite a man at a desk for what seemed like a lifetime. He had my play opened in front of him, and, every now and again, he would look up from casting a pityingly critical eye over the text, only to give the author an even more heartfelt commiserative look. Finally, I heard the expected comments. Who cared about the Cypriots? What was all this nonsense about Muslims being political? What was this caliphate business? And as for my writing? Well, maybe I should just stick to acting. Or perhaps my parents could buy me a kebab shop? Of course, this was the mid-1990s, and to imbeciles such as this, Muslims were just annoying exotic folk who came out in fancy dress every Friday and blocked up the traffic. The poor fool actually said it was like reading a foreign language.

I had a growing realization, as I stared into his face, that I was nothing but a foreigner to this man. In truth, there had been few examples of artists celebrating their ethnicity in Britain. Writers or actors who exposed their ethnicity would be cast as foreign. Unlike in America, where many artists became famous by celebrating their ethnicity, in Britain, ethnic minorities were at the bottom of the class ladder, after the white working class. You could move up the artistic ladder by shedding your ethnic identity, or be content as a mere archetypal alien. I walked out of his office, past the still-snickering assistant, and headed back to north London, knowing that the only *Fruitcake* that this literary numbskull had assessed was me.

★　★　★

Eight long years passed. By now, my wife had also dissociated herself from HT, and we had been blessed with two additions to our family. However, I had been less favored in my career path. The acting work I had obtained was mostly in repertory theater and, although it gave me the opportunity to prove myself as an actor, the little money I was receiving was hardly sufficient to support my family. And as for my play, after a few polite critiques from various theaters that said little more than what the literary numbskull had said eight years earlier, I stopped sending it out.

Then, one crisp sunny afternoon, I had just picked my children up from school, when another parent asked whether I had seen the news. An airplane had crashed into one of the Twin Towers in New York. I will never forget the way I ran home in an incredibly disturbed, and yet oddly perceptive, state of mind. I turned on my television to find that all of the channels were covering the horrific events as they unfolded. My wife was vacuuming, and I shouted at her to turn the machine off. Detecting from my tone of voice that something was wrong, my wife joined me in front of the television. Our eyes open wide in shock, we watched in silence as the second airplane hit the South Tower. Suddenly, we both drifted off into our own individual states of trauma. Mine was spurred on by the aerial views I was seeing. I had seen that view before, of course, on a similarly sunny day when the pilot announced that we should all look out of the windows to the right, and then tilted the aircraft to reveal the breathtaking view of New York. The disturbing, and yet natural link I was making between two separate emotional experiences was only overcome by one painful thought: I was going to benefit from this dreadful day. Turning to my wife, I uttered the first words that either of us had said in what seemed like hours: "My play is going to go on now."

The Theatre Royal Stratford East became famous in the 1950s under the artistic directorship of Joan Littlewood, and the management of Jerry Raffles. Having brought the company from the north of England to the East End of London, they concentrated on provocative class issues with their "people's theater." As a result, they not only gave the working class a platform to express itself, but also created many a star who would have otherwise had to cast off any personal characteristics in order to get work. Sound familiar? One day I received a telephone call from a close actress friend, who informed me that the associate director at the Theatre Royal was a Greek Cypriot, that she had told him about my play, and that he had showed great interest. Of course, this incredibly important piece of information—which I can only promise had a full, orchestrally accompanied choir singing "Hallelujah" in my head—was followed by the habitual insecure grumbling that all actors discharge when talking about the "business." By the time she had finished, however, I had a copy of my play ready to be mailed.

Before long, a meeting had been arranged between myself and Kerry Michael, the Greek Cypriot associate director. Kerry had enjoyed my play, but he said that it needed another draft. By the time the next draft was ready, Kerry was one of a few candidates being considered for artistic director. Needless to say I prayed hard, imploring whoever was listening to make sure he got the job. He did, and for the opening production of his artistic directorship he chose my play. It was as if, from the moment Kerry informed me of this monumental news, everything went into fast-forward. The publicity department at the Theatre Royal immediately started its work on our production, now entitled, *The Battle of Green Lanes*. Because of the subject matter, a lot of interest started to develop straightaway. But more was to come. The first interview I gave to the press was to the *Times* of London, over the telephone. I spoke for a minute or two to the journalist before mentioning HT. "Who?" she immediately asked. I was halfway through my explanation when I thought she had cut me off. "Sorry, just wait a minute," her voice came back. I was in Kerry's office, and I quickly notified him of what was going on and of my hunch that this was going to be quite a powerful article. I was right. As a result of that article we received a lot more attention, both from the British press, and from abroad, including Al-Jazeera.

However, it was when Kerry and I were interviewed on Sky News that I realized I really was making some noise. Sitting in the green room, I watched on the monitor as a journalist informed the English-speaking world of the forthcoming interview. Behind him there was a huge image of my head, and coming out from behind me was a masked Palestinian militant. I almost choked on my substandard studio tea. Who did they think I was? But watching the interview later, I was quite proud to see two north London Cypriots, one Greek and one Turkish, talking about their upcoming production.

The Battle of Green Lanes opened at the Theatre Royal Stratford East on October 15, 2004. The play was cast authentically, with Cypriot actors playing the Cypriot roles. I myself played the Turkish Cypriot protagonist. The curtains opened to reveal a community based in north London whose voice had never been heard before on the British stage. Of course, because the play was dealing with the tensions between the Greek and Turkish Cypriots, large numbers of both communities made the journey from north London just to hear what I was saying. Although this showed that we were doing the right thing by pulling a new audience into the theater, I was emotionally disoriented when I came out to the bar every night and saw large numbers of Cypriots. Had I pulled them into my world, or was I back at some wedding, just observing them whilst sitting next to the Hoca? But there was another voice on our stage, the voice of politicized Islam. It was because of this voice, that of the West's new foe, that the theater was full every night. Hearing the two "Islamist" characters explain away global injustices by condemning Western policies, the audience was intrigued. I think I showed the seductiveness of such rhetoric, and took the audience on the political journey of my protagonist.

It was at the end of my story that we saw the victims of such fixed convictions. On the night that the Hoca came and saw his son's play, he asked the author whether what he had deduced was correct. Was the Greek boy one of "them"? Indeed, my protagonist's Greek Cypriot best friend was one of "them." But to show that he was not allowed to express his orientation in the world that I was portraying, it was only suggested. We are informed by the Islamists that in an Islamic state, such characters would be thrown from the highest point in the land. The audience response to this punishment varied according to the audience makeup. Some nights they would gasp in horror. Other nights they would just laugh at the base ignorance of it. But there were nights when I observed all the actors on stage becoming unnerved by the ovation that those gruesome words received. There were also other victims at the end of my story. As nationalism raised its ugly head and everyone was pushed to extremes, families were torn apart and old friendships dissolved.

I thought I was going to be attacked for what I was saying with my play. I thought people would all think that the play was against them. Instead, people all claimed the play as their own. I was dumbfounded when I heard the Cypriot audience being self-critical and accepting how ignorant our internal feuds could be. Both Greeks and Turks recognized the hatred that was instilled from a young age, but they also acknowledged the resentment that we all carried for the host nation. Muslims also embraced the play, recognizing the extreme fringes that exist and the appeal they have to the youth. As for the Jewish community, one Jewish gentleman fought for my play to be part of the curriculum at a secondary school in East London so that his students could study it. I was invited to the school, and I saw that a class of mostly Muslim students was politically and creatively fired up after seeing our production. Their teacher informed me afterward that he had searched high and low for a play that they could relate to. The experience was nothing but humbling.

Yet sadly, there was a dark spot. Two weeks before we went into rehearsals, my old friend Chris was tragically killed riding his motorcycle. After every performance, as I observed the interaction between Greek and Turkish Cypriots in the theatre bar, I could not help but think of my old friend, and how much those precious adolescent years that we had spent in one another's homes had contributed to this "new voice" that people were now talking about.

★ ★ ★

Alas, even in my finest hour, the question of identity would not leave me alone. Much of the press referred to me as the "Turkish Cypriot" writer. People would talk of the "Muslim" or "Cypriot" play. Turkish Cypriot writer? I had been to Cyprus only four times in my life. I was as British as Shakespeare! A "Muslim" or "Cypriot" play? My play was as British as *Coronation Street*! My community is British, and we feel foreign when in Cyprus! If you teach a nation to have pride in its multiplicity of faces, then by celebrating one minority, you are showing that nation another part of itself. When I look at the Jewish community of Britain, I do not perceive them as something unconnected to myself. I think of it as "my" Jewish community. In the same respect, the so-called Muslim community of Britain is not "mine," but "ours."

Where do we start to establish communal rapport? For me, the answer to that question can only be in our schools, which is why I want my children to be at schools where they are surrounded by children from various communities, who practice different faiths. However, this has been discouraged in recent years because of the controversial issue of school uniforms and the religious attire of Muslim girls. A rush of restrictions and bans on religious clothing has been sweeping Europe. The ensuing discourse has led to new laws and legal judgments in such countries as France, Denmark, Germany, and our very own United Kingdom. The freedom to wear clothing that reveals a student's religious faith has been questioned, as has the right of governments and schools to impose restrictions. This hot subject has become a means of expressing the insecurities of all those who fear the changing face of our society. If in the very place where we encourage the growth and development of communication skills we say that such religious beliefs cannot be observed, we are instilling in our future politicians, lawyers, employers, and, indeed, teachers, the idea that such practices have no place in our society. Of course, such attitudes will only lead to a large portion of our population feeling alienated.

For the members of a group to feel responsibility toward the land they live in, they must see a reflection of themselves in its culture. It was only after I had graduated that I learned all about Europe's Islamic past, and discovered how much it had been enriched by the vibrant civilization that Muslims brought to the West. Made aware of the debt owed to Islam for its critical contribution to the European Renaissance, I had more of a vested interest in the culture that I could now truly call my own.

This is about familiarizing ourselves with the many groups that made contributions to the various fields of human endeavor, which allows us to realize how much we can relate to one another. I now know not only of the influential role the Jewish community has played in show business, but of their great contribution, from within the Islamic world, to the European Enlightenment. This, of course, is also the case with the Greeks and all the other donors to our culture. Only when separatist ideals are aired, usually through some form of nationalism, is the outcome divisive and marked by ignorance. I cannot help but think of the many times I heard Greeks and Turks arguing over whether the dark, strong caffeinated substance is "Greek coffee" or "Turkish coffee." Here were the heirs to two early civilizations, whose culture still affects our lives today in the arts, philosophy, science, mathematics, literature, and politics, and they were arguing about a few crudely ground and boiled coffee beans.

I am under no illusion that we will achieve a Utopian existence through self-exploration. Inevitably, where there are many opposing opinions, hot debates will arise. But instead of discouraging these conflicts because of political correctness, we, as a culture, should nurture analytical dialogue. Only with intellectual debate will we be able to tackle the external influences that penetrate our society. Only by refining our skills of political analysis will we be able to eradicate the more extreme viewpoints in our society. This refinement process must begin in our schools, where our children should be exposed to the diverse strands of political, religious, and social thought, and empowered with the skills of examining its partialities. Only in a culture that is proud of the many facets of its identity, and stimulated by intellectual rapport among them, will we be able to challenge the likes of Hizb ut-Tahrir.

★   ★   ★

After flying to Beirut in 2005, the infamous but charismatic Omar Bakri Muhammad was banned from Britain by the Home Office (Britain's interior ministry/department of justice), and detained by Lebanese authorities. Many critics believed this to be a victory, and have now called for the party itself to be banned, as it is in other European countries, and throughout the Middle East. I disagree, however, as by banishing such groups, we exclude their ideals from our intellectual debate and lose our ability to scrutinize—and defeat—their arguments. This will drive their ideas underground, where they will survive unopposed, and rot the foundations of any progressive achievements. We are not under any illusion that we will convince Hizb ut-Tahrir of the error of its ways, but by debating with it, we will provide its target population—the youth—with the ability to oppose its arguments.

In the current climate of political correctness, the so-called Muslim community has been charged with the sole responsibility of challenging such Islamist groups. In fact, this "community" consists of many subgroups that are often hostile to one another. The fact that these have lost a number of their youth to politicization only proves that their particular brands of "spirituality" do not meet the youngsters' needs, and that the problem cannot be solved by such community-based traditionalism alone.

This is a political issue; Hizb ut-Tahrir has won the hearts and minds of younger Muslims by providing an answer to global injustices, which they blame on "Western" interference in Muslim lands. The proposed solution is the caliphate that invests sovereignty in God but that is ruled in practice by a caliph who administers a political, economic, and social system. No imam telling Qur'anic stories in a local mosque can compete against this ideal in winning over restless and disaffected youth.

Unfortunately, Hizb ut-Tahrir's words are made all the more powerful and alluring because so many fear its message. HT tells the story of the Prophet Muhammad traveling from village to village to spread the word of Islam. His enemies would always go before him to tell the villagers to cover their ears, since the devil who was coming would win them over with his sweet words. HT appropriates this allegory for itself, and its critics play into the group's hands by refusing to allow its members to speak. Even if we expel it from all the mosques and deny it a public forum, its message will still be spread. Only when all arguments are out in the open will radical views be subject to denunciation by the very people that are targeted. I truly believe that we will never totally eradicate "Islamist" theories, nor should we.

But there is an alternative scenario that is just as frightening as an arena full of brawling zealots. The day may come when extremists of all religious denominations realize that they share similar values and can live together. What will then happen to those in our society who follow so-called alternative lifestyles? Throughout history, we have seen such groups thrive at the height of various civilizations. As is the case with all outsiders, their strength is to look at society from a different perspective, and to provide society with invaluable insights into itself. We cannot be so complacent as to think that such groups will not again be exterminated by extremism. Only from intellectual debate can reason prevail over such radicalism, and allow the outsiders' intuition to give us a better understanding of ourselves.

As for me? Gone are my days of playing kebab shop owners. I now sit in the waiting rooms of casting offices filled with other "ethnic" actors of all shapes, sizes, and ages. But although we are all born-and-bred Londoners, we never audition for the role of a Londoner. There is a new market for which we have perfected our accents—terrorists and Eastern European gangsters. But, hey, it is great work if you can get it!

CHAPTER SIX

Faces of Janus: The Arab-Muslim Community in France and the Battle for Its Future

SAMIA LABIDI

Born in Tunis in 1964, I am part of the so-called generation of Bourguiba, that is, those who grew up under the governments of Habib Bourguiba, the first president of modern Tunisia. Due to his historic reforms, he is also known as the "liberator of women." I was raised in traditional Sunni Islam for the first ten years of my life, until my family—along with thousands of other families throughout the Arab-Muslim[1] world—discovered political Islam. It was then that the Mouvement de la Tendance Islamique (MTI, Islamic Tendency Movement), better known under its post-1989 name, Hizb al-Nahda (Renaissance Party), began to emerge in Tunisia.

The religion of my mother and grandmother was the most beautiful form of Islam, in spite of the heavy influence of the male-dominated tradition that tends to obscure the humanism of authentic Islam. I remember a happy childhood in which religious holidays and celebrations strengthened family ties and sparked joy in our hearts. They were an opportunity to forgive those who hurt us—and to ask their forgiveness—so that love could triumph over hatred.

I never encountered a single instance of terrorism, fundamentalism, or fanaticism. Within this community, it was the elderly who most often practiced the five pillars of Islam. I can still see my grandmother diligently preparing for each of her daily prayers as if she had a date with God. Since children were not held back by any type of heavy-handed dogma, they were able to enjoy a happy and innocent childhood, without brainwashing or indoctrination. They were the "children of God," not the "soldiers of God." And in spite of continuing misogyny *outside* the home, women were the masters *inside* it.

This article was initially translated from French by Catherine de Vulder and revised by Emmet C. Tuohy for this volume.

It is tradition that requires a woman to take a husband—but it is Islam that gives a woman the chance to choose him. It is tribal Arab tradition that forbids her from going out alone, working, or driving—but it is Islam that grants her the *right* to make these decisions for herself. It would have been better to fight against this tribal tradition than to attack authentic Islam, which has had such difficulty putting an end to barbaric practices. Political Islam has gained ground by presenting itself as the sole custodian of the rights that Islam grants women, and it has since limited those rights.

The MTI arose within fairly close-knit university circles; in fact, one of its founding members is none other than my brother-in-law, who, by marrying one of my sisters, sparked an "Islamist mini-revolution" within my own family. Overnight, we witnessed a "regime change" in our home, from traditional Islam to political Islam, without so much as a word being spoken. There was talk of a "return to the original sources" and to "true Islam," to regain the identity and strength lost at the hands of the libertine and immoral West—which was, above all, the enemy of Islam and of Muslims. We abruptly left behind a world of color and entered a world of black and white.

The infiltration of the family, the basic unit of society, is an integral part of the Islamist strategy. It takes only one member to convert an entire family—willingly or not—to political Islam. Our metamorphosis took place because of my sister, who began by wearing longer and longer skirts and concluded by donning the veil and preaching to my other sisters, each of whom soon also began wearing this ostentatious sign of religion. Little by little, and under the indirect guidance of my brother-in-law, three of the four girls adopted the veil, before being "offered" the opportunity to marry Islamists. My older brother found himself encouraged to continue his secondary education in a military school, while the younger boys were sent to religious schools at the mosques.

My father rediscovered a sense of authority of which he himself had previously been unaware. But my mother refused to go along with this new approach, opting first for divorce and then for a move to France. In a short time, the family home became a bleak place. No more music, no more going out, no more summer trips to the beach, and no more friends, unless they also adhered to this revolutionary ethos. Everything in our family life had to be controlled, down to the smallest details, so we could be worthy of the brother-in-law who represented Hizb al-Nahda's military wing. Our family life was being undermined by Islamist dogma, revolving around nightly political gatherings directed at the overthrow of Bourguiba. Infiltration was carried out softly, by means of marriage and of religious diktat, within our family.

I put on the veil at age eleven because of the psychological pressure exerted in my family. I was taught that there was the side of "true Muslims," supposedly the holders of absolute truth and human salvation,

and the side of "false Muslims," who were considered traitorous supporters of the West. The idea of God interested me and pushed me to apply
myself in the pursuit of truth. Over the years, however, I realized that
God had been used by the Islamists as nothing more than a tool to achieve
purely political ends, that is, to attain power.

My family's situation is not an isolated case—far from it. This kind of
infiltration occurred simultaneously in thousands of families in Tunisia,
other parts of North Africa, and indeed, the entire Arab-Muslim world.
How did it happen? When I consider the case of Tunisia, especially my
family, and when I review my personal experience, I can say that this
transformation began in Tunisian universities.

Three factors helped Islamists expand their influence among Tunisian
university students. First, the Muslim Brotherhood (MB), the initial organization that launched the Islamists' drive for political power, was founded
in 1928 in Egypt, the center of the Arab-Muslim world's modern pop
culture, with its domestic movie and music industries. Egypt's flood of
cultural production exerted a strong influence on young people's minds
in Tunisia and its neighboring countries. It is no coincidence that Tariq
Ramadan, Europe's most popular cleric, is of Egyptian origin. The grandson of Hasan al-Banna, a founder of the MB, Ramadan is well suited to
reinforce the ranks of the organization—already one of the strongest links
in the Islamist chain, including in Tunisia—by winning over the North
African community.

Second, domestic politics made Tunisia ripe for political takeover by
Islamists, given the failing health of President Bourguiba, whom the
Islamists labeled the "Despot of Africa." Islamists thus considered Tunisia
to have the most vulnerable regime in the region. Moreover, Islamists
viewed Bourguiba as pro-Western, too secular, and too problematic due
to his record as a liberator of women.

Third, Bourguiba helped a new student elite emerge, ironically, due
to his successful policies aimed at increasing literacy, especially for the
population living outside the capital, Tunis. These southern Tunisians
have shown a tendency to convert more readily to political Islam. They
are young people who have experienced poverty but have nevertheless
succeeded in establishing themselves in the capital, to which all Tunisians
who wish to continue their studies at the highest level must move. Once
there, they generally marry Tunis-born women to advance up the social
ladder. Despite their intellectual growth and development in college, they
retain their skeptical and closed-minded approach to Bourguiba's ideal
of gender equality. The Islamist ideology and approach attracted these
students because it restored their masculine dominance. Political Islam
allowed them to conceal their traditional *machismo* behind a thin veneer of
sacredness and divine recognition.

In my own experience, marriage proved to be a tactic without equal for
Islamist infiltration of the capital's social scene. While the men are often

southern Tunisians of modest backgrounds and fresh converts to political
Islam, the women on whom they set their sights tend to be city-dwellers
from middle-class or even wealthy families. It is through these marriages of convenience that political Islam insinuates itself into Tunis families, to foment Islamist "mini-revolutions" that elevate Islamism along
Tunisia's social ladder by controlling society's most basic building block,
the family.

Once firmly ensconced within these families, the Islamists begin to
pressure the whole family to convert to political Islam. The splits within
the family, and its subsequent disintegration, can be seen in the fabric of
society as a whole. Generally, once an Islamist has married into a family,
the next step is to marry off the remaining sisters to Islamists and enroll
the boys in military schools to prepare for a coup. Infiltration also takes
place in the media, with materials produced by Egypt's Islamist press and
Muslim Brotherhood propaganda tapes; the military, ensuring that more
and more Islamists are found in the higher ranks (another brother-in-law
of mine rose as high as captain before being unmasked); and in education,
where preferential recruitment takes place throughout the entire system,
from kindergarten teachers up to university professors. By infiltrating the
education system, Islamists lay the foundation for an Islamic state from a
child's early life—hence the importance of women.

The veil is used as a symbol to spread political Islam among girls. Though
I was the only veiled girl in my class when high school began, within
seven years I convinced hundreds of girls to wear the veil. Eventually,
within converted families, the veil is required for all girls, and the beard
for all boys. Instruction in Islamist teachings is repeated throughout the
day, both at the mosque and at home. As in my own family, evening political gatherings with the movement's leaders become more frequent. Every
day, political Islam gains space to reshape society to its advantage.

⋆   ⋆   ⋆

My experience as a former Islamist allowed me to understand the scale
of the deception carried out in the name of God. I was eighteen when
I decided to stop wearing the veil. At that time, the veil was seen as a feminist gesture against the Western idea of woman as a sexual object; only
gradually did I come to understand the downward spiral in which we
were trapped, and the serious rethinking that was necessary to escape it.

It was then, in 1982, that I decided to go to France to join my mother.
I thought I had closed the book on Islamism and resumed a secular, freethinking life as a student of philosophy and sociology. But I was soon
confronted once again with Islamism, after the Islamists' coup attempt
failed (which was planned and ordered from France by exiled Islamists
such as my brother-in-law) and the would-be leaders were driven into
exile in France. In November 1987, with the transfer of the presidency to
Zine Ben Ali, the plot unfolded before our eyes. I could now see clearly

the full horror of the Islamist strategy, which I had sensed earlier. Leaving Tunisia in 1982, I could never have believed that I would face the very same struggle two decades later in the heart of the West, particularly France—the land where the modern concepts of human rights and citizenship were born.

In France, in the spirit of promoting the republican, secular values relevant to all segments of society, I founded From There or Here, But Together (d'Ailleurs ou d'Ici Mais Ensemble, AIME), an organization dedicated to increasing awareness of the Islamist threat among the young, especially those of North African descent. For more than ten years I have been sounding the alarm about Islamism in France, which, in the heart of its sworn Western enemy, has been able to operate with more freedom than it ever would be accorded in its countries of origin.

It is unfortunate that France did not react earlier to this dangerous, destructive phenomenon. France's Arab-Muslim community cannot be separated from its countries of origin, and the strength of these links means that what happens in France has immediate consequences on the other side of the Mediterranean, and vice versa. For example, Hizb al-Nahda's leaders moved to France and other parts of Europe after their failed coup attempt in Tunisia. They split up and moved to different countries to avoid being caught at the same time in the same country. In France, ex-Nahda leaders tended not to be very active after obtaining "political refugee" status, which, in principle, forbids them from resuming their political activities. Nevertheless, the "return to Islam" that is so evident both among the immigrant community (including the second and third generations) as well as among non-Muslim converts is due above all to the influx of these Islamist coup plotters who were expelled from their countries of origin.

It is quite difficult for the West to recognize the danger posed by Islamism because modern political Islam wears a mask of tolerance and openness in public. Islamists' dual morality works well in the West, whereas in Arab-Muslim countries it is harder for them to fool their fellow Muslims. In France, the Islamist immigrants exploit democratic and republican values to obtain rights—such as respect for cultural differences, freedom of belief, and freedom of speech—that they could only dare to dream about in a Muslim country.

While people in the West know very little about Islam and Muslims, Islamist Muslims know a great deal about the West. Many have studied in a Western country, and they know the West—and its vulnerabilities—very well. It is not difficult, then, to figure out the behavior of Islamists who, thanks to the doctrine of *taqiyyah* (dissimulation), can infiltrate Western environments without attracting suspicion. They project an image of seeking successful integration even as they foster division between Muslim communities and mainstream society in the West; anyone who dares to point out the flaws in this deceptive self-portrait is accused of racism, xenophobia, and Islamophobia.

The Western world has provided enormous benefit to the international Islamist movement, which has consistently expanded since it first established itself in the culturally Arab-Muslim communities of the West. By far the best recruitment locations have been public housing projects, especially the *banlieues* that are dominated by Muslim immigrants on the outskirts of major French cities. These projects are characterized by high unemployment rates and failing schools. These problems are all advantages for Islamists, as they foster alienation that makes it easier for Muslims to turn their backs on the West and join the ranks of the extremists. What is more, these Islamist advantages result from failed Western policies.

Beyond failed social policies in France and elsewhere in the West, the Islamists have perfected their strategies to feed on any problematic event that puts the West back on its heels. The Israeli-Palestinian conflict, Europe's extreme right, and racism and xenophobia strengthen hatred of the West, which is already being fostered by the Islamists and their preaching of the need to return to the "true values of Islam" as the only means of defending themselves against the Great Satan.

In France, Islamists have been on the move, establishing profit-generating businesses, publishing firms (including the renowned El-Tawhid, which launched the career of Tariq Ramadan), so-called charities, radio and television programs, political conferences, and even protest movements—all to enable a complete move away from the systems of their host countries. Even while working to separate themselves from mainstream society, Islamists present themselves as victims of dictatorships in their home countries and anti-Muslim discrimination in their adopted countries, thus garnering media sympathy and acceptance in French elite society. After several decades of disciplined Islamist work, the results are clear: a French Islamist presence can be felt at the highest levels, even under the patronage of the state.

Islamism's tremendous growth poses an unprecedented political challenge. The lenient negligence of the Left, in the name of religious freedom, allowed the situation to worsen. As for the Right, President Sarkozy made a deal with the devil, replacing the gang leaders of the *banlieues* with religious preachers to restore public order. Indeed, since the riots in 2005, more and more Islamists have presented themselves as the only way to improve the appalling situation in the troubled housing projects.

French political Islam's expansion has consequences for Europe and the rest of the world. Its leadership is comprised, for the most part, of North Africans, who are advised by Islamist political refugees. Although each group operates independently, they are unified by the goal of propagating political Islam as a way of seizing power in all areas, sooner or later. The mosque is the center for grassroots efforts. Extending from mosque networks are the so-called charitable or humanitarian organizations, which use charitable activities as a cover for their proselytizing and recruitment. These subversive and divisive efforts take place elsewhere "in the field," whether among criminals in prison or the future community elite in universities. Islamists can be found in employment agencies and in private schools as well—ensuring that France's Arab-Muslim community is surrounded by Islamists on all sides.

The Web of International Islamism

The Internet has been a tremendously useful tool for the global Islamist movement. Freedom of speech in Arab-Muslim countries remains more or less a myth that exists only to reinforce traditionalist approaches to Islam and to persecute remaining minorities. In such a context, political Islam—along with its largely apolitical nemesis, atheism—has turned to the Internet, and to the West, to ensure freedom of expression. The Islamists were the first to understand how best to exploit the vast worldwide network in the service of their own narrow interests. Soon after becoming firmly established in both Europe and America, they felt the need to gain mastery over the latest technologies, starting with the Internet. Now, there are countless Islamist websites throughout the world that allow high-quality work on a global scale, free of government oversight. The Islamists' undisputed professionalism in information technology has given them the means to monitor and sabotage sites that oppose their views, such as AIME's site, which was completely hijacked on the eve of its "Islam against Islam" conference in October 2004.

Moreover, the means used by political Islam to express its reactionary doctrines publicly are not limited to the Internet, or to its television networks, which are no less formidable tools. They include the Islamists' countless radio stations and print outlets, which produce material in every language. International Islamism, in short, has no right to complain about any limitations on its freedom of speech, since it has the ability to express itself globally in virtually any form.

Finally, it is clear that Islamists can rely on a certain degree of collusion from the public and the private sector. Far too many policymakers and other noteworthy people are willing to allow Islamists to use media freedom and other core values of secular democracy to claim a monopoly on the interpretation of Islam. In contrast, Islamists' moderate opponents have limited resources to communicate their message of tolerance and Islam's compatibility with universal values. In fact, even those limited means of communication are subject to constant surveillance as well as sabotage by the Islamists, with the result that only the "soldiers of God" can speak.

★   ★   ★

Just how far should we go in the name of freedoms of speech and belief? Should all ideologies be given a platform, even the most extremist, which seek to terrorize those who disagree with them? Should all expressions of religion be routinely placed above suspicion? (This is the case in France, which should know from its own history how formidable powerful religion can become.) Should Islamists be allowed to oppress and scorn atheists in the name of the proclaimed superiority of the sacred over the profane? Can freedom be defined unilaterally? To all these questions, Islamists answer yes, when this freedom serves their interests and allows them to eliminate differences—and even the right to be different—within the Islamic community. Yet, Islamist leaders oppose freedom of speech when such liberty retards their ability to compel fellow Muslims to commit themselves to a globalized Islamic world.

Islamism now seeks to increase its power even further, with the blessing of the French state, by claiming the absolute necessity of developing a "French Islam." It is because of the Islamists' use of this expression—which in their hands turns into a potent weapon—that we now see the Islamic headscarf in secular schools; the right to gender segregation in the public pools of certain cities; the demands of women that their husbands or eldest sons be present during doctors' visits or medical procedures; the unrolling of prayer rugs in government offices by officials who swore an oath to the republic that they would "never engage in any religious or political prose-lytizing in the context of their duties"; and the parades through the streets of Paris, featuring anti-Semitic and anti-France chanting.

As the Islamists establish their control over a "French Islam," they will seek to impose the notion that "the laws of God supersede those of the Republic." Their quest is an Islamic state in the heart of Europe, which, they hope, will eventually lead to the replacement of secular governments around the globe.

At what exact moment should secular, republican, and democratic states firmly declare, "Enough is enough"? Perhaps now would be a good time; these harmful activities are carried out in the name of values that became enshrined in law only because at one time citizens who objected to reli-gious interference in their political affairs were willing to pay with their lives to end it.

It may already be too late, since political Islam is now attempting to infiltrate all of Europe—and the West— at all levels. The problem is not that Islam is the second religion of France, but rather that political Islam is exploiting the Muslim community as a whole to both expand and exert its influence.

We cannot bring about true integration of Muslims into mainstream Europe by reducing a diverse community to a single religious label. Among all minorities in France, only Arab-Muslims seem to be automat-ically associated with a religion.

It is imperative that we work to change this prevailing view of the various Muslim communities. We must no longer give the spotlight to that handful of reactionaries and impostors who, with the state's com-plicity, seek only to aggravate an already critical situation, which could explode at any time. The long-desired goal of integration will not be achieved by means of the French [State] Council for the Muslim Faith (CFCM), in which Islamist cells that obtained a majority through trickery can exercise their right to "freedom of speech" by muzzling secular voices. These secular and moderate voices among French Muslims are at great risk because of their opposition to the new status of the Islamists, who are considered "partners" for the government because they promise to "control" the Muslim communities and prevent violent actions, as in the *banlieues*.

The West, in general, is sacrificing freethinkers to the likes of the Muslim Brotherhood. Rather than ally itself with progressive Muslims, the West prefers to cut deals with reactionary Islamists to allow the dictatorships in those countries to be replaced by even worse regimes, all in the hope of securing peace in those lands by preventing more terrorist attacks in the West. Yet what these governments do not realize is that by affording extremists increased legitimacy and room to maneuver, they have helped the international Islamist movement gain an even stronger position from which they can wreak further havoc.

The French government is not familiar with its Arab-Muslim citizens or their culture as it should be. The silent majority of French Muslims are still trying to make themselves heard, despite the difficulties. They seek to propose truly secular solutions that will repair the damage to their reputation that has been caused by ignorance, by hatred, or by self-interest. We seek to unite the voiceless into a single force more representative of our diverse community—especially compared to the CFCM, which at most represents itself.

I see no reason why the universal rights of freedom of expression and freedom of conscience can be exercised only in one direction, a direction that favors religious and political fanatics. The silent majority of French people of Arab-Muslim origin are increasingly eager to express their own point of view on Islam, and to distance themselves from the negative image of their religion in the media and popular opinion. Active in many areas, this silent majority remains unnoticed and underrepresented, because it keeps a low profile and aspires to be integrated. It nevertheless represents the ideal solution for slowing the rise of Islamist fundamentalism. Its understanding of the Islamist mentality could allow it to expose, and then oppose, this fundamentalism. It embodies the future and the stabilization of the Arab-Muslim world on both sides of the Mediterranean.

For more than ten years the AIME has tried to encourage this true majority to band together so it can speak for itself. Although we have been subjected to the same dogmatic and cultural influences, our paths have permanently diverged from the Islamists, and we now stand on opposite sides of the divide between liberty and slavery.

The AIME has adopted the goal of uniting all secular and freethinking people of Arab-Muslim origin under one banner, with the aim of engaging in constructive self-criticism about Islam and its origins. We want to publicize our suggestions for freeing our community from the intellectual and cultural stagnation with which it is struggling. Our deep familiarity with Islam also makes possible our struggle against fundamentalism and Islamic terrorism.

Certainly, we cannot replicate the Islamist success overnight. But if we could have access to the same means and methods as they do—such as media, government support, and institutions—we can confront them in a fair fight. We must fight them with their own tools: faith, Islam, the *hadiths* (Prophet's sayings and deeds), and the Qur'an.

Law of the Family, or Law of Infamy?

Closely tied to the discussion of freedom of expression and of conscience—especially in my own life and work—is the state of women within Islam. It is important to recognize that in many ways, the Prophet Muhammad was a liberator of the women of his era. At a time when newborn girls were buried alive and adult women were treated like furniture—pieces of property that could be included as part of a man's estate—his message gave them protection. We also should not forget Muhammad's last words before his death: "Take care of the women."[2]

However, it is also undeniable that the *sharia* legal system, as interpreted and written down by men after Prophet Muhammad, is against women. It is also against the spirit of Islam, since no institution created by mere humans has the right to proclaim itself the representative of God's interests on earth. With this understanding, many Muslim-majority countries have abandoned man-made *sharia* law in favor of a truly Islamic law, one that takes care of women and protects them. While many Muslim organizations in the West struggle against political Islam regarding *sharia*, the Islamists' religious tribunals continue to pursue women around the globe, so as to force them to submit to men, on behalf of God.

Throughout world history, male religious and political figures have oppressed women. In France and across Europe, sexism, and even misogyny, continues to exist. What *is* new is how self-declared "progressives," including feminists, have come to justify gender inequality in Arab-Muslim countries on the grounds that it is a fundamental part of local culture. One must respect cultural differences, they say, and avoid imposing a (Western) model on Muslim countries. This idea has been endorsed by Islamists, since it serves their purpose so well. In France, Islamists have been able to find other groups as well to relay their message, forming unexpected political alliances, most notably with leftist militants.

This "cultural differences" argument is, in fact, a reflection of a colonial or racist mindset, for two reasons: first, because it implies that only Westerners value justice and that Muslims are barbarians to be civilized someday; second, according to this idea, there are certain people who are programmed to live in unjust conditions and we should not "shake things up" for them, as they are not yet ready. Basically, what is good for Western women is not good for Muslim women. The corollary to this is that anything goes, and all is flexible; justice or injustice, democracy or dictatorship, freedom or deprivation. This cultural relativism is very worrying.

In France, the confusion among Muslims, Islamists, and fundamentalists is carefully maintained, both by the media and by identity-politics activists. As a result, many culturally Muslim young people view any demand by women as an act of aggression against Islam. Even the term "feminist" has become extremely pejorative. "Islamic feminism," which was created to promote progress in these conditions, is as hidden as the faces of covered women.

The issue of women is an indispensable component of Islamist strategy. In the 1970s, Islamists overlooked this point and told women recruits, after promising them everything under the sun, to return home and raise the next generation of God's soldiers. Nowadays, primarily in the West, the strategy is reversed, with veiled women presented as exceptionally modern and compatible with the values of the host country.

Islamists have learned more than enough lessons from their previous mistakes. They know that Islam is particularly criticized in the West, largely with reference to gender inequality and the position of women. For this reason, the approach to veiled Islamist women in France aspires to be respectful of women, according them virtually all the rights of Westerners, with a "bonus": chastity and faithfulness to God. French Islamists seek to demonstrate to the West that a Muslim woman who dons the veil is free because she has chosen to do so, without any deference to male authority. Even in political demonstrations, Islamist women can be found in the front ranks, defending the right to wear the headscarf.

The Muslim woman in the West thus becomes a formidable weapon of war for the penetration of Western society. She has a career, she is capable of leadership, and she occupies high positions in the Islamist movement. However, we must distinguish between the brain behind international Islamism, and the sincere, practicing individual Muslims who strengthen the Islamist side without realizing it. Of course, we should not prevent anyone from living a fully spiritual life, but it is, nevertheless, society's duty to remain vigilant in seeking to slow down this unprecedented rise in religiosity, which is a harbinger of a fanatical fundamentalism.

Given the Islamist advances, a secular opposition should be introduced to create an alternative for young Muslims in search of identity and approval. Currently these Muslims, viewed as second-class citizens by their governments, have only one source of help in this crisis: international Islamism. Caught between the dictatorships of their countries of origin and the hope-filled promises of the Islamists, how are they supposed to avoid yielding to temptation in the absence of any other viable option?

The Islamic revolution—exemplified by the completely veiled figure of a woman, representing the least negotiable of its differences with the West—has made a political symbol of the veil in its revolt against the West. A woman in a black chador is the most aggressive sign of the Islamic idea of civilization, the most obvious banner of a revolution that defines itself both *by* women and *against* women.

I have observed that many veiled students come from modest families that live Islam in its traditional, fairly superficial, form. Their decision to don the veil is often criticized by their families, pushing them further into the radical philosophy that seeks to create an alternative system, opposed equally to Muslim traditionalism and Western modernism. The veiled urban Muslim student symbolizes this form of radical Islam.

In France and most other parts of the world, these veiled women have not appeared in backward, highly traditional rural enclaves far from the influence of modernization. Instead, they are to be found in urban spaces, in universities where "modern" values such as these can be heard expressed regularly: "A Muslim woman who chooses the veil chooses virtuousness." "One must be veiled to avoid attracting the gaze of men." "One must hide one's beauty in order not to create social disorder." A well-educated veiled woman is a paradox, although young Islamist girls defy existing categories. The image of the well-educated Muslim activist is a direct challenge to the Westernized elites.

Whether it consists of a "top-down" re-Islamization of society, characteristic of the Iranian model of 1970–1980, or a "bottom-up" effort, such as the cultural Islam of the 1980s, radical Islam offers women an entirely new identity. This political trend promotes women equally as combatants—consider the images of Iranian women in chadors brandishing Kalashnikovs—and as the mothers of large families.

Political Islam empowers women by giving them an identity and a consciousness that is independent of men or children. Their newfound self-confidence also enables them to demand the right to a private life. Thus, a seemingly paradoxical conclusion is reached: the veil, which expresses submission to God, strengthens the transformation of their inner world. Ironically, it is Islam, a communitarian religion, that serves as support for this shift in identity stemming from individual spiritual life. The veil protects women from "modernity" and symbolizes their fidelity to Islam. It reminds us that a veiled woman remains "inside," even when she leaves her house. Entering public life with a motto of "personality, not femininity," she emphasizes her "sacred" body over her aesthetic one, while simultaneously strengthening her sense of "otherness" in the face of Western modernity.

★   ★   ★

Europe is faced with the difficult task of managing a dynamic characterized by two simultaneous phenomena: the failure of social integration, and the transformation of the religious or spiritual landscape. It must make room for new religions, manage a diverse society, fight against discrimination, and promote integration—all while continuing to fight against extremism. These challenges cannot be overcome by Europe alone; it must be able to rely upon the involvement of all citizens—inside or outside Europe's borders—who together aspire to a more just world. This world can be brought into being only according to a democratic model that protects rights for men and women alike.

In this context, then, we are entitled to ask ourselves whether Muslim women represent an opportunity for Europe. Unquestionably, women have often been an engine of emancipation and progress. Women will be in the front lines of the war that must be waged against those who debase humanity by denying women their dignity, in the name of a misguided interpretation of Islam. They will fight not only to defend democracy, as worthy a cause as it might be, but also to defend their individual right to pursue the happiness to which we all fundamentally aspire.

Passed down through the generations from mother to daughter, as naturally as one day follows another, the traditions of peaceful Islam are today being woven into a complex and rich tapestry that includes the most beautiful elements of the religion and its deepest humanist values. Just as Judaism and Christianity once adapted to the modern world, it is now Islam's turn to reform itself. In the struggle against this scourge of our century, the role of women from Arab-Muslim culture will be decisive.

The terrorists have so disfigured Islam and so stigmatized pacifist Muslims that more and more of them prefer to present themselves as ex-Muslims or atheists so as to dissociate themselves from the stench of reactionary thought. As for myself, someone who was immersed in traditional Islam before lapsing into secularism, I now identify myself equally as a believer, an agnostic, a secularist, and a reformer. And as for those who accuse me of apostasy because I dare to think for myself, let me remind them that one needs to only say the profession of faith out loud to be a Muslim. So, in my own way and in my own interpretation, let me say it: "There is no God but God, and Muhammad is his Prophet." This in no way prevents me from speaking up for the atheists of our culture, for, as Voltaire put it so well, "I may not agree with what you say, but I will defend to the death your right to say it."

It goes without saying that freedom of expression must be exercised in a peaceful framework. Fanaticism and fundamentalism—to say nothing of terrorism—must, first of all, be condemned by every participant in the debate. This is a war of ideas that will spill ink, rather than the blood of innocents. In this sense, the Islamists have the right to freedom of expression and belief only once their violent and reactionary ideology is confined to thought alone and no longer affects public order, either domestically or internationally.

Solutions

The government can begin changing the status quo by putting the silent majority in the public eye, instead of constantly spotlighting Islamists and their crimes against humanity. Instead of helping secular Muslims to develop their networks and maintain a presence on the streets without fearing for their lives, however, the state continues to fund and to strengthen an enemy that threatens all of humanity.

The constant media focus awarded to Islamists enhances their claim as the sole legitimate interpreters of Islam, while suggesting that we moderates do not exist. This needs to stop. We, the reformists and the secular, especially women, were the first victims of political Islam; we need to be able to establish a network to combat this plague from within, since we are familiar with its cause. We can achieve this objective only if we are no longer ignored; we need a platform, and the means to speak out against a danger that is universal.

For now, we receive only a few words of support and consider ourselves happy if we escape a *fatwa*. Nevertheless, it is saddening to experience life this way in the West. Even on the Internet, reformist and secular Muslims are afraid to reveal who they are, preferring to use pseudonyms instead.

It is vital to remember that what is happening in the Arab and Muslim countries has immediate repercussions for Muslims everywhere, including those second- and third-generation born and living in the West. The social problems in those countries are found, in more or less similar form, in France as well, and thus the solution must be implemented simultaneously in both. The institutions of secularism and democracy must take root and bear fruit in those countries so that the impact can be felt in the West as well.

However, if in Europe secularism was necessary to separate the church from the state by removing religion from the realm of politics, in the Arab-Muslim countries the problem is completely reversed. There, conflict is not between the spiritual and the temporal powers, but rather between the power of religious scholars who tightly censor writings of a religious nature, and the weakness of the uneducated masses who are reduced to reading only a single book, the Qur'an, without any guidance.

In the West, in the name of respect for freedom of conscience, religious practice should be restricted to the private sphere. In particular, the law against the display of headscarves and other outwardly religious symbols should be applied much more rigorously. Preventing girls from being educated is untenable. The state must refuse all compromises with the Islamists. If it does not, where will "respect for cultural differences" stop? With the acceptance of polygamy? With stoning as a penalty for adultery, or amputation for thievery?

A course in civic education should be introduced in the school curriculum. Young French people of Muslim culture should be able to identify and recognize themselves as fully French, which would close another avenue of Islamist recruitment.

The reduction of a diverse community to the single label "Islamic" must end. Better communication is needed with this segment of French society. We must overcome the prejudices and stereotypes that automatically imply that someone named "Muhammad" or "Fatima" is a devout Muslim, if not a potential extremist or terrorist. A Muslim by birth is not the private property of religious fanatics, but someone who has the choice of any one of the many spiritual paths, or none. Do we associate all cultural Christians with Christianity? No, we call them French, English, or German and refer to religion only if the person is outwardly devout.

A truly French Islam that respects women and universal freedoms must be established to represent the practicing Arab-Muslim minority. Such a French Islam would not tolerate the practices of oral divorce of women by men or polygamy, on the Islamist pretext that one should respect an unchanged text. It is only by following the national law that integration will take place.

In contrast to the CFCM, which is limited to the religious sphere, a secular cultural body is needed to represent the community of French citizens of Muslim cultural background, regardless of individual beliefs. Such an approach could unite all who share this culture, believers or unbelievers, practicing or non-practicing, secular or reformist. In this approach, the Arab, non-Arab, French, Maghrebi, and African perspectives on this cultural identity are included, without harming anyone or infringing upon freedom of expression and conscience. It would feature talk not about religion, but about creating a citizenship criteria that is worthy of our origins. It would be directed not at discussion of people's innermost thoughts and beliefs, but at developing some badly needed consensus views on managing relations with other groups.

When government seeks a specifically Muslim interlocutor, it should separate religion from politics. Instead of insisting on linking religion with culture—thereby further dividing a community already subject to considerable internal factional division on religious grounds—it can set a positive example. Questions on organizing the *Hajj* or constructing mosques would be primarily handled by the CFCM, although ideally after asking the opinion of the secular community. When the secular body is tasked with the management of social conflicts, no advice would be called for from the CFCM. In other words, the current situation would be reversed so that the secular would include the religious, whereas the reverse would not be true. The secular involves the entire community, while the religious includes only part of it.

The struggle against racial discrimination in hiring and the fight for the right to decent housing, quality schools, and literacy training must continue; it is wonderful when an illiterate person becomes able to read the scriptures, without needing to resort to reactionary Islamist interpretations. Yet integration has many aspects, and focusing exclusively on one dimension will not bring about a solution. Just as we are justifiably wary of Islamists' professed desire for integration, we must be encouraging in promoting goodwill among Arab-Muslims who want to be accepted as fully French.

The right to criticize Islam constructively from within the community must be protected. It is true that the more Islam is attacked from the outside, the more Islamism strengthens itself by posing as defender of the faith. However, Islamism's greatest vulnerability is internal; thus, the well-intentioned laws forbidding criticism of Islam and the Qur'an leave the Islamist position unassailable, and its "Islamophobic" opponents harassed and without the right to speak.

We must clearly distinguish an Islamist-phobe from an "Islamophobe." There is nothing Islamophobic in tackling the problem of political Islam and international Islamism, and it has nothing to do with the pacifist majority that finds itself the first casualty in this nameless war. To allow someone to criticize a doctrine, sacred though it may be, does not affect anyone who follows it in good faith. And questioning whether a person's activities are, for example, directed toward advancing the Islamist agenda has little to do with the Arab-Muslim community as a whole.

Today, the solution is in the hands of Muslims who want to take part in this battle to avoid the worst. Certainly, those who declare themselves to be in this camp are few, as their lives are at stake. But if a credible, secure institutional structure is created, there would be countless supporters who would invariably dare to speak up.

Notes

1. "Arab-Muslim" refers to Muslim Arabs, as opposed to non-Muslim Arabs (such as Christian Arabs) and non-Arab Muslims (such as Iranian Muslims).
2. Sahih al-Bukhari, *Hadith* 7.114, narrated by Abu Huraira: The Prophet said, "Whoever believes in Allah and the Last Day should not hurt (trouble) his neighbor. And I advise you to take care of the women, for they are created from a rib and the most bent portion of the rib is its upper part; if you try to straighten it, it will break, and if you leave it, it will remain bent, so I urge you to take care of the women."

CHAPTER SEVEN

The Lamp and the Candle

MOSTAFA HILALI

My name is Mostafa Hilali, and I am a major in the Royal Netherlands Army. I grew up in the same Amsterdam neighborhood as Mohammed Bouyeri, who murdered the Dutch filmmaker Theo van Gogh in the name of Islam. His parents and mine were acquaintances, and some friends of mine grew up in his apartment building.

I have often asked myself why he and I traveled such different paths. Why did two Muslim men with similar social, cultural, and ethnic backgrounds make such radically different choices in life?

A lot has been written about Mohammed Bouyeri and the other members of the so-called Hofstad Group. Their motives, their interpretation of Islam, and their terrorist tactics were analyzed in great detail during their court case in books, articles, and television reporting. There is not much I can add to that.

My story is a different one. By telling it, I hope to show that there is no contradiction in being a Muslim, a Dutch Moroccan, a critical thinker, an independent character, a loyal son, and a professional soldier at the same time.

I was born in 1973 in Morocco in the imperial city of Meknes. This was an extraordinarily difficult period in my parents' lives, even though I was blissfully unaware of that. My father had gone to the Netherlands in 1971 as a guest worker, and spent only the holidays in Morocco.

I am the product of one of those visits. When I recently asked my parents how they managed to keep their faith in each other without seeing each other, they told me that their faith in God had helped them through it. For them the separation was God's test of their love for one another, and they were very proud of having stuck together. It made me wonder why my own marriage ended in divorce. Had I failed that same test?

By 1976 my mother had had enough of God's tests, and made it clear to my father that it was time for the family to reunite. That prompted him to rent a larger house in Amsterdam, and at the tender age of three I moved with my parents and four siblings to the Netherlands. Later I would frequently ask my father why he moved to a country that has so many rainy days. Usually he would reply that there are even wetter countries than the Netherlands. But in more serious moments, he would say that a person only travels the path that God has chosen for him.

It is at these times that I see the strength that my father's faith gives him. And again I wonder, Do I believe this too? Is my faith just as strong? Could I set upon a path, without any idea about the end result, and do this with the absolute conviction that I am only doing what God wants me to do? And what is left of free will if it is God who determines the route I should take?

Yet there we were, a group of immigrants in Amsterdam. My father had arranged everything for us, and we settled in quite easily. It was, of course, much harder for my brother and sister, who were both older than me. They had been to school in Morocco, and now had to adjust to a new system. I was in the luxurious position of getting a fresh start in this new country. I do not remember experiencing any differences with Dutch kids. Going to Christian schools probably had something to do with that.

In fact, reading from the Bible was one of my favorite things at school. I also recall the Christmas plays, where I always had a role. At that time I had a full head of black curly hair, and I did not mind wearing a robe, even though the other boys said it was a dress. I saw my father wearing robes many times and had one myself. I usually was one of the shepherds. It was a good role, because I always had a lot of stage time and did not have to say much.

There was nothing special about being Muslim during my school days, except for Wednesday afternoons or weekends. It was then that I had to go to "Qur'an school," the same one attended by Mohammed Bouyeri. It was a horrible experience, and helped shape my ideas about Islam in a very negative way. It is not that I was too stupid to memorize *surahs* (the Qur'anic chapters). On the contrary, while I was a small kid with big glasses, I had one advantage: I was better at memorizing texts than most other children. And this was a great asset to have at Qur'an school, because the curriculum consisted of memorizing *surahs* and reciting them for the teacher. The teacher was quite a character, with a special way of encouraging his pupils not to make mistakes: a two-meter long, thin wooden rod. I will not go into details, but his methods did motivate me to really concentrate on my scholastic endeavors. Truth be told, I hated the man, and it became difficult not to hate Islam, especially given the fact that my Dutch teachers educated us about Christianity in a kinder, quieter manner.

Looking back, I am not surprised I developed a certain antipathy toward my own religious heritage. While most other kids started to pray at the age of ten, I refused to learn the rituals despite having memorized parts of the Qur'an. I identified more with my Dutch friends than with Moroccan or Muslim friends. In my secondary school, there were very few children of non-Dutch origin or of Muslim background. It was not until the age of sixteen, during a vacation in Morocco, that I learned to pray, but I did not become a strict practitioner of the rituals.

Doubts remained. I did not think the rituals had much point and, like so many other second-generation Dutch-Moroccan boys, I found that relations with my parents were deteriorating. They were the last people I could talk to about my religious doubts.

★   ★   ★

All of this changed when I met my ex-wife. Even though our marriage ended in divorce, it still remains a formative part of my life. It was during my marriage to a Christian girl that I learned much about myself, Islam, and life. But my feelings for her came at a price. When I was eighteen and very much in love with her, I was confronted by the harsh reality that not everybody in Dutch society appreciated relationships between Muslims and non-Muslims. A group of well-dressed, middle-aged Dutch men beat me up for having the nerve to date a Dutch girl, breaking my jaw. I spent a night in the hospital and contemplated what had happened. It was a rude awakening to realize that even though I saw myself as a Dutchman, others did not. Whether I liked it or not, I was different and would always remain different in the eyes of some.

Using a straw for six weeks to get your nutrition is not very enjoyable, but my mind had suffered the bigger blow. I felt a very strong and deep anger, one that could have tipped the scales and made me hate Dutch society. If I think back and ask myself why I retained my belief in society and my place in it, it must have something to do with the Dutch nurse who comforted me when I cried my bitter tears. And, of course, it also helped that the girl I loved only loved me more for it, and decided she wanted to be my wife.

Being beaten up and getting married are two profoundly different experiences, but they both helped shape my religious identity. My fiancée was a Dutch Christian. We were nineteen years old, full of optimism, and confident that our different religious backgrounds would not pose an obstacle to marriage or happiness, even if others might disagree. For now, the question I faced was how to tell my parents I was getting married to a Christian girl. I foresaw big problems, but it turns out that I need not have worried. What I did not realize is that, even though I saw myself primarily as a liberal, secular Dutchman, I was also in a way acting on the basis of my Muslim upbringing and values. I proposed to my girlfriend because I did not want to live together without being married. And for her as a Christian it was the same: her values meant she wanted to marry me. There is a saying in the Netherlands that when two religions sleep on the same pillow, the devil lies in between. We both tried hard to prove it wrong and out-of-date. And, I might add, we succeeded.

I went to my parents in a very determined mood. I intended to tell them about my marriage, and warn them there was nothing they could do to stop me. They would simply have to accept that she was Dutch and Christian. Then came the big surprise. My parents struck a conciliatory tone. They said, "She is a nice girl and you will not find a better wife. But are you not a bit too young to get married?" That was an eye-opener. Here were my parents, first-generation immigrants, illiterate, and hardly taken seriously by mainstream Dutch society, and they did not make an issue about me marrying a Christian. They gave us their blessing.

Even though a part of me was very happy with the way things were going, another part had not fully recovered from the beating. It triggered questions like: What had I done to deserve the beating? Had God punished me for not fulfilling my religious duties? I held to most religious rules: I fasted during Ramadan, professed the faith, did not eat pork, and abstained from alcohol, even though I did not pray the five proscribed prayers every day. I thought that perhaps the answer was to pray regularly, and to avoid making excuses.

But every time I tried, my critical self would hold me back, thinking, Why am I doing this? I was missing something, but I did not know what. There seemed to be a gap in my knowledge and understanding of Islam that was keeping me from experiencing true communication with God, without any static or atmospheric clutter, just like my parents seemed to experience when they prayed.

As I was pondering the meaning of Islam, the wedding came closer. My fiancée wanted to get married in her church. That made me wonder, Is that possible? I had a conversation with my father, and he told me that being blessed in a house of God was a blessing. "And you cannot have enough blessings in your life!" he said. This was one of those moments that made me understand the profound wisdom of my parents. They were traditional Muslims who had made many sacrifices to give me and my brothers and sisters a chance at a better life. They had done this by working at jobs that many Dutch people felt were below them, all the time holding on to their dignity.

This was the defining moment in my life, when I learned that faith and free will could be allies. We went to a feast in our neighborhood where an elderly Moroccan man confronted my father and me about the wedding. The man said that it was forbidden for a Muslim to marry an infidel. Since I had expected people to ask this question, I had done some research and was ready to tell him that the Qur'an allows a Muslim man to marry a Christian or Jewish woman. But before I could say anything, my father told the man, "Well, she is a Christian, so she is not an infidel. And even if she was, at least my son is marrying her. Your son does not bother to do that with his Dutch girlfriend!" I was very impressed. My father, who had dropped out of school at the age of twelve, showed what real enlightenment means.

We got married on a cold November day in 1993. I still have the pictures, and when I hear people speak about the intolerance of Islam I look at those pictures. I see my father in the front row of a Protestant church, holding a little songbook with Christian psalms and hymns and trying hard to sing along. I see my mother with her headscarf on trying to do the same, and looking proudly at her son. These are the pictures that remind me, if ever I doubt it, that true faith and tolerance are two sides of the same coin.

I began to think more positively about my own religion. My father-in-law would ask me difficult questions about Islam and Muslims, helping me to discover my own heritage. I began to study Islam as a religion and culture so I could give better answers. Sadly, my marriage ended in divorce after six years. When people ask me about it, they naturally assume that the cultural or religious differences were too great—two religions on one pillow. They are wrong. Each year, we fasted together during Ramadan and went to church together on Christmas Eve. But for young people, living apart for most of the week is hard.

★   ★   ★

The reason we spent so much time apart was that I had become a soldier and was stationed in Germany during the week. Joining the military was a decision with profound consequences for my personal development as a human being and as a Muslim.

I had to overcome a few bureaucratic hurdles to be able to enlist. Some years back, when I turned eighteen, my father had suggested I apply for Dutch nationality. My answer was that if I did that I could be conscripted into the Dutch Army, and at that time who wanted that! A few years later, the army had become an all-volunteer army, and I was unsatisfied with my job and thinking hard about my next step. I decided to join the ranks. The recruiting officer asked me whether I had Dutch nationality. I did not, and was told I could not enlist until I had it. I asked my father for some original Moroccan documents, and he asked me why I needed them. When I told him that I wanted to apply for Dutch nationality because I needed it to enlist in the army, it made him laugh. I wondered if he had a crystal ball.

Enlisting also made me think about the likelihood that I would face religious dilemmas when deployed abroad. It was 1996, and Dutch peacekeepers were deployed in Bosnia-Herzegovina to oversee the implementation of the Dayton Agreement. I could not imagine any problem arising from my Islamic background in this particular situation.

It did not take long to find out that being a Muslim does make military life in a Western army harder. The first time I was confronted with being a Muslim was during my basic training. I was in the "Orthodox" phase of my life, praying five times a day, but this did not interfere with my training. My colleagues respected my beliefs, and they would actually keep everybody quiet in our dormitory when I was praying. It was later, during my last field exercise, that I really had to think about what to do. This exercise was like a final exam, and I was required to pass it.

It was, however, also the month of Ramadan, and therefore time to fast. The Qur'an states that soldiers do not have to fast during wartime, but an exercise hardly counts as wartime. The weekend before this exercise started I spoke with my father, who said that I should have the intention of fasting and start the day accordingly. If I felt that I could not proceed responsibly with my work, I should break the fast.

So I began the exercise, and in a strange way fasting actually made me more capable and alert. One of my colleagues was also Muslim, and he also had to go on this exercise, but he decided not to fast. I remember other colleagues asking me why I was fasting, and he was not. I told them that it was a personal choice, and I did not feel obliged to tell him to fast or not. This satisfied them, but it did not stop our platoon leader from kidding around. He assembled the platoon and told them that since I had *Jammerdan* (a play on the word "Ramadan" that can be translated as "tough luck"), they would also have to fast with me! Now the entire platoon was going to go without food for the next twenty-four hours. Later I discovered that this was actually a planned part of the exercise, but it says something about the relaxed attitude toward Muslims in the Netherlands at that time that our lieutenant felt he could link it to Ramadan.

When I finished my initial training I joined the Forty-First Light Brigade, which was stationed in Germany. There I had to attest my loyalty to the army by swearing an oath in front of my superiors, my peers, and my family. It is tradition that religious people finish their oath with the words, "so help me God." Non-religious colleagues would finish their oath by saying, "I promise thus." I would have had no problem with the first oath, but I came in contact with a chaplain at that time who told me that Muslim soldiers were allowed to take their oath by saying, "In the name of Allah, the most gracious, ever merciful." He explained this was a tradition in the Dutch armed forces, dating back to the days when Indonesia formed part of the Dutch colonial empire and many of the soldiers in the East were Muslims. I was impressed. When my commanding officer asked me how I wanted to affirm my oath, I told him I wanted to swear the Muslim oath. He first doubted the possibility really existed, but after some research, agreed it was possible. Thus was I sworn in, in front of everybody, in a way that was in accordance with my religious beliefs. When I hear Muslims claim that Western armed forces are by definition anti-Islam, I always think of the oath I took. I cannot think of many Islamic countries that would allow non-Muslims to serve in the armed forces, let alone have them sworn in using their own religious terminology.

Not everything went smoothly, however. Finding *halal* food was a problem. I would always bring a can of vegetarian macaroni with me on exercises, because the supply officers would sometimes forget to arrange for food without pork. Around the time of Ramadan it would be difficult to make arrangements for Muslim servicemen, since they would want to have breakfast much earlier than their colleagues, and not every mess hall would open up so early. I was a private, and rank does count in the army. Every year there was a debate with the stewards in the mess hall; sometimes it was an easy debate, and at other times it was a hard fight, but in the end, it would always work out.

After my deployment to Bosnia, I decided to apply to the Royal Military Academy in Breda to become an officer, and I was accepted. Being Muslim had no effect on my time there, except when I was asked to give lectures about Islam because the staff and cadets wanted to know more about it. After my education there, I was commissioned as a second lieutenant in the infantry and returned to Germany to serve with an infantry battalion. Here I found that being an officer made the debates with the mess hall staff around Ramadan much easier, so it seems there is a subtle relationship between power and tolerance.

Army humor would sometimes rear its head. One day, coming back from a meeting with my company commander, I saw that some of my soldiers had parked the APC (Armored Personnel Carrier) with the ramp down. They had placed a small rug in front of it and put their shoes outside it. The main gun was aimed toward the east, and a sign on the APC read "Field Mosque!" In today's more heated atmosphere, no doubt some of my fellow Muslims would cry "discrimination!" but for me this simply meant that my colleagues felt relaxed enough about my religious beliefs—and about me—to pull this practical joke.

★　★　★

Unfortunately, relations became much more tense after 9/11. I was on a live-fire exercise that day and on the ranges for hours, so I did not see the awful pictures until I returned to the barracks. The events were terrible, but I did not feel a special responsibility; so when a colleague of mine confronted me the next day, it came as a shock. He shouted at me, in front of other people, "Why do you Muslims always attack us?" I tried to remain calm, reminding him that during the attack he and I had been on the range together. What, exactly, I asked him, was the link between those terrorists and me?

I was still inclined to think this was an isolated incident, to be forgotten as quickly as possible. But then a Muslim private in a different company approached me and told me he was having second thoughts about taking the Muslim oath. I replied that this was, of course, a matter of personal choice, but I was curious to know why, given that he had been very certain only a few weeks earlier that he would use the Muslim oath. He told me that he had been the subject of a great many remarks from his colleagues, and that he expected a good deal more if he were to show his religious background openly during the ceremony. By then I was no longer certain that these were isolated incidents. Was there an invisible undercurrent dividing the ranks into "us" and "them"?

After a while, things cooled down. Neither of the incidents had involved physical harassment. We evaluated them within the unit, and I wrote a short letter to the *Defensiekrant* (which is the newspaper for the Netherlands armed forces), describing them as isolated incidents resulting from emotions running high in the aftermath of the attacks.

A little while later, we were preparing for deployment to Afghanistan. We had been briefed about Islam by an Iranian woman who had fled her homeland because of the Islamic revolution. Her experience with religious fanatics had understandably influenced her in a negative way, similar to my experience in the Qur'an school. But hers were lasting scars, and the Islam she taught us was not the Islam I had learned to love. Nor did I feel she was preparing my colleagues very well for our mission in Afghanistan, where building relations with local tribal elders would be of crucial importance. She made it seem that most Muslims would prefer to live in an Islamic theocracy. I took issue with her, arguing that religion itself was not to blame but the people who misused it for their own power plays. My colleagues, intrigued by our sometimes heated discussions, asked me to give a briefing of my own. I did the best that I could, but felt embarrassed by how little I still knew. In many cases I could not explain why certain practices had developed, and I decided to continue building up my knowledge of Islam.

★   ★   ★

In Afghanistan, dilemmas for Muslims became real. For instance, what would happen if I were to die? Who would make certain my remains were washed according to Muslim customs and the appropriate rituals followed? In those days, the International Security and Assistance Force in Afghanistan (ISAF) was led by the Turkish armed forces, who do not have imams in their ranks; so I made a deal with a Dutch-Moroccan corporal. We promised each other to take care of the rituals if one of us were to die. If both of us died at the same time, that would constitute a problem, but there is only so much a person wants to think about and arrange for. Fortunately, we both survived.

The Ramadan dilemma also came up again during this time. The Qur'an says that in a war a Muslim does not have to fast, but we were participating in an international peacekeeping operation, not a war. I consulted an imam in Amsterdam, who told me that it was a difficult case and the choice was mine. I should try to fast, but if I could not keep it up I could break the fast and continue my work. So that is what I did, and fortunately all went well again.

I continued to be deployed to Afghanistan and other Islamic countries in the years afterward, and I found that my background, in fact, worked well in my interaction with the local population. In one particular case, an Afghan chief whom I had to talk to about some incidents in his area proved not very cooperative, and maintained that there was nothing he could do.

When my colleague pressed him on the subject, he became angry and said, "If there was a Qur'an here [in the field] I would swear on it!" I got my Qur'an from the front pocket of my uniform and offered it to him. He looked at me as if I were crazy, and then he backed down. Suffice it to say that the end of the conversation was more productive than the beginning.

These deployments convinced me that the army needed reforms that would help Muslims combine their military duties with their religious convictions. I sent a letter to army headquarters and was invited to discuss the matter. There seemed to be a sincere willingness to make progress on this issue.

By 2004, the time seemed ripe to push through some of these reforms. Under the auspices of the Multicultural Network of the Department of Defense (MND), we organized a seminar to formulate concrete steps to improve the position of Muslims in the armed forces. One key issue was the absence of religious support for Muslim servicemen by a person with the same religious background. The armed forces employed ministers, rabbis, and Hindu priests, but no imams. The seminar participants agreed this had to change, and that is when the search for imams began, but finding imams was easier said than done.

★   ★   ★

That same year, Mohammed Bouyeri set back Muslim emancipation in the Netherlands by several years. It is astonishing what a destructive effect the murder of a single man can have on a society. Measured by the psychological damage to the fabric of Dutch society, Bouyeri's act was a success. The impact was amplified because Bouyeri chose his target so carefully. van Gogh was an outspoken defender of the right to free speech, and had seemed to revel in insulting Muslims. He had also cooperated with the Somali-Dutch parliamentarian Ayaan Hirsi Ali to make their notorious movie, *Submission*. Bouyeri added to the impact of his crime by butchering Van Gogh with two knives, as one would slaughter a pig.

Shocked and angry, the Dutch felt they needed to take a stand against Muslim radicalism. In their desire to defend their tolerant society, confusion reigned. How do you defend a tolerant society against intolerant Muslim extremists? And how can you distinguish between "good" Muslims and "bad" Muslims? How can you be sure that not all Muslims are secretly trying to turn the Netherlands into a Muslim theocracy and subjugate all non-Muslims? As ridiculous as these questions seem, many people had real fears and began to look at Muslims with suspicion. There were calls for a collective Muslim apology for Bouyeri's act. Some politicians poured fuel on the fire and began to suggest that Dutch Muslims could not be trusted. It made me wonder how resilient the famed Dutch tolerance really was.

Dutch Muslims felt increasingly isolated and exasperated, especially those who had tried hardest to play a meaningful role in Dutch society.

Proud of their religion, they could not accept being held responsible for the deed of one man. Even my father temporarily lost his cool, and began to doubt that he and his family would ever be accepted as true citizens of the Netherlands. He had lived in the country for over thirty years and had never been out of a job during that time. He and my mother had raised six children who all contributed to society. My parents had always been proud of me serving in the Dutch Army and supported me, even during deployments to Islamic countries.

It made me sad to see their pain but it was also heartwarming to see how they kept their faith in the Netherlands and decided to stay, instead of returning to Morocco as they could have done. It was as if God was again putting them to the test, and they were again determined to pass it. My mother simply said, "This is the country where we came to build our future. Our children live here, and this is where our grandchildren were born. We are Dutch, and we have as much right to be here as anybody else."

Paradoxically, one of the reasons Muslims did not turn their backs on Dutch society was that to some degree, they *did* feel responsible. While an entire group should never be held responsible for an individual's act, the problem was that Bouyeri committed his crime in the name of their religion. In some perverse way he believed that he was God's instrument, and this created a dilemma for many Muslims. Some maintained that speaking out would only confirm for non-Muslims that one Muslim could indeed be held accountable for another Muslim's crime. I personally, however, had some sympathy for those calling for Muslims to show that Bouyeri had not acted on their behalf. While there is no such thing as collective guilt, I did see the need for Muslims to distance themselves from Bouyeri's interpretation of Islam. Fortunately, I was not alone; the same day that van Gogh was murdered, a collective of Dutch Muslim organizations condemned the act during a televised press conference.

In the army, van Gogh's murder triggered a replay of the incidents that occurred after 9/11. Colleagues asked me whether I would fight side by side with non-Muslims against Muslims in places such as Afghanistan. It was a relevant question, but addressed to the wrong person. During my deployments I have been involved in numerous dangerous situations, and at no time did I hesitate to do my duty because my opponents may have been Muslims. When you are under fire, your religious affiliation matters less than distinguishing between those who want you to stay alive and those who want to kill you. Dutch pacifists and Dutch Muslims would sometimes criticize my career choice, to which I would always retort that their liberties and rights could only exist because there are so-called macho types like me who are willing to put their lives at risk.

★   ★   ★

Just as the tension had subsided after 9/11, tensions eventually subsided after the van Gogh murder. However, the search for imams had been placed on the back burner, and by 2006 no imam had been appointed. That year, a group of Muslim soldiers organized an *iftar* dinner during Ramadan, the first within the Netherlands armed forces. This dinner was a positive surprise and an eye-opener for many senior officers and non-Muslims. Speaking to the guests, the assistant secretary of defense made a firm commitment that imams would soon be instated. It took us two more iftars, but in April 2009, two imams were commissioned into the Royal Netherlands Army—five years after the subject was brought to the attention of the army leadership; better late than never.

One reason it had taken so much time to commission imams is that we wanted to make sure that the imams who were appointed did not belong to the same "school" as the Qur'an teacher who reveled in beating young boys for failing to memorize *surahs*. I am confident this will not happen. One good thing about the Netherlands is that its people, including its Muslims, seem to be always able to find a consensus, even amidst the greatest of controversies. The organization that nominates the imams for the army, the CMO (which stands for *Contactorgaan Moslims en Overheid* and can be translated as the Organization for Contact between Muslims and the Government), is an umbrella organization composed of different Muslim organizations which, in turn, represent different religious schools and ethnic groups and it acts as a mediator between the Dutch government and the Muslim communities in the Netherlands. In good Dutch *poldermodel* fashion (a model for consensus decision-making, which is said to be typically Dutch), the CMO makes sure a consensus is achieved about candidates, which makes it very difficult for an imam with extremist ideas to slip through the cracks. Most Muslims in the army are aware and vigilant, and so is my father. When I told him I was attending a meeting about the new imams, he said, "That is good news. Just make sure you don't get the bad ones."

★   ★   ★

In 2005 the next stage of my education began, as I started to study history and Islamic studies at the University of Leiden while continuing my work in the Defense Ministry. The University of Leiden has a centuries-old tradition in Islamic studies, and an incredibly rich library. A new world opened up for me and I learned more about the Shia and Sufi traditions, which differed from my own Sunni background. Learning about the mystical side of Islam was particularly gratifying.

It had taken me many years, but it was at the University of Leiden that I finally learned to speak to God in my own way, without static clutter, while at the same time feeling more confident as a social scientist. During my studies I learned to question many things that I had accepted as truths before, and I discovered that I was not alone in my doubts or questions. Many Muslims before me had struggled like me and found their way. I also realized that many of my fellow students had the same questions, and that debate is a healthy thing.

In Leiden, I learned perhaps the greatest of all lessons. To other, more enlightened souls than I, this may seem obvious, but to me it was an eye-opener: I finally understood that there is no such thing as one Islam. Instead, there are many different Islams, and while my ideas about Islam will have little in common with those of a person from certain other parts of the world, we both call ourselves Muslim, and both believe we should try not to disregard God's will. And with that I finally found a kind of inner tranquility. I know that I do not always do what the Orthodox deem obligatory, and that I sometimes do things that literal believers see as forbidden. I still have many doubts about my religion, but I realize that it is all right to have these doubts, because it means that I am thinking about how to be and how to act as a human being.

Now that my confidence in my version of Islam has grown, so has my faith in science. I know that I truly believe that God is out there, and that He or She is looking down at us. But it is up to us as individuals to make something of our lives here. God may shine on and illuminate the path, but we still have to walk it ourselves. We cannot hide behind ideas about destiny, predestination, fate, and other notions that take responsibility from us as individuals. Those who hand over to God all responsibility for their acts in fact become robots. And it is impossible to be a robot without will and a true believer at the same time. I also realize that my parents might have walked the path they believe God set out for them, but it has not stopped them from actively shaping and changing their lives!

It is up to us to use our God-given gifts and talents to try to make the world a better place, which brings me to my final words. A few years ago, I wrote an article about the roots of the radicalization of Dutch Muslim youth. I said that non-Muslims should try to change some negative attitudes about Muslims. I also said that Muslims do not bear sole responsibility for combating radicalization, but that it is the job of all of us. I would like to add that there *is* a responsibility that Muslims do have, one we cannot share with our non-Muslim countrymen.

That responsibility is to take a stand against those who use, abuse, and besmirch our religion. The real heretics are those who claim that only they know what true Islam is, and that others are at best hypocrites, and at worst apostates and infidels. These are the people who threaten, hurt, maim, and kill other people, and in particular, innocent bystanders, in the name of Islam. It is these people who make a mockery of the true message of Islam, and I must say that we have given them this power. By "we" I mean those Muslims who for too long have been silent, and have let these fanatics corrupt and abuse our faith to further their political agendas. We do have a responsibility to break the silence, raise our voices, and say that we cannot condone these acts of violence and intolerance. Many young Muslims in the West have identity problems, a low socio-economic status, and difficulty in communicating with their parents, and are very susceptible to radical, extremist Islamists.

It is among these second- and third-generation Muslims that we see a revival of Islamist ideology, and the search for the so-called pure Islam. That is why Muslims who have struggled, like these youths, and found a way forward, must speak up and help them to understand that there is an alternative to closing your mind: opening your mind, and seeing Islam in all its facets.

When I talk to boys in my Amsterdam neighborhood, I sometimes tell them the following story. A Sufi teacher is asked by his students which is the one true religion. He answers that there is no such thing, but there is only one true *faith*. When asked to explain the difference, he tells them that faith is like a candle: it gives light and illuminates its surroundings, and thereby shows people the way. It also warms and comforts those who feel cold or sad. He goes on to say that this one faith is universal, and not exclusive to Islam. He explains that religion is like a lamp with many pieces of colored glass, and that a person who looks through this glass will say, "The light is this or that color, and that is the true light." The others will disagree, saying that their color is the one true light. In doing so, they become so obsessed with the discussion that they cannot feel the warmth of the candle any more, and can see only part of the light.

This story is important to me. It symbolizes how faith is more important than religion, how being Muslim is about openness and tolerance. Islam is not a doctrine, nor an absolute truth. It has helped me to feel confident about being a Muslim and an individual at the same time. For me, it was a long struggle to get to this point, and I am grateful to all those who helped me to get there, from the men who beat me up, to the nurse who looked after me, to my ex-wife and father-in-law, to my military colleagues, to my Dutch friends, and to my professors and fellow students at Leiden University.

But most of all, I feel immensely proud to be my parents' son. They came to the same conclusion without the benefit of an institution of higher learning, without extensive travel to other countries, and without all the self-questioning that I experienced. It does make you wonder whether all roads lead to Rome, or to Mecca.

Was Mohammed Bouyeri destined to become a murderer? Was I destined to become a soldier? I think not. Many social, cultural, and economic factors played a role, as did family. Bouyeri became radicalized after his mother's death. Maybe he was treated badly at crucial points in his life. Who is to say? But it is my firm conviction that all of God's children have their own responsibility as individuals, too. I fear that, at heart, the explanation is shockingly simple: Bouyeri became so obsessed by one particular facet of the lamp that he could no longer see its other facets and colors, let alone feel the warmth of the candle. And then he fell into a deep darkness. I thank God and count my lucky stars that I have been able to stay focused on the candle itself.

PART III

Looking Ahead: Islam's Renaissance and Coexistence with Secular Democracy

CHAPTER EIGHT

Reading the Qur'an in Paris: The Case for a Secular Democracy

GHALEB BENCHEIKH

The "Islam question" has emerged at the center of the world's strategic and political agenda. Like the "Eastern question" of the early twentieth century, it has profoundly critical implications for all the key issues confronting the international community. Unfortunately, both in Europe and in other parts of the world, a climate of tension, fear, and misunderstanding affects the way people approach this question. This negative climate has been further exacerbated by the way the media have treated the issue. Neither the voluminous (and often insidious) commentary in the popular press, nor the prolific but tendentious output of amateur "analysts" has succeeded in clarifying matters, much less in reducing tensions.

The attacks in New York, Madrid, and London seized the world's attention. Cases such as the wearing of headscarves in France and the murder of filmmaker Theo van Gogh in the Netherlands have quickly polluted the debate and muddied the waters. The unfortunate caricatures of the Prophet Muhammad, as well as Pope Benedict XVI's blunder in Regensburg,[1] have compounded the misunderstanding between Muslims and their fellow citizens in European countries. A kind of mass hysteria has set in, with exaggerations from a whole slew of poorly informed observers. This hysteria has affected the entire spectrum of Western public opinion, from those who are merely suspicious of Islam to those who attack Muslim places of worship. Examples such as the dispute over the mention of Christianity in the preamble to the European Constitution and declarations by British authorities that thousands of Muslim citizens are under heightened surveillance have done nothing to reduce tensions or to put minds at ease. Instead, they point to the widespread nature of Islamophobia—a psychosis that is at times almost palpable.

This article was originally written in French and was translated by Emmet C. Tuohy for this volume.

This phobia is due, in part, to tremendous ignorance. In the minds of Europeans, the mere sound of the word "Islam" conjures up dark images. This fear of Islam is exacerbated by the indefensible attitude of a small minority, who view themselves as "God's prosecutors" and the sole defenders of His rights, while readily flouting the rights of others.

To be fair, some highly placed Muslims also bear responsibility. Their weak-mindedness and timidity have at times bordered on outright cowardice. Their silence has amounted to approval of the extremism that has corrupted the Islamic community for many years. Though a few notable intellectuals and religious leaders have spoken out, most rational, moderate Muslim leaders in positions of influence have been unwilling to make their voices heard in public, thus allowing the shrill sensationalism of the radicals to dominate the public square.

Unfortunately, the steadfast commitment of democratic Muslims to peace and dignity is little noted in a media climate dominated by superficiality. Yet these strong-willed people work tirelessly—both inside and outside the Muslim world—to bring about freedom and the transparent establishment of democracy, law, and justice in respect for the diversity of religions and traditions. Democratic Muslims engage in cultural dialogue and defend secularism, even though they are ignored and only marginally understood by those who stigmatize all Muslims as rebellious opponents of modernity and progress. It is curious that the inhabitants of what is called the "Muslim world" are the only ones who are categorized by their faith alone, despite the great diversity of languages, cultures, and traditions in this "region." Rarely do we hear the Argentineans, the Irish, and the Filipinos lumped together as "Christians," or all Japanese reduced to "Shinto followers." Why do we not hear about the impact of African animism on international relations?

The catch-all term "Muslims" is used to refer to a wide range of people, whether Indonesian or Senegalese, Uighur or Hui Chinese, Slavic or Latin American, Ingushetian or Tatar. Yet Tunisians are more similar in customs, lifestyles, and values to the Maltese than to Pakistanis, and Pakistanis have more in common with Indians than with Tunisians. The Jews of North African or Turkish cities have more in common with their Muslim neighbors than Muslims from Senegal or Indonesia have with each other.

Whether he is observant or lapsed, a devout believer or a proud agnostic, a resident of a Wahhabi monarchy or a secular republic, *homo islamicus* will always be perceived as a natural sympathizer with the actions—acceptable and otherwise—of the other members of this "species." He may not be a fundamentalist, but he is always a potential terrorist—so that we feel the need to add "moderate" when describing Muslims who act with goodness and decency. Radicalism, it seems, is the rule, and moderation the exception—at least for Muslims. Terms such as "open-minded" or "moderate" are not used to describe followers of other religious traditions, because "fundamentalists" or "extremists" are assumed to be the exception among Christians or Hindus. Yet for many "well-informed" and "enlightened" observers, it seems, the difference between a Muslim and an extremist Islamist is one of degree, never one of nature. The slope from Islam toward Islamism is slippery indeed.

To avoid seeming like the bearer of yet another *chikaya* (Arabic for "complaint"), let me reiterate that the larger part of the blame falls upon Muslim leaders. In the complex process of ideologization of religious tradition and practice, these leaders have had different reactions, and adopted highly contradictory approaches. Three main trends have emerged:

First, there are intellectuals and religious leaders who subscribe to an emerging Islamist pseudo-intellectual system that defends Muslims against perceived injustices from the West. Convinced of the pragmatic necessity of using fundamentalist arguments in the struggle to reestablish "equilibrium" in the regional and international balance between the Muslim world and the West—even if they themselves do not agree with these arguments—these intellectuals and religious leaders refrain from directly criticizing any of the participants in the struggle against the West—not even the extremists—in the view that to do so would be tantamount to betraying the entire "resistance." They reject violence and terror—if at all—only after first condemning at length the atrocities of the Serbs in Bosnia and Kosovo, the Israelis in Palestine and Lebanon, the Russians in Chechnya, the Indians in Kashmir, and, of course, the United States and United Kingdom in Iraq and Afghanistan. The need for this kind of "tit for tat" criticism might be legitimate from the perspective of an ordinary citizen, bruised and embittered by the denial of rights and justice suffered by a sizeable number of his co-religionists, but it is very difficult to accept from religious leaders, who engage in intellectual haggling and moral blackmailing rather than attaining what a healthy education should provide: an elevating, humanistic transcendence with an unwavering commitment to justice and peace.

The second group is composed of scholars (*ulema*) in state service who are unwilling or unable to escape from the shadow of royal or presidential palaces. Committed above all to the state, they sacrifice religion to government policy by approving the decisions and wishes of the president or emir. They support rulers whose self-contradicting speeches are full of apocryphal *hadiths* and Qur'anic verses taken out of context to serve the occasion. Depending on what the ruler wants, they condemn correct actions and approve incorrect ones; all is tailored to fit domestic and foreign political objectives. We simply cannot expect anything good to come from these zealous servants of a politico-religious agenda. Instead of guiding people and educating them so they can take control of their own destinies with vision and insight, these clerics add to the burdens faced by the people and prolong their subjection to the state. These dignitaries have failed in their educational mission and betrayed their religious vocation to serve mankind. By their actions, they demonstrate the desiccation and hardening of whatever moral conscience they may have had.

Finally, there are some sheikhs, imams, and muftis, along with upstanding, honest intellectuals, who refuse to distort their religion or corrupt its noble precepts. These independent, freethinking individuals profess Islam loudly, often risking their lives in the process. Caught between the governmental hammer and the fundamentalist anvil, their room for maneuver is limited. Subjected to harassment in many countries, they are often forced into exile. Nevertheless, these progressive thinkers remain committed to the principle of freedom of conscience, which they not only profit from in their own work, but also defend on behalf of others—even non–Muslims. Writing and speaking with great courage and determination, they have begun the long process of redeveloping Islamic thought by equipping themselves with a formidable intellectual arsenal. To do this, they first try to learn to think for themselves, which requires mastering the appropriate methodological disciplines, from sociology and ethnology to semiotics, hermeneutics, philology, historiography, and analogy. These are the keys needed to reopen doors of *ijtihad*[2] closed for centuries, and transform the very structures of modern thought, with the goal of reviving an Islam of beauty, intelligence, and light.

The absence of any central authority or clerical hierarchy—which has been both an incredible blessing and source of freedom, and an obstacle and handicap—has not, alas, allowed a voice representative of faithful Muslims to make itself heard. As we see from the three categories outlined earlier, it is difficult to identify an "official" position of the Muslim *umma* (community).

The intellectual hodgepodge of modern European Muslim thought *must*, therefore, be clarified, and a policy agenda established. We should start by evaluating the major problems facing the Muslim community in Europe, particularly in France. After pinpointing these problems we must establish a list of priorities, and then get down to business, since the task of resolving these problems is a massive one. This titanic burden falls primarily on Muslim intellectuals, who must meet the challenges and demands of modernity. The objectives include pluralism, secularism, equality, individual autonomy, and the de-sacralization of violence. For this effort to be successful, we need an atmosphere of calm and serenity for reflection and intellectual production.

The current debate in France about the incompatibility of Islam with secularism is an example of the work that has already begun. Democratic Muslims have started with a rereading of scriptural references, attacking the bedrock foundations of Islamist ideology, which rest on very shaky grounds. The argument at the core of Islamism is that society ought to be governed exclusively according to Islamic precepts and the teachings of the Prophet. This issue has long been a stumbling block in relations between Western Muslims and their fellow citizens, and is one of the most serious misunderstandings between the two sides.

Muhammad's death marked the beginning of a new era in which society would no longer be governed by God through his chosen Prophet, but by fallible human beings. All Muslims, other than those fortunate enough to live in the time and place of the Prophet, share the responsibility of governing themselves. Muhammad was silent on this issue, as is the divine revelation of the Qur'an, which says not a word about politics. The Qur'an in the *surah* Consultation (Surah 42, ash-Shura, verse 38) simply says: "And their affairs are by counsel among themselves."

This verse, which has given rise to numerous debates, has been invoked equally often by those supporting the secularization of Islamic societies and those defending a system founded upon the famous concept of *shura*, or consultation. It is also part of the sophistry utilized by Islamists, who argue that anything *beyond* consultation and deliberation—such as the democratic electoral process—is sinful and forbidden.

I would suggest that the passage can be understood on two levels:

On the first level—that of classic modernist secular thought—it is clear that the Qur'an delegates to mankind the authority to direct all public activities through dialogue and consultation. Because these thorny, but crucial, issues are extremely complex and cover a vast area that cannot be adequately understood or resolved by a single person without prior discussion and debate, free engagement with other members of the community is essential for managing the community's future. In this reading, a political structure based on democratic principles of popular sovereignty is not inconsistent with the Qur'an.

On the second level, beyond this interpretation, it should be understood that no verses are necessary to support the separation of the temporal and the spiritual, because they are epistemologically distinct. While moral and spiritual content is desirable, and perhaps even natural, for formulating general principles of harmonious and fraternal relations among human beings, the formal and technical organization of society is a neutral, and exclusively human, enterprise. These questions will, in a sense, always remain "profane," as they are different in nature from questions of the sacred.

This second level, which is a higher, more refined, exegetical approach, holds in essence that the Qur'an gives license to Muslims not to refer to Qur'anic discourse *at all* while managing their worldly affairs. Thus, there should not, and cannot, be a political doctrine that is reducible to the Qur'an alone. This does not mean that the Revelation should be marginalized or devalued; on the contrary, this separation restores it to its elevated status as a source of profound truth. The Qur'an is a message providing direction, with an ethical and spiritual emphasis, stemming from the "unknowable," inviting mystery, but requiring a commitment from humanity to use its reason and intellect. With this separation, Islam becomes the religion of the escape from politics.[3]

The fundamentalists' intellectual position and underlying logic are different, of course, since they wish to extend their faith to all areas of life. For these Islamists, there cannot be any policy, law, science, or economy other than an Islamic one. Any argument thus ends before it is even raised. They do not see that the principle of "render unto Caesar" actually *strengthens*, rather than weakens, the monotheistic belief in the omnipotence of God. God holds supreme power in the universe, and reigns over all worlds, all life, and all things; to ascribe the workings of minor government ministers to His will is to ridicule Him. Divine Providence is of transcendent value, and cannot be reduced to procedural protocols or bureaucratic formulas.

It is therefore curious to read and hear so often that there is no clear distinction between the profane and the sacred in the writings of the Qur'an, as there is in Christianity—as exemplified by the tribute coins that Jesus asked his followers to "render unto Caesar." In point of fact, Matthew 22:15–22, the passage in the Gospels that refers to the payment of tribute, was "rediscovered" as the foundation for the separation of religion and state at a very late point in the history of the Church—a development that should be applauded by everyone. This is because, after the Church's political involvement in the Arian controversy of the first part of the fourth century, and above all, after the triumphantly political Christianity of the Emperor Theodosius (reigned 379–395), there is no further mention of Caesar's tribute.[4] Saint Augustine of Hippo, the "shield of faith and scourge of heretics" and the first great Christian philosopher, does not quote from Matthew 22 in his *City of God*. Augustine's "city of God" and "city of man" are not divided by a strict line between the spiritual and temporal. For the Bishop of Hippo, the celestial kingdom must make its mark on the terrestrial one. In spite of Matthew 22—which in contemporary Christianity is seen as so straightforward that its meaning is no longer even questioned—defenders of the link between the sacred and the profane in Christianity, especially in the East, have never given up temporal power of their own accord.

Even as late as the seventeenth century, when Bishop Jacques Bossuet and theologian François Fénelon were theorizing about absolutism and the divine right of kings, they did not invoke Caesar's tribute.[5] However, this does not mean that the passage remained obscure or hidden. On the contrary—renowned preachers of the time, such as Louis Bourdaloue and Jean Baptiste Massillon, as well as the nineteenth-century bishop Félix Dupanloup, referred admiringly to the finesse and political acumen that Jesus displayed in escaping the trap laid for him. He did not wish to agree to pay the tax and be seen as a collaborator with the Roman occupiers, or refuse to pay it, and be seen as a rebel.

While the separation of ecclesiastical and temporal power had been confirmed in practice over centuries of history, this never received official religious sanction. The Church continued to hold that the prince holds his power from God, because, as St. Paul wrote, "there is no authority that does not come from God," and "the authorities that exist have been established by God," with the mediation of the Church (Romans 13:1). The temporal was accordingly placed under the protective shadow of the spiritual, and would remain there for centuries, because the Church claimed not only its rightful authority over the transcendent, but also immanence in its relations with the world.

Thus, even the idea of separation was vigorously condemned by Pope Pius X in his 1906 encyclicals, *Vehementor nos* and *Gravissimo officii*, the latter forbidding, among other things, the formation of the worship associations endorsed by the French Parliament as part of its 1905 separation legislation. The controversy proved to have a dramatically divisive impact on society, and was deeply traumatic for the Church. It almost goes without saying that the members of Parliament who voted for the law were all excommunicated. It was only after nineteen years of silence that the Church announced its assent, in an appendix to Pope Pius XI's encyclical, *Maximam gravissimamque*, and even then, it conceded only on the point of the diocesan associations. Like his predecessor, Pius XI was opposed to the separation law both in principle and in practice, viewing it as unjust, discriminatory, and a means of plundering the Church's property. At no point during this tumultuous period did Caesar's tribute emerge as a way of easing tensions. In fact, it was not until the Second Vatican Council that the Holy See's position underwent a metamorphosis. The new doctrine was reflected in the beautiful texts drafted at the Council, especially *Gaudium et spes*, which tells us that "the Church and the political community in their own fields are autonomous and independent from each other." Moreover, noted Jean-Pierre Richard as president of the French Council of Bishops, "this independence and autonomy do not prevent a healthy cooperation [between church and state] for the good of all."[6]

★   ★   ★

The reason for this detour through the Christian experience is only indirectly pedagogical. It does not detract in the slightest from the respect we should have for the faith of the men and women who belong to this great religious tradition. Rather, the fundamental idea behind this discussion is that a relatively clear text can be interpreted in different ways by scholars, according to their individual circumstances, and as a function of the evolution in the mindset of believers. The new reading of Matthew 22 enshrines the Doctrine of the Two Swords, established by Pope Boniface VIII in 1302, which holds that power is divided into two cooperating dimensions, the spiritual and the temporal. It also, after centuries of uncertainty, finally puts an end to the Investitures Controversy, the eleventh-century struggle between the Vatican and the Holy Roman Empire over the power to appoint church officials, which led to a lengthy civil war in Germany and the permanent weakening of the Holy Roman Empire. (The issues it highlighted were not fully resolved until the twentieth century.) This new reading develops a sound framework, rooted in the Gospels, for providing credible and solid grounds for separation of the Catholic Church from secular governments. It is a readaptation of Christian teaching that raises it to the level required by modern times.

There is no reason whatsoever not to make the same intellectual effort—this famous concept of *ijtihad*—to have a modern exegesis for Islam, one that establishes a clear dichotomy between religion and politics. Neither is there any good reason why sincere and pious Muslims should not speak out against the politicization of their religion and call for a clear separation of the two. Moreover, logically speaking, the absence of the formal idea of separation does not necessarily imply the idea of unity between them. Aside from the fact that the Qur'an had no reason to speak of Caesar or what should be rendered unto him, it does not mention anywhere that the spiritual and secular should be somehow interwoven. God, the Omniscient and Omnipotent, has by His will delegated questions of the secular to those who are, from the perspective of the faith, servants of that will. All this is part of the dignity that the Creator grants to His "property manager" on Earth, humanity. It is a guarantee to mankind of its freedom of thought and action. It is up to human beings to deploy their political genius to determine the best system of government for themselves, taking into account the particularities of their time and place. They need to give free rein to their creativity to imagine how best to do so. They do not require a spiritual adviser to dictate to them how to run their affairs, nor a predetermined reductive framework that must serve mankind for eternity.

Unfortunately, it is precisely the absence of a clear separation between the spiritual and the secular that leaves so much room for manipulation and distortion. We individuals, who enjoy equal rights to interpret our religion without any intermediary between ourselves and God, must simply say no! Religion should not interfere in politics, just as religion should never submit to politics. The Qur'an is not intended to be confined to the narrow role of a constitution for a so-called Islamic state. That would diminish its universal message, which should be presented to people as a free choice, not imposed on them by the chains of an étatist system. Moreover, why would we want a denominational state? While a modern, democratic state is the guarantee of free exercise of any kind of religion, a state with the Revelation as its fundamental constitutional law simply deforms the word of God.

Yet, in perhaps the most appalling example of the Islamists' distortion of the Qur'an, even many non-Islamist Muslims believe that the word of God does support this concept of the state. What is surprising about the success the Islamists have enjoyed with this interpretation is how little they have had to work with. There is only one appearance of the Arabic word *dawla*—which in contemporary Arabic means "modern nation-state"—in the entire Qur'an. Surah 3, Al-i-Imran, "The Family of Imran," verse 140 declares "And these are days We rotate among humanity so that God may know those who have believed" as "Islam is religion and state." Of course, Islamists use only these last five words as their slogan—but even out of context, they do not lend support to their arguments. Arab philologists have pointed out that the traditional sense of the word *dawla* was first "circulation," then "alternation," and finally "dynasty," in line with the changes in the ruling family after a conquest or a palace coup. Thus, if Islamists had respected the word's etymology, their slogan would instead be, "Islam is religion and alternation." This sounds almost farcical, considering how far it is from the fixed idea of a pseudo-theocratic state governed by a *vali-e faqih*, literally, an "Islamic jurist who governs," a title used by the supreme leader of Iran.

Moreover, a "first level" reading of another Qur'anic verse reveals support for separating the secular and the spiritual, assuming again that it is prudent to go back to the Qur'anic text to place a theory of secularism in an Islamic context. As democratic Muslims, we cannot properly deny Islamists the use even of misinterpreted Qur'anic verses to establish their all-embracing political agenda, while we do the very same thing to address clearly political themes that concern the organization of society. Even if we claim to have the *correct* interpretation, our respect for intellectual rigor and awareness of the limitations on human knowledge tell us not to base our arguments on the Qur'an, especially in public affairs, because of the Qur'an's demonstrated neutrality on these issues.

Remaining on this "first level" of exegesis so as to satisfy those who prefer to debate—or even to fight—each other with verses on the level of primary exegesis, as well as those who prefer to debate using competing quotes from scripture, it is appropriate to reflect on the Qur'anic passage that calls believers to obedience: "O you who believe! Obey God and obey the Messenger, and those from among you who are invested with authority" (Surah 4, An-Nisa, "Women," verse 59).[7]

This listing of those to whom obedience is owed shows clearly that there are two kinds of authority (besides the obvious authority of God, who is by definition the Almighty): an authority of the spiritual order, exercised by the Prophet, and a temporal authority, exercised by those who hold power. The coexistence of the two powers in a single verse demonstrates vividly that religious authority should not be confused with political authority. In addition, the duty of obedience corresponds directly with the duty of the person being obeyed to consult in every matter with those concerned. In a beautiful passage addressed to the Prophet, the Qur'an reminds him that "It was by a mercy from God that [at the time of the setback] you [O Messenger] were lenient with them [your Companions]. Had you been harsh and hard-hearted, they would surely have scattered away from about you. Then pardon them, pray for their forgiveness, and take council with them in their affairs [of public concern], and when you are resolved [on a course of action], put your trust in God. Surely God loves those who put their trust [in Him]" (Surah 3, Al-i-Imran, "The Family of Imran," verse 159).

If, as early as the time of the Prophet, the two types of authority could so clearly coexist, we should not allow them to be blurred fifteen centuries later. The only valid principle is that the exercise of power must be subject to the consent of the governed through consultation and deliberation.

The government of men must come from their votes. Once the legitimate power is established by democratic means and secular procedures, obeying the person who exercises it becomes a civic and religious duty for believers.

★ ★ ★

The precepts of the Qur'an and its moral commandments are general; they do not establish any particular policy norms, let alone a general theory of the state. The silence of God in this regard is instructive. He is "silent" out of respect for those He created as free beings, to whom it is left to work toward salvation by delivering justice and promoting universal brotherhood. Whether the "city" is ancient or forbidden, whether ideal or of God, whether virtuous or of the sun, whether Muslim or of the Gospel,[8] it belongs, above all, to humanity—and it is humanity, and humanity alone, that must in the end organize that city in its general interest. In this brief listing of the different adjectives used to describe the city, we realize the major importance it holds in the development of political theories on the relationship between man and the *res publica*, both in our time and throughout the centuries.

Of course, the metaphysical and spiritual reference points that form the religious beliefs of each member of the city are also recognized and respected. The member gains the right to draw inspiration from this city the moment that—whether in a public declaration or in the privacy of his own thoughts—he participates in the establishment of universal laws that allow people to live in concord with others who do not profess the same faith and who may not even share the same basic philosophical ideas. In a modern pluralistic society, no one should impose his religious beliefs on others, nor rely on them as the sole basis for law. Society promotes the common good when it creates positive law, while scrupulously respecting the dignity of man and his fundamental rights. Only a secular framework that promotes the distinctive values of humanism permits society to come as close as possible to this ideal of harmony in diversity.

Political thinking must be alive and progressive in order to adapt itself to the hazards wrought by the constant passage of time. It cannot be confined within a rigid framework, with immutable rules that are dictated once and fixed forever. Reflection, carried out within the *umma*, can and should bear fruit in a mild climate in which the freedoms of belief and inquiry are respected.

There is also a need for an academy in France for *ulema*, religious scholars well versed in theological study. It should include serious, competent imams of a Gallican[9] spirit, which is needed everywhere, not only in France. Their training is not just an issue for Muslims to resolve. The Republic must work with the relevant ministries and local government authorities to ensure that once built, the institute of Islamic theology is guaranteed both financial autonomy and operational independence. It is in the nation's broader interests to do this, instead of boldly assuming direct political responsibility in this delicate situation. It is particularly important that the state ensure *financial* support to this Muslim endeavor, above all for reasons of fairness—whatever it gives to Catholics, Protestants, and Jews should also be given to Muslims. The specious argument against state support for Islamic religious bodies, based on the absence of the Muslim faith from the concordat system, simply does not hold.[10]

We cannot continue to brag about *laïcité* as a wonderful exception to the confused situations in other countries, while also arguing that the legacy of the concordat is an exception to the exception—thereby ensuring that Islam, the only major denomination excluded from the concordat, is the exception to the exception to the exception! *Laïcité*, properly understood, allows ideas and doctrines to encounter one another. It establishes a basis for calm, objective, and constructive public debates. It is the catalyst for what we are alchemically trying to bring about—it takes ingredients from different sources and makes it possible for them to coexist.

★　★　★

Meanwhile, the Muslim community in France is itself in constant flux. Without lapsing into either victimization or bleak pessimism, it is disoriented and confused and often feels itself adrift. It is perceived as an alien life form that has invaded a host body, and is most often referred to in terms of its "otherness." This perception is reinforced by the famous contrast between "Europeans" and "Muslims," which is further fueled by the Muslims themselves. This strange new phenomenon is rooted in the semantic slide in European languages, which in French is seen in the way the initially predominant term "immigrants" was replaced by "Muslims," then "Arabs," and then "*beurs.*"[11] All this previous terminology has been replaced by the increasingly frequent use of imprecise and inappropriate terminology, such as a "Muslim governor" or a "suspect of the Muslim type."

Yet far from being the monolithic bloc or unified mass that these terms suggest, the Muslim community is, in fact, buffeted by strong contradictory currents, from the most secular (whose adherents are by far more numerous) to the most fundamentalist. Heterogeneous, pluralistic, and diverse, Muslim society is composed of two asymmetrically sized groups.

Members of the first group, a minority of French Muslims, are wealthy, mostly of Arab stock, and they speak with the trademark harsh, grating accent that is used to stereotype them. Their children attend the best public and private schools in France—that is, when they are not away studying at Europe's most prestigious boarding schools and colleges. They are never suspected of radicalism, and will never be tarred with the label "Islamo-thug"; the average Frenchman never worries that he will have to give these Muslims the contents of his wallet if he meets them after dark. In fact, with no small amount of hypocrisy and duplicity, Monsieur

Average will flatter them as much as possible—after all, they are ensuring that the race horse industry does not go bankrupt. The top fashion houses set up special shows for their wives—or their mistresses. They support the employees of Paris's palaces, either as owners or as big-spending customers. The counts and duchesses of the *Almanach de Gotha*, the "Who's Who" of European nobility, fall all over themselves trying to get invited to their mansion parties, while the jet-setters try just as hard to score an invitation to their yachts.

The second group, the majority of French Muslims, are proletarianized, marginalized, disadvantaged, impoverished, ostracized, despised, and, above all, de-Islamized. There is currently a re-Islamization of those new to the religion, who use it as a way to claim a political identity. With the virtual Talibanization of their outlook, a whole generation of young people is clinging to fads in dress or cuisine. They hold on obstinately, reassuring themselves with things they consider to be essential to the correct practice of their faith. When will they realize that there is no such thing as "Islamic clothing"? The way Afghans dress should in principle concern only the Afghans. In Rome, after all, Muslims live like Romans, and in Bourg-la-Reine they live like locals.

Since Europe directly imported some members of *homo economicus* from the Atlas and the Djurdjura Mountains—the Moroccan and Algerian equivalents of the economically marginalized Appalachian Mountains or Welsh Valleys, respectively—it should come as no surprise that it later produced the problematic *homo islamicus*. The question of how the peasant workers of the Rif desert can be "integrated" would have emerged just as sharply had they been "imported" to the major urban centers of Morocco, rather than Marseille and Mainz.

As long as human beings in situations of significant distress find—or think they can find—a means of recentering and balancing their identities, they are easy prey for the escalating extremism that to them represents a miracle cure for their situation. Similarly, so long as the so-called *jeunes en mal de vivre*[12] continue to inhabit an extremely hostile environment where only the *sharia* prevails, they cannot help but be receptive to the fundamentalists. They are also susceptible because they will always be considered products of immigration,[13] and they think that they carry the stigmas of rejection, exclusion, and discrimination at work, at home, and at play. Moreover, as long as Muslims continue to practice their religion clandestinely, in unhealthy places unsuitable for worship, such as cellars and sheds, the crypto-Islamism that runs rampant in the suburbs of major French cities will target them.

Once again, it is self-proclaimed, untrained imams who step in and take responsibility for these young people at a bleak point in their lives. All it takes to feed their resentment is to mention the kind of place they are praying in. Moreover, hardline preachers from abroad, not at all aware of French realities, try to sell their readymade, off-the-shelf viewpoints to those who are eager for action and unwilling, or unable, to reflect. It is much easier to win people's hearts and minds, and to capture their consciousness and imagination, when they are mired in serious social problems. An identity of substitution is offered them, and they accept it.

For these reasons, it is incumbent on European Muslim leaders to invest in training imams. They must establish seminaries to ensure that religious ministers achieve mastery of the humanities and social sciences separately from, and in addition to, the theological competence they develop. In this way, they, too, will one day be able to enter the ivory tower and, in France at least, raise the traditional toasts to the immortality of departed professors. Then they will go out into the community and, in their authoritative sermons, bless their country and encourage love for their homeland. At ease in the democratic institutional framework of their country, whether a republic or a constitutional monarchy, they will be committed to the secular ideal and will carry out the *aggiornamento*[14] that is necessary to cure the stagnation that afflicts much of the *umma* around the world. This group of European imams will stand up, most of all, for liberating the practice of religion from the guilt-inducing shackles of the past.

On the other hand, the French state needs to come to terms with the fact that, along with other European nations, France has for decades been experiencing a profound shift in the very nature of its identity, through a process in which the Arab-Islamic element of the population has played a central role. The "Islamic question" is inseparably bound together with the French nation, and has been since before France became France. Today, Muslims make up fully one-tenth of the population. It is up to French schools to recognize this and develop a careful and informative approach to teaching about it, and there has already been some encouraging progress in curriculum development. Happily, we are no longer confronted with sentences laden with consequences for how we view each other, such as this: "In 732, Charles Martel (the Hammer) wiped out the Arabs near Poitiers." This mythical historical episode was magnified and glorified to suit the political and ideological circumstances, first of France, and then of other parts of Europe. For example, the English historian Gibbon erupted with passion in evoking what would have happened to his country and to Christendom without the victory of Charles Martel.[15] Even today, discussions of this subject are marked by references to Muslims as "the other." Islamic civilization—a term that now properly includes Europe—is reduced to some tired clichés about polygamy, "holy war," and Allah as "Muhammad's God."

It is also time for schools—and society as a whole—to recognize that the frequently cited ties between "Judeo" and "Christian" are much more recent, historically speaking, than those that link just as closely the "Judeo" with the "Islamic," and the "Islamo" with the "Christian." The great Judeo-Islamic tradition occupied history's center stage for more than a millennium; our young Frenchmen should learn this and integrate it into their own mental frameworks. As for the rest of the French, we possess a dual genealogy, belonging to a broader Euro-Mediterranean civilizational zone, with its separate Roman and Greco-Arabic influences. No longer can any serious Western school teach that there was no such thing as astronomy for the fourteen centuries between Ptolemy and Tycho Brahe. Nor can they maintain the claim—also still found in some textbooks—that the science of medicine that emerged from the schools of Salerno and Montpellier developed directly from the works of Hippocrates and the practice of the Roman physician Galen, without any progress whatsoever in the intervening 900 years.

★   ★   ★

For reasons such as these, historians are seeking to lend support to the idea that the culture known as "Western" has, for a long time, been enriched by the culture known as "Muslim." To recognize this, teach this, and have it accepted as "normal," not controversial—this is sought not only to restore a scorned sense of pride or to cure a dying identity, but to support an effective pedagogical strategy that presents culture as sedimentation that collects on a layer of bedrock, enriching it with contributions that help consolidate the entire stone.

Young people in France can, and should, learn in school how to cultivate a sense of patriotism and to nourish a love for France's entire cultural and religious heritage. Their attachment should be to the entire wide range of this heritage, from the majesty of cathedrals and their beautiful stained-glass windows to the great motets and sacred chants, the "biblical"-style paintings, and the works of Marc Chagall. This collection is further consolidated with the inclusion of the heritage of Voltaire and Rousseau.

Similarly, France must also try to stop seeking a vanished mythical past, or fainting in awe at the wonders of the Ancients, and without any apologia at all, leave behind its damaging, incomplete, selfish, and Eurocentric vision of history by recognizing the Arabs' contributions to the body of universal knowledge, and paying a debt of gratitude to al-Ghazali, Alhacen, Ibn Bajjah, Ibn Tufail, Abu al-Qasim, and the many others whose names were Latinized and whose ideas were appropriated.

Islam did not rediscover Athenian classicism, as is sometimes claimed, because it was never lost in the first place! Islam was, instead, a direct inheritor of Hellenism for reasons of geographic proximity and historical continuity. Muslim philosophers such as al-Kindi and al-Farabi were more than passive copyists who preserved Greek works for later European use; they had a decisive role in the expansion and development of concepts and knowledge throughout the entire range of the Greek *oeuvre*.

As for the renowned Andalusian master Averroës, though known primarily as the author of introductions and commentaries on the works of Aristotle, he was far greater even than this. Through his followers and successors Nissim ben Moses and Moses ben Joshua (who happened to be Jewish), Averroës was the single guiding spirit behind Western thought for centuries—even taking into account the so-called Father of Humanism, Petrarch, in the thirteenth century—continuing, in fact, up until the dawn of the Renaissance with the late fifteenth-century work of Giovanni Pico della Mirandola. Whether one was a partisan of his—such as the Low Countries' Siger of Brabant—or an opponent, such as Albertus Magnus or Saint Thomas Aquinas, Averroës and his works left no one indifferent.

For over eight centuries, Arabic was the vehicle of knowledge from Pamplona and Zaragoza in modern-day Spain, all the way to the lands beyond Transoxiana. Translators such as Constantine the African, Dominicus Gundissalinus, Domingo de Soto, Petrus Alphonsi, Gerard of Cremona, Herman of Carinthia, Adelard of Bath, Daniel Morley, and Michael Scot dedicated themselves to accurate rendering of the subtlety and precision of Arabic. Following the example of Holy Roman Emperor Frederick II or of Pedro of Castile, both of whom spoke fluent Arabic, Westerners have continued to study the language—and many more have spoken it without even realizing it. Consider the following short fictional narrative:

My dear *abbot*, sit down on the *divan* underneath the *alcove*; I will join you on the *sofa* shortly. Would you like to try a *syrup* drink, or to taste some *sherbet*? Perhaps you'd prefer *coffee*? It is excellent both bitter, and made with *sugar*. It is fine if you'd prefer a stronger drink distilled in our own *alembic*, rather than in some factory somewhere. As for me, I will stick with my usual favorite, the *apricot* nectar.

While waiting, you can take a look at these *alchemy* and *algebra* texts; you will find many *algorithms* in them. You may want to review the book I bought for my children on basic *ciphering*; even if your interest is *zero*, the intellectual workout should get you ready for our *chess* match—I do suggest having some coffee if you want to avoid *checkmate* this time!

Ah, why don't we open the *moucharabies* so we can feel the fresh breeze; can't you smell the *jasmine*? And look across the bay at the admiralty building, with the flagship surrounded by *feluccas*.

If you're feeling tired, change out of that *gauze* shirt and try on these *muslin pajamas*. You can stretch out on the mattress—it's a wonderful *baldaquin*, a real four-poster canopy bed! You'll recognize it by its *crims*on-colored *taffeta* covering.

And don't worry about thanking me! That's what friends are for.

All of the words in italics are derived from Arabic. This is refined Arabic that has been lightly Anglicized. These are not small, symbolic influences, either—not like the merguez sausage and couscous, which the average person sees as "authentic Moroccan food." These are wide-ranging influences that can be found in all major European languages.

Schools should offer their students every possible opportunity to open their mental horizons to a more poetic universe by learning a lyrical and suggestive foreign language. For this and other reasons that have nothing to do with religion—such as its official UN status—Arabic is a very advantageous language to study.

It is also worth noting that the introduction of official poetry to Europe—done with the patronage of royal courts across the continent—also drew inspiration from the etiquette of the caliphate. King Roger II, the Norman—and thus French-speaking—king of Sicily, chose for his coronation an elaborate coat, adorned with verses of Arabic poetry embroidered in golden thread. Five centuries after Roger was crowned, the Prussian University of Konigsberg awarded the degree of Doctor of Philosophy to a successful candidate, and the diploma given to the student—the great philosopher Immanuel Kant—had a heading in Arabic calligraphy featuring a Qur'anic verse that lists the names of God and commands the reader to acquire knowledge.

Islamic cultural influences are also reflected in opera, in Mozart's *Il Seraglio*, in which Selim Pasha magnanimously returns a fiancée to her betrothed, or Rossini`s *L'Italiana in Algeri*, and of course, we cannot forget Rimsky-Korsakov's *Shéhérazade*, or the arabesques of Claude Debussy.

The visual arts also reveal the passion that great painters have shown for romantic Orientalism; both Eugène Delacroix and Eugène Fromentin had great success with this style. Equally successful was Jean-Etienne Liotard, who painted Marie-Adélaïde of France in Turkish costume after completing his own turbaned self-portrait. It was the height of fashion in its day.

As for writers fascinated by Islam, a *very* non-exhaustive list must include Montesquieu and his *Persian Letters*, or Goethe's *West-Eastern Divan*. And it was Victor Hugo who, in *Legend of the Centuries*, wrote about Muhammad: "Oh Chief of true believers, Soon as it heard thee earth believed thy word; the day that thou wert born a star appeared, And fell three turrets of Chosroe's palace."[16] Finally, the French Romantic poet Alphonse de Lamartine once rhetorically asked, "Of all the scales by which one can measure, which man has been greater than Muhammad?" He was a committed monotheist who recognized the authenticity of Muhammad's revelation.

One cannot help but think about the honest man—as recent centuries have defined him—who takes an equal interest in Chimú art in Peru or primitive Maasai art in Kenya; who becomes enraptured by Japanese engravings of a figure such as Utamaro; and who yet can blithely ignore the beauty of Persian miniatures, and remain blissfully unaware of the very basics of a centuries-old civilization.

For our hypothetical European, the civilization in question is not a distant one, but one that is close and accessible, familiar and understandable. We can see traces of it in place names along the southern trade routes, from Ramatuelle, near Nice, to Valladolid in Spain, through Perpignan.[17] Its former presence is reflected in the names of the great rivers of the

Iberian Peninsula.[18] In fact, all of the regions of southern Europe retain the indelible marks of the Muslim presence throughout the centuries.

In the end, it is only by means of science, knowledge, learning, and teaching that the oncoming tide of obscurantist opponents of knowledge and thought can be held back. And it is only through culture, literature, the fine arts, and aesthetics that we can refine the human soul. Music and poetry can complete the upbringing of our young fellow citizens. This is the noble mission of educational institutions—and let us hope it will always be.

An optimist believes that the future of French Muslims will see a gradual calming of tensions and an increase in normalcy. Despite current tensions and recurring crises, Muslims in France will continue to struggle, to the best of their ability, to pave a way forward. To the extent possible, they will strive to participate in the political institutions of their country without paying the price, either in victimization or self-flagellation, and will do so until they obtain full citizenship and contribute to national prosperity naturally, according to their merit and their ability. The pessimist, in contrast, sees a future of radicalization and response that in the end will lead to confrontations, clashes, and provocations that exacerbate tensions to the utmost. This is not what we desire, and it is certainly not our wish. If this fate is not to befall European Muslims, we must ourselves take responsibility for avoiding it in accordance with our values of love, mercy, solidarity, justice, and peace, which go hand-in-hand with those of the French Republic.

Notes

1. Editor's note: In a speech at the University of Regensburg in September 2006, Benedict touched off a firestorm of controversy by quoting the critical remarks about Islam made by the fourteenth-century Byzantine emperor Manuel II Paleologus. While Benedict later clarified that he did not personally share the emperor's view that "only bad and inhuman things" were brought by the Prophet Muhammad, the damage had been done; Vatican-Islamic relations have yet to recover fully.

2. Editor's note: *Ijtihad* is the process of establishing new (legal) norms by applying deductive reason to the Qur'an and Sunnah.

3. I am alluding here to Christianity, which Marcel Gauchet has described as "the religion of the escape from religion."

4. In an effort to promote unity, Constantine exiled the heretical bishop Arius in 325, only to reverse himself ten years later, when he declared Arianism to be the orthodox faith and ordered the Trinitarian bishop Athanasius into exile. Successive Arian emperors exiled Trinitarians and vice versa for the next several decades, until Theodosius settled the question forcibly at the end of the century.

5. I go into further detail on this in my *Alors, c'est quoi l'Islam?* (So Just What Is Islam?) (Paris: Presses de la Renaissance, 2001), p. 92.

6. Testimony before the Stasi Commission, which was tasked by President Jacques Chirac with investigating the application of the principle of *laïcité*, October 24, 2003.

7. Editor's note: The English Qur'an used in translation is by Ali Unal. *The Qur'an: With Annotated Interpretation in Modern English* (New Jersey: The Light Inc., 2006).

8. There are a number of references to the "cities" in the works of renowned thinkers. In order the references are to *The Ancient City*, by nineteenth-century French historian N. D. Fustel de Coulanges;

the Forbidden City of the Chinese dynasties in Beijing; the "Ideal City" described by Plato in *The Laws*; *City of God* by Augustine of Hippo; *Ideas of the Citizens of the Virtuous City*, by medieval Muslim scholar al-Farabi; *The City of the Sun*, by the seventeenth-century Italian priest Tommaso Campanella; *The Muslim City*, published by the French Orientalist Louis Gardet in 1954; and the New Jerusalem of Christian teaching; according to St. John, Armageddon will be followed by the creation of a city as an earthly paradise for believers (see Revelation 3:12 and 21:2).

9. Editor's note: The word usually refers to the late French monarchy's approach to relations with the Vatican, in which it successfully gained control of the appointments of priests, control of church property, and even specific prayers.

10. Editor's note: Even though the concordat between the Vatican and the French government was repealed by the 1905 separation law, that law had what would be called in American English a "grandfather clause," and continued to provide funding for the maintenance of religious facilities (churches, synagogues) of the "included religions" (Catholicism, Protestantism, and Judaism), so long as they were built before 1905. This means that despite huge demand, Muslim immigrants have to raise funds to buy basic prayer facilities, but empty village churches are fully paid for by the state.

11. Editor's note: Originally *beur* was considered fairly offensive, but (as happens more frequently in the United States or Britain) the group originally designated by it, the second-generation Maghrebins, have embraced it, and the meaning has changed.

12. Editor's note: This buzzword appears in most French works on the *banlieues*, the low-income housing projects on the outskirts of French cities whose population is heavily Muslim. The most accurate translation is "disaffected youths" or "alienated youths."

13. While normally one speaks only of "first-generation" or "second-generation" immigrants, and for subsequent generations avoids mentioning foreign ancestry, this segment of the population has been treated differently; already writers are referring to "fifth-generation immigrants"!

14. Editor's note: The term means "bringing up to date" in Italian, and usually refers to the reforms carried out in Vatican II that brought the Catholic Church into the twentieth century.

15. Editor's note: The very memorable quote he mentions is as follows: "...the Arabian fleet might have sailed without a naval combat into the mouth of the Thames. Perhaps the interpretation of the Koran would now be taught in the schools of Oxford, and her pulpits might demonstrate to a circumcised people the sanctity and truth of the revelation of Mahomet."

16. Victor Hugo, *La légende des siècles* (The Legend of Centuries), trans. George. S. Burleigh, *History Brief Epics* vol. 1 (New York: printed privately, 1867), pp. viii–351.

17. All three cities' names derive from Arabic. Ramatuelle is from *rahmatullah*, "God's grace"; Valladolid is from *balad al-wahid*, "newborn land"; Perpignan is from *birbunian*, "city well."

18. Such as the Guadalquivir, from *wadi al-qabir*, "big valley."

CHAPTER NINE

Euro-Islam: An Alternative to Islamization and Ethnicity of Fear

BASSAM TIBI

Although the history of interaction between Islam and Europe is as old as both civilizations, Islam's return to Europe in the late twentieth century in the context of global migration has ushered in an entirely new phase in their relationship. Together with other factors, the growing Islamic diaspora on the continent has brought about a dramatic shift in European demographics.[1] This not only correlates with a changing composition of the European population, but also represents a challenge to Europe's secular identity, since most diaspora Muslim leaders do not approve of the separation of religion and politics. The challenge, moreover, is not unidirectional; Muslims who move to Europe also find their own worldviews and identities questioned. While neither Europeans nor immigrant Muslims seem to be willing to come to terms with the new reality and the challenges it brings, they must nevertheless make a choice among the options they have; refusing to deal with this reality is not one of them. This chapter discusses their predicament and rejects self-censorship, whether because of political correctness, or what is called "Muslim sensitivity."

Introduction

It is deplorable that most Europeans continue to view Muslims living in Europe—even those who were born there—as aliens. European states identify Muslims as immigrants, or "people of migratory backgrounds." Some view even European-born Muslims as intruders, fostering Islamophobia. Conversely, most of these Muslims do not feel at home in Europe, nor do they identify with European values; they compensate for their alienation by establishing their own ghettos. This becomes a great challenge to Europe, when Islamists view these separate neighborhoods as an extension of *dar al-Islam*, the "land of Islam," in Europe.

Ethnic enclaves in Europe itself, like Turkey in Germany or Algeria in France,[2] become the focal point for a religionized politics reminiscent of the *amsar* (the settlements during the classical Islamic *Hijra,* the migration to spread Islam).[3] These enclaves function as parallel societies that are located in the West but are not of it.

My own life as a Muslim immigrant is illustrative of this. I moved to Europe from Damascus in 1962 at the age of eighteen, and retired in 2009. In the past decades I have not succeeded in being accepted as a European citizen, nor in obtaining equal treatment or equal opportunities in my academic career. My accomplishments include my embrace of European civic values and even of the civilizational idea of Europe, as well as the publication of twenty-eight books in German that have enriched German literature and culture. Yet none of these accomplishments has enabled me to be seen as a European in any sense other than a European Union (EU) passport holder (a *Syrer mit deutschen Pass,* or "Syrian who holds a German passport"). Both Islamists and European liberals accuse me of being "Europeanized," and both ultimately legitimatize the view of the Islamic diaspora and Europe as two different worlds. Europe is not the meeting point of Muslims and ethnic Europeans embracing democracy, as some Western academics like to believe. This is wishful thinking, a kind of self-delusion. How can this be changed?

Islamists are very active in the diaspora, and are obsessed with the Islamization of Europe.[4] To be sure, every Islamist is a Muslim, but not every Muslim is an Islamist; there is a great distinction between the two. Islamists are not interested in integration. The European failure to help migrant Muslims become "citizens of the heart"[5] gives Islamism its greatest boost. Is there hope for change? I believe that there is, and that it is called **Euro-Islam**. To paraphrase Martin Luther King, I have a dream of a European Islam. This, however, is not a dream shared with Hasan al-Banna's grandson Tariq Ramadan; I wish to Europeanize Islam,[6] while it has been argued that Ramadan supports the "Islamization of Europe."[7]

This study is concerned with Euro-Islam, not with Tariq Ramadan or the politics of doublespeak.[8] Nevertheless, many factors compel me to set the record straight: I am the originator of the concept of Euro-Islam, not Ramadan—despite his supporters' claims to the contrary. The issue here is not about copyright, but about the meaning of the concept. At issue are different agendas. That is what separates Ramadan's work from my own. Euro-Islam means no more and no less than a Europeanized Islam, and not a "mission of the Muslims in Europe,"[9] as Ramadan asserts. My core argument is that if a secular European Islam is accepted by both Europeans and Muslims, then both parties may live together in peace. This would avert not only the cultural imperialism of Islamization, but also the potential for ethno-religious strife that could develop into an "ethnicity of fear."[10] An ethnicization of the Islamic diaspora may become a source of violence and even civil war in Europe, along the lines of the Kosovo model. There, among the Albanian and Serbian populations, one can see the impact of an ethnicity of fear—where ethnic divisions become a driving factor behind cruelty and violence. Although the ethnic identities of European Muslims are unlikely to vanish, their continued existence does not have to lead to such a bleak outcome, provided that Islam can be "Europeanized," thus allowing Muslims to become European citizens "of the heart." This requires that people on both sides cease to "ignore predictions they dislike," as they do at present.[11]

There have been many warnings, beginning with March 11, 2004 in Madrid. Yet the warnings were overlooked and predictions ignored; Europeans continue to engage in rhetoric about mutual understanding, and to downplay significant tensions by calling them "misunderstandings." For instance, the Spanish government replaced the dreadful term "clash of civilizations" with the benign formula "alliance of civilizations." In France, the government, media, and opinion leaders continue to deny that the turmoil of 2005 has anything to do with Islam. The rioters' use of the term *intifada* (uprising), as well as their chanting of the jihadist slogan, "*Allahu akbar*" (God is great), as they torched thousands of cars, are completely ignored.

Between Islamization and Europeanization

The competition and rivalry between these two scenarios for Europe's future are the background to the vision of a "Euro-Islam for bridging." By this I mean a Europeanized Islam that could become a part of Europe, a continent that has its own secular civilizational identity. Europe's civilizational identity is not Islamic, and Islam was never a source for it.[12] With his concept of "the Muslim mission in Europe," Ramadan seeks a space for Islam in Europe. He attributes some Islamic traits to Europe, and even concludes that Europe is *dar al-shahada*, another term for *dar al-Islam*. Clearly, this notion implies religious imperialism, because Europe is not a part of this realm; indeed, I hope that it never does become *dar al-Islam*. All Islamists, including Salafist Muslims who believe that they are following the *salaf*, or early companions of the Prophet, identify Europe as *dar al-harb*, the "house of war." By his use of the term *dar al-shahada* to describe Europe, Ramadan is not shifting to a more tolerant mindset, as some naïve Europeans want to believe. The new notion indicates instead a belief in a peaceful takeover of Europe via (im)migration. One Muslim author summarizes Ramadan's thinking about *dar al-shahada* thus:

Tariq Ramadan, a theorist of what he calls "European Islam," argues there are five fundamental rights that are secured within European/Western societies:

- The right to practice Islam.
- The right to knowledge.
- The right to found organizations.

- The right to autonomous representation.
- The right to appeal to law.

Where these rights exist, he argues, that place should be considered an "abode of Islam."[13]

However, this is not part of an effort to make incoming Muslims Europeans, but to make Europe part of the "House of Islam," or *dar al-shahada*. This is an agenda for the Islamization of Europe, part of the history of Islamic expansion, what historian Efraim Karsh calls "Islamic imperialism."[14] My concept of Euro-Islam is a Europeanization of Islam, not an Islamization of Europe, which is how the liberal Muslim German scholar Ralph Ghadban describes Tariq Ramadan's approach (see note 7).

★ ★ ★

I came to Europe as a student who never considered becoming an immigrant. I belonged to the post-1967 Arab Left[15] and engaged with Edward Said and Sadik Jalal al-Azm in thinking about a better Arab world,[16] in which, during the late 1960s at least, I was planning to pursue my future. My years of study at the University of Frankfurt, under great minds such as Theodor Adorno, Max Horkheimer, Jürgen Habermas, and Iring Fetscher were intended to be limited to acquiring knowledge.

However, the rapid rise of political Islam that began in the early 1970s in the context of the struggle between Islamism and authoritarian secular neo-patriarchy had dispelled all the illusions fostered by critics within the Arab-Muslim intelligentsia. In this battle, the Arab Left—myself included—was marginalized to the point of insignificance. In the late 1970s, as political Islam was rising,[17] I chose Europe as my permanent home. It was then that I started to care about Islam in Europe, and to think about civilizational bridging.

In the summer of 1982, I visited West Africa and saw a non-Arab Islamic cultural space for the first time in my life. My thinking about Europeanization of Islam was stimulated by the West African experience of the Africanization of Islam. In Senegal, I encountered a highly positive variety of Islam with no veiled women, no *sharia* (Islamic law), and no gender apartheid.[18] There, too, I watched how Wahhabi Arabs were employing all possible means—above all their petrodollars—to purge this wonderful African Islam of its most precious feature: diversity and being African. I asked myself how Islam—based as it is on an Arab, not an African, culture—could set down roots there. The answer was that Islam had been Africanized.

Ten years later, in 1992, I was invited to join a historical process in France: abandonment of the French model of assimilation and adoption of "integration" which was limited to acceptance of the civic values of the French Revolution and France's secular republic.[19] Of course, this is the model, but the reality is an ethnic France in contrast to the civic

France that the state proclaims itself to be. In a short paper presented at the Institut du Monde Arabe (Arab World Institute) in Paris, I proposed my concept of Euro-Islam. A report about the Paris meeting published in the *Frankfurter Allgemeine Zeitung* in December 1992, together with the conference paper and a French book that emerged from that project in 1995, document clearly that Euro-Islam was a new concept at that time,[20] and that this was the first public pronouncement of a vision for integrating Muslims in Europe through Europeanization.

Time magazine's special issue on Islam in Europe had the following to say on this subject:

> Bassam Tibi...who coined the term Euro-Islam, insists that the integration of Europe's Muslims depends on the adoption of a form of Islam that embraces political values, such as pluralism, tolerance, the separation of church and state, democratic civil society and individual human rights. The options for Muslims are unequivocal, says Tibi, there is no middle way between Euro-Islam and a ghettoization of Muslim minorities.[21]

I have just one clarifying comment to add to this fine and accurate summary: those Muslims who demand a cultural space for Islam in Europe end up endorsing not Euro-Islam in the meaning defined above by *Time*, but instead "ghetto-Islam."

Subsequently, other people used the term with no acknowledgment of the source and with an entirely different meaning that completely distorts the concept. It was therefore a great consolation that in the late 1990s, the University of California at Berkeley launched a project, inspired by my approach, on "Islam and the Changing Identity of Europe." The findings of that project were published in *Muslim Europe or Euro-Islam: Politics, Culture, and Citizenship in the Age of Globalization*. One of the chairpersons of the project, who served as an editor of the volume, says this:

> Bassam Tibi attempts to rethink Muslim identity in Europe by devising a new form of Islam, one Tibi calls Euro-Islam.... Tibi writes that the point of departure for the understanding of Islam in Europe is the recognition that Islam is...rich in cultural diversity.... Tibi argues [that] Euro-Islam is the effort to devise a liberal form of Islam acceptable both to Muslim migrants and to European societies, thus accommodating European ideas of secularism and individual citizenship.... Tibi points out that Euro-Islam is directed against both ghettoization and assimilation.... Tibi advocates the democratic integration of Muslims into European society.[22]

Despite this and other positive responses, my work has also attracted considerable opposition. Whether from Islamists who fear the effects of public criticism of their agenda, or from Europeans who refuse to confront the danger faced by their society and its principles, the flood of aggressive criticism of the concept of Euro-Islam and of me personally has not abated.

Nevertheless, I continue to discuss the fundamental incompatibility that has presented so many difficulties for the Europeanization of Islam: that between the Islamic faith and cultural modernity. This tension between Islam and (European) modernity is not a new one; although the details are obviously different, it has been a central feature of earlier Euro-Islamic encounters.[23] Today, spurred by the formation and growth of the immigrant diaspora—and fueled also by conversion—Islam now has a significant presence in Europe. Moreover, this presence is in large part an Islamist one. "Persecuted" political refugees have successfully obtained asylum in Europe, and are then able to politicize Islam in an attempt to "return to history," that is, to regain Islam's lost dominance.[24] This conflict between the Europeanization of Islam, and the Islamization of Europe, is often blurred through Islamist doublespeak.

Some may dismiss this discussion as panic-mongering. As a Muslim living in Europe, no such thing could ever be my intention. My aim is rather to find ways of living together in peace, without proselytizing. My goal is to replace the spirit of conquest by one of consensus, based on universal support for civil society and its values. Euro-Islam is an attempt to prevent the clash of civilizations.[25]

A Europeanization of Islam, restricted to Europe, underlies the concept of Euro-Islam. We must begin with an uncensored look at the existing inter-civilizational conflict.[26] The Islamists are not a "crazy gang," as asserted by Edward Said, but a powerful, organized movement that must be taken seriously. Those who sound an alarm should not be silenced, dismissed, or defamed as "Islamophobic." Europeans are prejudiced against Islam, something I struggle against, but "Islamophobia" has become a weapon in the Islamist war of ideas used to undermine any criticism of Islamism. I propose to replace this term by the notion "Islam-bashing," with its meaning restricted to prejudice.

Determining the Issues

In 1950, only about 800,000 Muslims lived in Western Europe, largely in France and the United Kingdom. Their presence in Europe was related to the British and French colonial legacy. At the turn of the twenty-first century, not only had the figure risen to 15 million, but their distribution had also changed. In 2008, there were an estimated 20–23 million Muslims in the European Union. These figures are only estimates, as for a variety of reasons there are no verified statistics. Scholars who insist on using official statistics lag behind the facts, citing, for instance, a figure of about 13 million.

In addition to immigrant Muslims living in Western Europe, there are also some 12 million native European Muslims in the Balkans. My focus, however, is Western Europe, where the pertinent question is whether these new immigrants are integrated into the European polity. The answer is clearly no.

A documentary broadcast in January 2008 by the European television station Arte aired verbatim and at length the inflammatory speeches made by an influential Moroccan imam at the al-Quds mosque in Hamburg. It is well known that the Hamburg cell of 9/11 frequented this mosque and used it for its meetings, as well as for indoctrination and recruitment. This imam warned migrant Muslims against exposure to Europeanization, and told them of the perils of losing their faith. He exhorted them not to interact with Europeans, whom he called "*kuffar*" or "unbelievers." This happened in a major European city, and it is not exceptional, but in fact rather typical.

Those who demand that Muslims live separate lives and follow *sharia* law resemble this imam and his agenda. The feature was followed by a televised debate about Euro-Islam in which I participated. I argued against the imam and advocated integrating Muslim immigrants as equal European citizens. In this context, I cited the French riots of October–November 2005; most of the perpetrators in these riots were born in France.

The conflict is determined by a mix of cultural and socio-political factors, and is not a religious one. It arises from the social marginalization of most Muslim immigrants to Europe, but they articulate their protest in religious-cultural terms. The result is religionized politics and an intractable conflict, because what is religionized is not negotiable. It is true that a tiny Muslim middle class is very slowly emerging in Europe. The sample presented by Jytte Klausen in her study of this small minority ends up wrongly generalizing from the findings, with the result that her conclusions are misleading. The fact is that "integrated Islam"[27] is a delusion, not an empirical finding.

Again, conflicts about religion become intractable because religious issues are not subject to negotiation. This is the major implication of the notion "religionized politics." By contrast, Euro-Islam is a secular concept. The Europeanization of Islam has a secular dimension aimed at averting this already unfolding scenario. For this reason, the cultural concept of Euro-Islam must make a secular contribution to facilitating Muslim integration in Europe. The concept must also be paired with a social policy that can bring an end to marginalization. Based on my own experience as an immigrant Muslim, I can state that the discrimination is not merely a matter of social class but also has a cultural dimension that increases the incentives toward an Islamic identity politics. The self-ghettoization of Muslims in European cities implies an ethnicization of the diaspora as a cultural phenomenon, not merely a social one. The roots of Islamization are to be found in this soil.

The European Union clearly lacks a policy framework within which to develop an appropriate continent-wide response. Islam is changing Europe, but most Europeans, particularly politicians, are reluctant even to recognize the existence of this issue, let alone to deal with it.

As a devout Muslim and an immigrant to Europe, I challenge those who speak of successful integration. Europeanization could make Islam compatible with the model of a secularized religion and with an ethnicity-blind secular identity in Europe. Muslims can achieve this compatibility through religious reforms, educational channels, and social policies. Europeans, too, must be involved in this venture. Though I do not exclude the state as an actor, I believe that civil society should be the primary framework for making Euro-Islam a reality in Europe. An honest Muslim-European cooperation is needed, one that transcends *iham* (willful deception), prevarication, and the dishonest pronouncements of harmony and convergence.

To be sure, Euro-Islam is a secular concept, but it admits religion as a source of political ethics while strictly separating faith from politics. Euro-Islam can also replace the security-based approach used today, in which huge amounts of police time and resources are devoted to monitoring and thwarting radical Islamists' activities—because under the principles of Euro-Islam, Muslims would not tolerate criminals in their midst even if they share the same religion, but would instead support the rule of law above all. The message to Muslim immigrants must be conciliatory and accommodating in order to avoid the perception—and the reality—of exclusion.

*   *   *

A major challenge is the integration of Muslims who live in parallel societies. The Islamic culture in these "ghettos" makes people more susceptible to Islamism and to Wahhabi Islam sponsored and promoted by Saudi Arabia at home and in the diaspora in Europe. The American scholar of Islam John Kelsay aptly describes these ghettos as "enclaves existing in Europe, but not of its culture."[28] Can this be changed and, if so, how? Among the necessary remediary policies is a halt to the ongoing ethnicization of the Islamic diaspora in Europe (see note 10); integration cannot occur when the Muslim community is not only separated from the rest of society, but also divided within itself on ethnic grounds.

Islam in Europe is a challenge, not a muse for romantic fantasies. A free and unbiased debate is needed. Instead, there are two extremes among those who deal with Islam in Europe. The first subscribes to a populist, Islamophobic view, while the other advocates multiculturalism and an "anything goes" policy. No prudent person can turn a blind eye to the emergence of parallel Islamic societies, which are enclaves within Europe that give rise to political, cultural, economic, and social problems. The events in Madrid, Amsterdam, and London between 2004 and 2006, in

Paris in 2005 and 2007, and in Copenhagen in 2006, were an indication of severe conflict.[29]

Well-informed politicians and experts acknowledge the need for a politics of integration to avoid worst-case scenarios. In contrast, some postmodern scholars preoccupied with multiculturalism deny that there is any conflict of values in a long-term perspective. To be certain, assimilation, on the one hand, and xenophobic exclusion, on the other, are extremes to be dismissed in favor of civic integration, in which consent to shared cultural values is combined with economic integration. A request that Muslim immigrants share some core values and live as citizens in peace and mutual recognition is not to be confused with assimilation. This requires also social and economic integration in the workplace. Migration that results in a net drain on the welfare system, common in Western Europe, creates social dynamite.

Salafist leaders of the Muslim community, as well as other Islamists, reject Euro-Islam because it runs counter to their agenda. There are also racist Europeans—predominantly those in the lower-classes, who are motivated by a fear of socio-economic competition—who do not want to see any Islam in "old Europe."[30] Then there are the benign multiculturalists who confuse apartheid with the right of cultural communities to autonomy. This creation of an Islamic space is clearly a step in the Islamization of Europe. We should apply Karl Popper's notion of an "open society" and speak instead of an open Islam.

In 2004 when the Dutch held the EU presidency, I was asked to propose a model for a reasonable integration that would allow Muslim immigrants to truly feel European. A conference on "Europe: A Beautiful Idea?" was supposed to set guidelines for thinking about a post-bipolar Europe that includes a significant Islamic component. In a presentation in Rotterdam, later published in Amsterdam,[31] I argued for an inclusion that cannot be achieved either by a multiculturalism of "anything goes" or by the "space for Islam in Europe" that Ramadan wrongly calls "Euro-Islam." I made the case that while assimilation is neither feasible nor desirable, the inclusion of Muslims in Europe is imperative. For their part, European Muslim leaders must be willing to engage in a reformist interpretation of Islam. The background to this story is Islam's difficulty with cultural modernity,[32] which must be addressed with both candor and vigor.

Europeanization of Islam will facilitate a worldview that allows an embrace of secular democracy, individual human rights, pluralism, civil society, and tolerance. This requires both religious reform and cultural change—two things brought by Euro-Islam. There can be no half-solutions. If Muslims live in their own enclaves—a development that Tariq Ramadan seems to advocate—then they will never become members of European civil society, and will never be viewed as Europeans. Ramadan's approach is not only resistance to integration, but also entrenchment of the existing divided enclaves, and a more permanent establishment of the *dar al-Islam* in Europe, albeit under the different but synonymous name of *dar al-shahada*.

Can Islam Be Europeanized?

Islam was an Arab religion that was born in the seventh century in an Arab environment and cultural context. In the course of the ensuing centuries, Islam spread to Asia and Africa. In West Africa and Southeast Asia, Islam was incorporated into local cultures. In these non-Arab parts of the world of Islam an adjustment took place, not a reform.

Today, Europe is the place where Islamist neo-absolutism and European cultural relativism meet. More needs to be done in Europe because Islam is still based on a premodern value system. Some Europeans say that Islam is archaic and can never become European (see note 30). I reject this view. Muslims, for their part, cultivate in their identity politics an essentialized, allegedly immutable Islam. I reject this, too. Some imams in Europe seek to purify Islam of any European influence, while at the same time claiming a cultural-political space for Islam in Europe. These preachers do not allow for accommodation, let alone reform. In arguing against both points of view, I would say that there is *no* essential Islam, and *no* essential Europe. The two can be brought together on the grounds of cultural modernity (see note 32). This is a reason to press for more change in Islam so as to make its presence in Europe harmonious with cultural modernity.

Europe is one civilizational entity, but it is characterized by diversity. Nevertheless, the situation in Germany does not much differ from the situation in the United Kingdom. My fellow Muslim (living in the United Kingdom), Hanif Kureishi, came to a similar conclusion, based on an experience that is worth quoting at length: "The mosques which I visited were dominated by fanatical preachers, one following the other in inflammatory preaching. In an endless torrent, these imams incite hatred against the West and the Jews.... This happens not only in mosques, but also in most other religious institutions."[33] This is reminiscent of the Hamburg imam cited earlier. This kind of inflammatory Islam alienates not only Europeans, but also many non-Muslim immigrants (although in certain populations, such as the economically marginalized Caribbean groups in Britain and the Netherlands, this kind of Islam has attracted many converts as well). Muslims in Europe constitute 40–50 percent of each country's total immigrant population. Any *sharia*-based Islam is not acceptable to Europe's non-Muslims or to liberal Muslims. Islamism and Salafism should not be admitted in the name of diversity.

Three principles are necessary for the successful integration of Muslim immigrants: First, citizenship, which is the easiest requirement to fulfill; second, complete social and economic participation in society and in the labor market; and third—the most difficult requirement—cultural integration into Europe based on the acceptance of civil and open society.

If they are to accept them, Muslim immigrants need to be shown that there exists an Islamic basis for each of the following five pillars of civil society:

- Democracy, not only as an electoral procedure, but as a political culture that entails acceptance of the related values
- Separation of religion from politics
- Individual human rights in the specific understanding of entitlements of individuals vis-à-vis state and society (in Islam there are *faraid*, duties, not *huquq*, rights in the meaning of entitlements)
- Cultural and religious pluralism, which places all religions on an equal footing
- Tolerance, not in the Islamic sense of treating Jews and Christians as *dhimmis* (protected minorities with second-class status) but tolerance based on equality on all levels

To be sure, there can be no reconciliation between Europe and Islam if Islam is based solely on the three Salafist pillars of *da'wa* (proselytizing), *jihad*, and *sharia*. If Muslims fail to embrace the five core values outlined earlier, and if Europe does not maintain its civilizational identity (see note 12), then Euro-Islam will never succeed.

Europeanizing Islam

As stated earlier, Europeanizing Islam in Europe resembles Africanizing Islam in Africa. I have visited and lived in Islamic parts of West Africa, as well as Southeast Asia, where I familiarized myself with Indonesia's "civil Islam."[34]

Clearly, African Islam is very different from Arab Islam. In Africa I often asked, "Is this really Islam?" and added, "This is not the Islam I know." The self-confident answer was always, "This is African Islam, this is our Islam." The same thing happened in Indonesia. The indigenization process explains why Islam in West Africa and Islam in Southeast Asia are at home. While the situation in Africa comes to mind every time I think about Europeanizing Islam, it is also clear that Africa and Southeast Asia do not provide a model for Europe. Though Islam is in its origin an Arab religion, in Africa Islam became part of African culture, adapting the *adat*—traditions—of Islam to the *adat* of local cultures. In Indonesia and Southeast Asia, a similar process of accommodation took place. In contrast, in Europe, Islam has not yet adapted itself to local conditions, or the *adat* of Europe. Moreover, Muslims in Europe—unlike Muslims in West Africa—are immigrants, not indigenous local people. Thus, not only is Islam alien to Europe, but so are its followers.

If Muslim immigrants display an honest willingness to become European citizens of the heart, and if Europeans demonstrate a true spirit of inclusiveness, then an Islam that comports with the values of cultural modernity would be feasible. But the realization of this vision of Euro-Islam requires some work. Neither Muslims nor Europeans seem to welcome it. Although multiculturalism is a dead end, many Muslims prefer it because it allows them to live under *sharia* law, which amounts to legal apartheid. It would be wrong, by all means, to qualify multiculturalism as pluralism. It is not; it separates communities from one another.

History is the best source for learning lessons to shape the future. I refer to Belgian historian Henri Pirenne's thesis, "no Charlemagne without Muhammad,"[35] to explain the roots of the relationship between Islam and Europe. What Pirenne states is that without the challenge of Islam, Charlemagne's Christian Occident would never have come into being in the way it did. Pirenne shows that both of these civilizations—Europe as Western Christendom, and Islam as a religion-based civilization[36]—have a shared historical record. From the very beginning, this relationship consisted of challenging one another through jihad and crusade, and of cross-cultural fertilization as well. This fertilization was described by the late Maxime Rodinson as "*la fascination de l'Islam*,"[37] the fascination of Islam.

How does this affect the present and the future? And why is the historical record important to the Euro-Islam project? The reference to Pirenne supports an interpretation of Islam's relationship to Europe as a century-long mutual "threat and fascination." Each of these civilizations has threatened the other, with jihad wars, crusades,[38] or colonization. At the same time, each has enriched the other in cultural and civilizational terms. This is documented in medieval Islam's borrowings from Hellenistic philosophy and science, and in the influence of Islamic rationalism on the European Renaissance. These processes have continued up to the present. The perhaps 23 million Muslims living in Europe today may be placed in the overall context of threat and fascination. Is it now possible to find a bridge between Kelsay's "enclaves in Europe, but not of its culture," and Europe, just as bridges were found earlier? I propose that it is indeed possible. As a reform-oriented Muslim, I see in the Europeanization of Islam in today's Europe a parallel to the Hellenization of Islam in medieval times. In the past, the Islamic *fiqh* orthodoxy undermined the institutionalization of that Hellenization of Islam. Will Islamism today also succeed in undermining the Europeanization of Islam?

★   ★   ★

At present, in Europe, the debate on "Europeanization versus Islamization" cannot be held freely, due to the taboos of political correctness. This culture promotes prevarication and avoidance of key issues. I have enjoyed greater freedom of speech in the United States than in Europe. It was at Berkeley and Cornell, and later at Stanford, that I was able to develop my concept of Euro-Islam as an inter-civilizational bridge.[39] In Europe, however, false argument of "Islamic sensitivities" is continually used to undermine freedom of speech and of academic research.

Notwithstanding the discouraging comments and the accusations of polarization, I carry on in my venture, inspired by the tradition of cross-fertilization in Islam. In my contribution to *Preventing the Clash of Civilizations: A Peace Strategy for the Twenty-First Century,* by the former president of Germany, Roman Herzog, I provide ideas for averting the clash of civilizations. I continue this work to revive medieval Islamic rationalist humanism. The earlier Hellenization of Islam is a precedent for Europeanizing Islam to prevent its "sharia-ization."[40] It is not my work that promotes "polarization," but rather Islamism itself.

Europeanization Means Adopting an Inclusive European Identity

Unlike Europe's universalist ideology of Westernization, which replaced missionary Christianity, the Europeanizing of Islam is not universalist but is limited to Muslims settled in Europe and to Turkey, which seeks full European Union membership. With Europeanization, Muslim immigrants are expected to recognize that Europe has its own civilizational identity—one that it has the right to preserve. Respect for the identity of immigrants must be coupled with respect for the identity of Europe. The same applies to countries that want to join the European Union.

It is ridiculous when some liberal Europeans, such as Timothy Garton-Ash, confuse the demand for reform of Islam in Europe with a demand that Muslims abandon their faith. A reform of Islam is simply an effort to bring the religion into terms of compatibility with cultural modernity (see note 32). Europe does not need Europeans who do not defend European values when they are challenged by Islamic proselytizing that is aimed at—and is leading to—an Islamization of Europe.

Although unfortunately not yet a reality, Euro-Islam presents a model of an inclusive identity that can underpin Europeanization of Islam in Europe. I have learned to appreciate the idea of Europe as an "island of freedom in an ocean of despotism" from my Jewish teacher Max Horkheimer.[41] Horkheimer was a survivor of the Holocaust, and only too familiar with the other, darker side of Europe. This ugly face of totalitarianism and racism should not detract from the freedom and enlightenment of the other Europe.

The Europeanization of Islam rests on a cultural synthesis. Europe as a beautiful idea, free from the past horrors of colonialism, two world wars, and the crimes of totalitarian regimes (equal credit to the USSR as to Nazi Germany), is a Europe of freedom, individual human rights, democracy, pluralism, and civil society. This beautiful idea can also be shared by non-European immigrants, including Muslims. Euro-Islam is an attempt to make the idea of a European identity palatable to Muslims through a cultural synthesis with Islam. Citizenship in the law for Muslims will remain incomplete if it cannot be expanded to a citizenship in the heart by appropriating European values (see note 5). In the context of a Euro-Islam, migrant identity could be shaped by multiple identities with both European and Islamic components.

In the context of this discussion, the distinction between Islam and Islamism is especially pertinent. Islam is a religious faith as well as a system of cultural values—one, as I have argued, that is highly adaptable to different cultures at different times. Islamism, by contrast, is a totalitarian ideology. Islamism contests Europe's universalist values—which, being neither ethnic nor religious, are inclusive—in favor of Islamist universalism. Therefore, Islamism, in contrast to Euro-Islam, is a threat to the civilizational identity of Europe.

Despite common assertions to the contrary, European identity is not Christian, but secular. This distinction is highly important, because European identity can be inclusive only if it is secular. Among its sources is humanist Hellenism, as mentioned earlier. At the high point of Islamic civilization, Hellenism was among the sources that gave rise to medieval Islamic rationalism. These historical facts point to a record of a bridge linking the two civilizations, and it is imperative that this bridge must be rebuilt. In principle, a Muslim or a Jew can be European without being Christian and without having ethnic roots in Europe. In this model, the sole precondition for sharing European identity is adoption of the basic European civic values of liberty, equality, secularism, and democracy that emerged from the Renaissance, the Reformation, the Enlightenment, and the French Revolution. This is how one can remain Muslim and wholeheartedly become a European citizen. This cannot be done, however, without reforming and rethinking Islam.

The Islamists in the Islamic diaspora reject a Euro-Islam, claiming that integration of Muslims in Europe is only camouflaged Christian proselytizing. Clearly, these Islamists are not pursuing integration because it thwarts their vision of an Islamized Europe. Introducing *sharia* in the name of multiculturalism matters more to them. The problem is not only Islamism, but also European opinion leaders. While they advocate inclusion, their words are not followed by deeds. European inclusiveness is, like Euro-Islam, a blueprint for future action, not a description of current reality. In other words, to bring Islam and Europe together on European soil, both Muslims and Europeans must transform their approaches.

European civilizational identity and the historical record of cross-cultural fertilization should be the basis for the encounter between Islam (not Islamism) and Europe. For non-Western peoples, it is a positive sign when Europeans abandon their Eurocentrism. It is, however, unfortunate that this is happening as part of a trend of renouncing European core values. The debate we are concerned with here, in which the Enlightenment has been written off and attacked as a type of fundamentalism, not only demonstrates intellectual confusion but also a lack of awareness of values of any kind. Postmodern relativism is not what Europe needs if it is to open up to others. The vision offered by Euro-Islam contrasts with the relativism of today's Europeans.

Conclusions

I have argued here for a cultural synthesis involving the Europeanization of Islam, since this is required if Islam is to be successfully included in the political culture of the European Union. Today, since EU countries are home to people from all over the world, they must share a value system to establish peace and harmony. Europeanization separates identity from religion and ethnicity, linking it solely to the values of cultural modernity, which consist of secular democracy and individual human rights, based in civil society.

In conclusion, I would like to relate Euro-Islam to a concept developed by the last great philosopher in Islam, Ibn Khaldun, who died more than 600 years ago in 1406. Ibn Khaldun coined the term *asabiyya* (esprit de corps, or better, "collective civilizational identity") to measure and assess civilizational self-awareness, which indicates the strengths and weaknesses of a civilization. How strong is the European *asabiyya*? Only when the Europeanization of the newcomers succeeds as a democratic response to the Islamic challenge will it be possible to speak of a strong European *asabiyya*, in Ibn Khaldun's sense.

Going beyond the confines of Eurocentrism, it is crucial today to integrate Europe as a continent of the old world, and also as a civilizational entity, into a pluralistic world at large. This entity must have its own *asabiyya* as well as a clear sense of self. If it is not exclusionary, a civilizational self-awareness will not prevent Europe from remaining open to those who come to live there. The incorporation of immigrant Muslims through a politics of Europeanization involves a concept of Europe far broader than the economic or common space as it is often understood. If it were to be reduced to an understanding of a multicultural home to diverse cultural communities claiming space for their culture, then there would be no integration. Diverse communities need to be related to one another by shared values. I insist that Europe is a "beautiful idea." It is a community of values based on cultural modernity. The concept of Euro-Islam suggests Islamic participation in this project of a new Europe.

The task of preserving Europe with Islamic participation is a peace project for the twenty-first century. The opposing concept, the Islamization of Europe, is a recipe for repeating what happened in Kosovo. Liberal Muslims and democratic Europeans must thwart this agenda through civilizational bridging between Islam and Europe, within the territory of the European Union, which is not, and should not become, *dar al-shahada*.

Notes

1. On the Islamic diaspora in Europe, see the two volumes that emerged from a research project at the University of Leiden: W. A. R. Shadid and P. S. van Koningsveld, eds., *Muslims in the Margin: Political Responses to the Presence of Islam in Western Europe*, and *Political Participation and Identities of Muslims in Non-Muslim States* (Kampen, Netherlands: Kok Pharos, 1996). *Muslims in the Margin* includes the author's chapter, "Islam, Hinduism and the Limited Secularity in India: A Model for Muslim-European Relations in the Age of Migration?" pp. 130–144. The conclusion to the question posed is negative.

2. Paul A. Silverstein, *Algeria in France: Transpolitics, Race, and Nation* (Bloomington, IN: Indiana University Press, 2004); the author's *Mit dem Kopftuch nach Europa: Die Türkei* (Darmstadt: Primus, 2007).

3. In early Islamic history, Islam was spread through the *futuh*at-conquest. In conquered areas Muslims establish colonial settlements they called *amsar*. These *amsar* were related to the Islamic *Hijra* (migration) for the spread of Islam by force.

4. See Chapter 10, "The Islamization of Europe," in J. Millard Burr and Robert Collins, *Alms for Jihad: Charity and Terrorism in the Islamic World* (Cambridge: Cambridge University Press, 2006), pp. 237–262. Following a Saudi lawsuit this book was withdrawn from the market. The notion of Islamization means transforming Europe into an Islamic space as part of the "House of Islam."

5. See the author's "A Migration Story: From Muslim Immigrants to European 'Citizens of the Heart?' " *The Fletcher Forum for World Affairs* 31, no. 1 (2007): 147–168 and the chapter: "The European Diaspora of Muslim Migrants and the Idea of Europe: Could They Become Europeans by Choice?" in *Political Islam, World Politics and Europe: Democratic Peace and Euro-Islam versus Global Jihad*, ed. Tibi (New York: Routledge, 2008), pp. 188–215.

6. See the author's "Europeanizing Islam or the Islamization of Europe: Political Democracy vs. Cultural Difference," in *Religion in an Expanding Europe*, ed. Peter Katzenstein and Timothy Byrnes (New York: Cambridge University Press, 2006), pp. 204–224.

7. Ralph Ghadban, *Tariq Ramadan und die Islamisierung Europas* (Berlin: Verlag Hans Schiler, 2006).

8. Caroline Fourest, *Brother Tariq: The Doublespeak of Tariq Ramadan* (London: Encounter Books, 2008).

9. According to the printed program of the Johnson Foundation, this is the title of Tariq Ramadan's presentation at the Swedish conference held on June 15–17, 2006 near Stockholm. I was among the speakers, but after the ordeal of listening to such doublespeak, I felt compelled to leave.

10. See the author's "Euro-Islamic Religious Pluralism for Europe: An Alternative to Ethnicity and to 'Multiculturalism of Fear,' " *The Current* 11, no. 1 (2007): 89–103, and also Roland Hsu, ed., *Ethnic Europe* (Stanford: Stanford University Press, forthcoming). These texts developed out of research conducted at Cornell and Stanford.

11. This quote is from the front page and editorial heading of the *Financial Times* of December 30, 2008, and is supposed to answer the question of why the financial crisis was so unexpected. Though "crisis" here refers to the economic situation, and not Islam in Europe, I believe there is a parallel between the two.

12. See the author's *Europa ohne Identität? Die Krise der multikulturellen Gesellschaft* (Munich: Bertelsmann, 1998).

13. Ramadan as presented by Abdullah Saeed, "Muslims under non-Muslim Rule: Evolution of a Discourse," in *Islamic Legitimacy in a Plural Asia*, ed. Anthony Reid and Michael Gilsenan (New York: Routledge, 2007), p. 25. The volume includes an approach that is different from Ramadan's, as it is based on an Islamic embrace of cultural modernity. See the author's chapter, "Islam and Cultural Modernity: In Pursuit of Democratic Pluralism in Asia," in the same volume, pp. 28–52.

14. See note 4 and Efraim Karsh, *Islamic Imperialism: A History* (New Haven: Yale University Press, 2006).

15. For more details, see Fouad Ajami, *The Arab Predicament: Arab Political Thought and Practice since 1967* (New York: Cambridge University Press, 1981). On pages 28–29, Ajami refers to my place in the Arab left.

16. See the author's chapter, "The Genesis of the Arab Left: A Critical Viewpoint," in *The Arabs Today: Alternatives for Tomorrow*, ed. Edward Said and Fuad Suleiman (Columbus: Forum Associates, 1973), pp. 31–42.

17. On this subject, see Nazih Ayubi, *Political Islam* (London: Routledge, 1991), and two monographs by the author, *The Challenge of Fundamentalism: Political Islam and the New World Disorder* (Berkeley, CA: University of California Press, 2002), and *Political Islam, World Politics and Europe* (see note 5).

18. See the chapter on "Islam in Africa" in the author's *Crisis of Modern Islam: A Preindustrial Culture in the Scientific-Technological Age* (Salt Lake City: University of Utah Press, 1988), pp. 68–80.

19. On Islam in France, see Alec Hargreave, *Multi-Ethnic France: Immigration, Politics, Culture, and Society* (New York: Routledge, 2007).

20. See the author's article, "Euro-Islam oder Ghetto-Islam," *Frankfurter Allgemeine Zeitung*, December 7, 1992, and also "Les conditions d'un Euro-Islam," in *Islams d'Europe: intégration ou insertion communautaire?* ed. Robert Bistolfi and Francois Zabbal (Paris: L'Aube, 1995), pp. 230–234. The whole story is told in the chapter on "Euro-Islam," in the second edition of the author's, *Im Schatten Allahs: Der Islam und seine Menschenrechte* (Munich: Ullstein, 2003), pp. 491–529.

21. "Special Issue: Islam in Europe," *Time*, December 24, 2001, p. 49.

22. Nezar Al-Sayyad, "Muslim Europe or Euro-Islam: On the Discourse of Identity and Culture," in *Muslim Europe or Euro-Islam: Politics, Culture, and Citizenship in the Age of Globalization*, ed. Nezar Al-Sayyad and Manuel Castells (Lanham: Lexington Books, 2002), pp. 9–29, here p. 19. The volume includes the author's chapter "Muslim Migrants in Europe: Between Euro-Islam and Ghettoization," pp. 31–52.

23. W. M. Watt, *Muslim-Christian Encounters: Perceptions and Misperceptions* (London: Routledge, 1991).

24. See Robert Kagan, *The Return of History and the End of Dreams* (New York: Alfred Knopf, 2008).

25. See the author's chapter, "International Morality and Cross-Cultural Bridging," in Roman Herzog et al., *Preventing the Clash of Civilizations: A Peace Strategy for the Twenty-First Century*, ed. Henrik Schmiegelow (New York: St. Martin's Press, 1999), pp. 107–126.

26. See the author's chapter, "Jihadism and Intercivilisational Conflict: Conflicting Images of the Self and of the Other," in *Islam and Political Violence: Muslim Diaspora and Radicalism in the West*, ed. Shahram Akbarzadeh and Fethi Mansouri (London: Taures, 2007), pp. 39–64.

27. Jytte Klausen, *The Islamic Challenge: Politics and Religion in Western Europe* (New York: Oxford University Press, 2005); Jonathan Lawrence and Justin Vaisse, *Integrating Islam: Political and Religious Challenges in Contemporary France* (Washington, D.C.: Brookings, 2006); and Jocelyne Cesari, *Where Islam and Democracy Meet: Muslims in Europe and in the United States* (New York: Palgrave, 2004) belong to the same category of scholars who close their minds to existing conflicts.

28. The term "enclaves" is used by John Kelsay in *Islam and War* (Louisville, KY: John Knox Press, 1993), p. 118.

29. Akbarzadeh and Mansouri, ed., *Islam and Political Violence* (referenced in note 26).

30. See the German Islamophobic contribution by Hans-Peter Raddatz, "Antisemitism in (Contemporary) Islam: Europe in the Conflict between Tolerance and Ideology," in *The Legacy of Islamic Antisemitism: From Sacred Texts to Solemn History*, ed. Andrew Bostom (Amherst, NY: Prometheus, 2008), pp. 643–649.

31. See the author's articles on Euro-Islam and respectively on Islamic humanism published in the Dutch journal *Nexus*, issues 41 and 50 in the volumes 2005 and 2008.

32. See the author's book, *Islam's Predicament with Modernity: Politics, Religious Reform and Cultural Change* (New York: Routledge, 2009).

33. Hanif Kureishi, "Karneval der Kulturen," *Neue Zürcher Zeitung*, August 11, 2005.

34. Robert Hefner, *Civil Islam* (Princeton, NJ: Princeton University Press, 2000).

35. Henri Pirenne, *Mohammed and Charlemagne* (London: Allen & Unwin, 1939).

36. See Peter Brown, *The Rise of Western Christendom: Triumph and Diversity, A.D. 200–1000* (Cambridge: Blackwell, 1996), and Marshall Hodgson, *The Venture of Islam: Conscience and History in a World Civilization* 3 vols. (Chicago: University of Chicago Press, 1974).

37. Maxime Rodinson, *La fascination de l'Islam* (Paris: Maspero, 1980).

38. See the author's, *Kreuzzug und Djihad: Der Islam und die christliche Welt* (Munich: Bertelsmann, 1999).

39. On the author's work at Berkeley see the reference in note 22, at Cornell note 6 and 10, at Stanford note 10. In 2008/2009 the author completed while in residence at Yale the book *Islamism and Islam* (forthcoming: to be published in New Haven, CT by Yale University Press in 2010).

40. See note 25 as well as the author's article, "The Return of the Sacred to Politics: The Case of Shari'atization of Politics in Islamic Civilization," *Theoria* 55, no. 115 (2009): 91–119.

41. Max Horkheimer, *Kritische Theorie* 2 vols. (Frankfurt/Main: S. Fischer, 1966). A Cornell professor published a positive book on Islamism with a reference to the Frankfurt School of Horkheimer. Against this see B. Tibi, "The Political Legacy of Max Horkheimer and Islamist Totalitarianism," *Telos* 148 (Fall 2009): 7–15.

CHAPTER TEN

Americanism versus Islamism

M. ZUHDI JASSER

The conflict between Western liberal democracy and Islamism, or "political Islam," is the central ideological struggle of the twenty-first century. The personal stories of Muslims who love their lives in the West hold the key to understanding how to bridge the gap between the two.

It has been over eight years since 9/11, and we have finally begun to see a growing consensus about the obvious: the root cause of terrorism is the Islamist goal of establishing an Islamic state. Islamism is an ideology that seeks to create governments rooted in a legal system of *sharia* law (Islamic jurisprudence) in which the Qur'an is the constitution and clerics are the final authorities who write and interpret that law. Islamists vary from those who want to bring about that change by military force, like the Taliban, to those, like the Muslim Brotherhood (MB), who envision even a generational change of "Islamization" in free Western lands where Muslims are a minority. This global incremental change begins with Islamist plans for Islamization state by state throughout the region where Muslims are a majority, and then follows with their plans in the West. This was confirmed in the Holy Land Foundation trial, which uncovered a document of the Muslim Brotherhood in the United States that planned a "Civilizational-Jihadist Process" for the *Ikhwan* (Brotherhood) as a "kind of a grand jihad in eliminating and destroying the Western civilization from within and 'sabotaging' its miserable house by their hands and the hands of the believers so that it is eliminated and God's religion is made victorious."[1]

Ultimately many Islamists also seek the more global reestablishment of the caliphate (a transnational hegemony of Islamic states within one empire). Although only a small portion of Islamists are militant, this does not diminish the fact that all of them come from a larger pool of Islamists with a common vision regarding the Islamic character of the state.

For Islamist-inspired militants, terrorism is only a tactic. They are not simply criminal or psychotic; they are led by ideologues whose vision for the Muslim world and, in fact, the entire planet, is diametrically opposed to the type of society embodied by the free nations of the West. The tragedy of 9/11 woke many people up to this conflict, which had been brewing for over a century, if not far more.

Islamists seeking to deceive Western leaders will protest, insisting as part of a grand denial that political Islam is compatible with Western ideals. Or they will remain deceptively silent. Western leaders seeking shortcuts, and advocating blind multiculturalism and appeasement, will ignore the great divide, and downplay the danger of Islamism. They do so at our peril.

My Family Story: Understanding Nationalism and Identity

My parents fled Syria in the mid-1960s for Lebanon, ultimately immigrating to the United States in 1966. They escaped the political oppression of Syria's military dictatorships, which ravaged the Syrian population through the 1950s and 1960s and finally entrenched the totalitarian Baathist regime of Hafez al-Assad, one of the most corrupt, barbaric regimes of the twentieth century.

My grandfather, Zuhdi al-Jasser, a prominent Syrian businessman and newspaper columnist, was one of many outspoken intellectuals at constant odds with these regimes who trampled upon human rights. He spent his life in the 1950s, and into the early 1960s, fighting for democracy with his pen, at the repeated cost of his freedom. His son and my father, Mohamed Kais Jasser, fought a similar struggle. Fortunately for me, my father decided to leave Syria upon finishing medical school in Damascus and emigrated to the United States. The United States represented the ideals of freedom in which he so strongly believed. Though I have never been to Syria, the stories I heard from my grandfather and my family of the generations that challenged authority and stood up for freedom against the fascists and autocrats of Syria had a profound impact upon my appreciation and understanding of what the United States meant as a nation. My parents described to me how intensely American they felt immediately upon arriving in the United States in 1966, and how they left their failed Syrian nationalism unapologetically behind in Aleppo.

They easily traded Syrian nationalism for life in a nation that guaranteed them rights and freedoms, a life that, prior to their immigration, had seemed to be almost impossible for an individual to exercise. The regimes that controlled Syria from 1949 onward, with coup after coup, denied them the rights of assembly, free speech, representation, religious freedom, property, and other basic human rights. I learned through osmosis that their faith, their practice of Islam, was separate from their political struggle for human rights in Syria. My parents and grandparents instilled in me, if only subconsciously, an understanding that it was the power of the oppressive corrupt military that destroyed any possibility of a free

Syrian nation. The thugs of the military who took power through coups and terror soon after the French pulled out at the close of World War II ensured that the young nation of Syria never developed into a thriving and independent democracy.

This led me, in my youth, to marvel at the American experiment. As the son of immigrants, it was natural for me to compare the nation where I was fortunate enough to be born with the stories I heard about the nation from which my parents came. Of all the differences between the land of freedom in America that accepted them and the land of oppression in Syria whose government rejected them, the most poignant and impactful was the difference in the two countries' militaries.

The Syrian military had become a haven for thugs, which made military coups commonplace; that is, until one particular group of thugs attained enough military might, barbarism, and control to entrench itself for decades. The better-educated and more ethically minded Syrians largely avoided the military. This stands in stark contrast to America's all-volunteer military.

I learned during my years of service in the U.S. Navy that our military is a true cross-section of America. I saw Americans who enlisted in the service out of a personal sense of duty to the nation, or a deep personal sense of responsibility to protect the freedoms of their fellow citizens. I learned early on what my parents had known from their history in Syria. The broad access and cross-pollination in our military of people from all walks of life made it a strong American institution that was bound to succeed. The unique nature of the checks and balances in American government attracted my family and led me to feel obligated to serve in the armed forces.

My Islamic faith, upbringing, and personal relationship with God instilled in me a sense of purpose about the need to give back in a general sense for all the things for which I am thankful. My family, who saw so many spend their lives fighting the military of their own country, came to the United States, and not only taught me to love the American military, but also the personal responsibility to serve and give back to the nation that guaranteed my freedoms. I believe in giving back to God in prayer and service. I believe in giving back to family in love and sharing. And I believe in giving back to the nation in service and national responsibility. The U.S. Navy, in which I served for eleven years, gave me that opportunity.

No Conflict between Faith and Citizenship

There are many freedoms guaranteed by the U.S. Constitution, and preserved by our servicemen and women. Our First Amendment rights, most notably, preserve freedom of speech; freedom of assembly; and freedom of religion. This freedom to practice my personal faith of Islam in the way I choose, as an equal of every other U.S. citizen, has always been central to the absence of conflict between my American nationalism and my faith. I could feel almost palpably how my nation granted every citizen access to all levels of government and all levels of the legislation and the law. This was blind to faith (or to lack of faith), as guaranteed by the Constitution and made more sense to me than any other type of government in the world.

It was obvious to me that I was freer to practice my faith, and to be an independent human being with free will, than in any so-called Muslim nation. The essence of faith was, after all, the ability to choose its practice, its text, its scripture and its law. If government dictates religious law it is no longer a choice, but rather a coercive inhumane system of societal rules. Even *sharia*, the Islamic religious law, is human at its core when put into practice, unless the clerics claim to have direct, ongoing communication with God on interpretation and adjudication of Islamic law. Throughout my life, the separation of faith and government has been intimately related to my love of the United States, and our system of government. As I matured, I learned that Islamist ideology, which advocates the establishment of Islamic states that empower clerics to implement *sharia* law, was at odds with Western secular liberal democracy.

America is a place where all spiritual paths are supported. It is a country where God is freely talked about in the country's founding documents, which gives great support to all faiths, especially minority faiths, and which provides all people of faith with a sense that they belong. The United States has a special combination of the public defense of religion, and a separation between religion and government. In *Democracy in America*, the great French observer of life in early America, Alexis de Tocqueville, notes that despotism can "do without faith, but not liberty . . . what can be done with a people that is master of itself, if it is not subject to God."[2] Nevertheless, acknowledging God in our lives is different from implementing Christian Canon law, or Islamic *sharia* law.

A 2007 Pew study, "Muslim Americans: Middle Class and Mostly Mainstream," made many claims about the opinions of American Muslims. One that stood out was that, when asked whether they were American first or Muslim first, 47 percent of American Muslims said Muslim, and only 28 percent, American.[3] The study compared this to Christians, 42 percent of whom said they were Christian first. Naturally, American Islamist organizations such as the Council on American-Islamic Relations (CAIR) and the Islamic Society of North America (ISNA) claimed vindication, asserting that Muslims are no different from Christians in their identification with religion. Unfortunately, this comparison is not valid. A more telling question in the survey would have been: should the U.S. Constitution be "under God," "under Islam," or "under Christianity"? As a citizen of the United States who has lived his whole life in this country, it is clear to me that most Christians would say "under God," as outlined in the Constitution. As an American Muslim, who has contact with Islamists who now dominate Muslim organizations in the United States, I believe far more Muslims would say, "under Islam," reflecting a core tenet of Islamism.

The corpus of knowledge that is Islam today is infused with the ideas of political Islam. While unsupported by the Qur'an, the idea of government as the entity that enacts *sharia* thereby creating an Islamic state has yet to be formally reformed or defeated within the halls of academic Islam around the world. The Enlightenment and the American Revolution brought an end to theocracy in Great Britain's American colonies. In fact the word Christian does not even appear in America's founding documents. How many devotional Muslims would advocate for a government that does not use the word Islam in its founding documents? The American version of secularism did not eliminate recognition of the essential role of God and morality in guiding individuals who lead governments and write laws; it established a government that writes laws based on reason, not on the interpretation of religion (or of *sharia*, as Islamists favor).

In fact, the 47 percent of American Muslims who see themselves as Muslims first most likely have a very different understanding of the mixture of government, religion, and law from that of Christians who may see themselves as Christians first. This difference runs to the core of the disagreement between the ideologies and legal systems of *Islamism* and that of secular liberal democracies or *classical liberalism*.

Growing up in the American Midwest (Wisconsin) in the 1970s and 1980s, I thought that this debate was more accurately called "Americanism versus Islamism." This is especially true when considering the ends sought by radical Islamists—namely, an Islamist theocracy to replace our pluralistic democracy. The Pew study also showed that "13% of those who think of themselves primarily as Muslim believe that suicide bombing to defend Islam from its enemies can be often or sometimes justified compared with 4% of those who are American first."[4] Additionally, those who identified themselves as Muslim first were twice as likely to believe that Arabs did not commit the acts of 9/11 (40 percent vs. 20 percent). Those who saw themselves as American first were much more likely to accept that the acts of 9/11 were committed by Arabs (61 percent). Again, we see a significant correlation between religious observance, radicalism, and Islamism.

The Roots of My Anti-Islamist Ideas

My love for Americanism was not created in a vacuum, nor did it emerge as any kind of mutation. There were many heroes of the American Revolution and the European struggle against the Catholic Church's political ambitions who were pious Christians, and who wanted to get government out of their lives and live Jesus' message of love and compassion unencumbered by governmental interference. In the same way that many Christians opposed government interference, I too, as a religious Muslim, oppose the government interference that comes with Islamism.

I was born in Ohio and grew up mostly in Wisconsin, where my family settled when I was four. Until I matriculated at the University of Wisconsin-Milwaukee in 1985, I lived in the small town of Neenah, Wisconsin. There were initially only three other Muslim families in Neenah, and together we built the first mosque in all of northeastern Wisconsin. My parents, both the children of well-respected, knowledgeable Muslim *ulema* (scholars) in Syria, raised me in the Sunni tradition, with conservative family values that never conflicted with my American identity. I learned to love America for many reasons, not least of which was its central role in giving my family an environment where they could practice their faith free of government coercion, and equal before the law to every other citizen. My parents felt that they were "American" the moment they stepped on American soil. The day they took their oath and became naturalized was one of the most memorable days of their lives.

I was raised with the understanding that America was about pluralism and I was taught to respect our nation, its Constitution, and its laws. This was in my own mind, in harmony with my Muslim identity. I was also taught that Islamist theocracy conflicts with American freedom of religion, and with Islam—or, at least, "our Islam." In my youth, references to "home" always meant the United States, not the "motherland," as with some Muslim immigrants. Other than religion, the only aspect of our heritage we sought to preserve was our Arabic culture (food, language, and art). Syrian nationalism was left in Syria.

For my parents, the breaking of the cultural and national bond with their previous "home" was essential in forming a truly American identity. My father and grandfather's political struggles against the despotism and corruption of the Syrian government made that break possible. They were able to retain the morals, values, and ethics of Islam as a deep part of their soul while embracing the new political system of the United States.

My grandfather and father taught me that the all-volunteer U.S. military was a cornerstone of our democracy, so it was natural that I joined. I earned a commission as an officer in the U.S. Navy on a medical scholarship. For me, serving in the Navy was a responsibility, and in fact, a part of my personal identity, a drive I could not ignore.

In the realm of religion, I was taught that a personal relationship with God would nourish my soul and build my character. Through my formative years, in the 1970s and 1980s, as Neenah's small Muslim community slowly grew, the mosque was for me God's house, a place of worship and religious teaching, and a place for holiday celebration and socialization. The *umma*, as I saw it in our small very American community, was about prayer, family, education, and socialization. The *umma* as a political entity, a vehicle for the enforcement and promulgation of *sharia*, was not a part of my experience, not a part of the Islam I knew. Not until I was an undergraduate in Milwaukee did I begin to see a different side of Islam—a very political Islam.

I was quite fortunate to have grown up in a town that was not populated by Muslims with a different ideology. My understanding of Islam and the United States was not changed or clouded by a different understanding from the "Muslim ghetto." At the university I did meet large numbers of Muslims who left their motherlands for economic reasons. They saw in the West, and the United States, an opportunity to secure prosperity, away from the failed, oppressive dictatorships of the Middle East. Many Muslims in the United States had not been involved in the failed efforts at political reform in the Middle East, but in the Islamist responses to Middle Eastern dictators, like the Muslim Brotherhood. The MB, for example, fought Hafez al-Assad's regime violently at times, but did not try to understand what made Western nations successful. In fact, the MB often demonized the West in its propaganda.

For generations, the MB and other Islamist groups have exploited Western freedoms to disseminate conspiracy theories blaming the West for their countries' own failings. They dismissed secular governments as illegitimate, whether liberal democracies or oppressive autocracies, such as Syria. This grew out of a culture where Arab despots encouraged their subjects to hate the West as a way to divert their anger from the failed economies and political repression for which the despots were responsible. Dictators such as Assad silenced those who sought internal reform, and gave platforms to those who radicalized Islam while feeding anti-Western and anti-Semitic sentiment.

Radical Islamism's Ties to Arab Dictators

It should be no surprise, then, that Egypt's dictatorship has always had a close relationship with the radical Islamists and clerical leadership of al-Azhar University. Al-Azhar, still hailed by Islamists as the "seat of Sunni scholarship," has produced such dangerous clerics as Yusuf al-Qaradawi, the spiritual father of the MB, who was ultimately exiled to Qatar. Reformers such as Egyptian Mohammed al-Ashmawy, a superior court judge who took on the Islamist leadership of al-Azhar, were persecuted and punished for their support for liberty and pluralism.

Furthermore, it should not be a surprise that the Saudi monarchical dictatorship has developed a close relationship with the radical Islamists and clerical leadership of the Wahhabis, who now control the legal structure of the Saudi state; a truce between evils was reached after Wahhabi militants took over the Grand Mosque of Mecca in 1979.

Ultimately, these are but two of the most malignant and metastatic examples of how a secular fascist dictator or an autocratic tribal monarchy can exploit a direct relationship with radical Islamist groups and institutions to keep the "moderate" masses at bay. The dictators' love-hate relationship with radical Islam creates an environment where voices of reason are incapable of surviving amid this clash of evils. Thus, despots nurture radical Islam so that they can turn around and justify draconian attacks upon their population. This was seen, for example, in the Syrian despot's razing of the town of Hama in 1981 where over 30,000 Syrians perished as Hafez Assad claimed to be making an example of the MB. Similarly, the Saudi Kingdom fed the Wahhabis for years while turning around and claiming to be our allies in the battle against al-Qaeda, a Wahhabi byproduct. This symbiotic relationship between despots and Islamists is a primary reason we will not be able to bring Islam into modernity without first removing many of these governments. In some nations, such as Iran, or Afghanistan under the Taliban, radical Islamists were able to take over governments completely.

These despotic regimes, from Egypt to Saudi Arabia to Pakistan, do not have to be changed through military force. Communism collapsed without an invasion of the Soviet Union. But we, especially the Muslim diaspora in the West who believe in liberty, need to turn our attention to the dissidents in the countries from which our ancestors came. We need to turn our attention to those who believe in freedom and liberty, not only in the mechanical elements of democracy. The term "democracy," not coincidentally, cannot be found in America's founding documents of the U.S. Constitution, Bill of Rights, and the Declaration of Independence. Democracy alone implies an electoral process where the "majority rules." Western secular liberal democracy is about much more than simply "mob rule." American democracy is representative, meaning elected leaders have an obligation to exercise judgment and take decisions they believe are in the broad interest of the citizens who elected them into office, respecting and balancing the rights of individuals, minorities, and all citizens. William Dalrymple has warned that "democracy," in the absence of enlightened decision-making, can be the "engine of political Islam."[5] Thus, we must first help facilitate the building of "liberal" institutions within the Muslim consciousness before expecting a simple electoral process to usher in modernity.

If we align ourselves only with democratic movements in countries where the culture of democracy has yet to develop and Islamists seek to dominate political life, we risk elections that result in parliaments based on Qur'anic law, and that result in actually trading one set of autocrats for another. Hamas and the clerical regime in Iran are two obvious examples. It is not in our interest as Americans, or as Muslims, to facilitate the establishment of Islamist states that may, in the short term, appear to be more peaceful simply because of the promise of a cessation of violence on the ground. The cost of such a flawed approach is to weaken our position in the long-term battle against Islamism and in our quest to preserve universal liberty.

As important as the President George W. Bush's initiative to democratize the broader Middle East might have been, this approach reflects a lack of understanding of the scope of the entire conflict between Americanism and Islamism when viewed solely from the perspective of elected parliaments. Almost twenty years after the United States liberated Kuwait from Iraq's invasion, the Kuwaitis have yet to establish a legitimate parliamentary system, let alone one based on reason and not run by Islamist principles. In the long term, if secular liberal democracies were to take hold of political structures in the Muslim world and replace Islamic states that already exist, global stability would be greatly increased, for at the center of the Islamic state's vision is an expansionist dream of reestablishing the caliphate and promoting the spread of political Islam around the world.

At the core of Western liberal democracies' success is the defense of individual liberty and freedom, regardless of faith, and built upon the concept of inalienable human rights. This debate will lead us into a number of areas that many of us have taken for granted living in the West, but which are undercurrents to the major ideological chasm. I have begun to appreciate, in my lifetime struggle against Islamists and their ideology, the multiple layers of this conflict almost like peeling an onion. Each layer reveals part of the clash of cultures, civilization, and political systems that could be only described as *Americanism vs. Islamism,* or alternatively, an internal war within Islam between liberty and Islamism. They are best summarized in the table below:

Americanism	*vs.*	*Islamism*
Individualism	vs.	Tribalism
Individual ideas (questioning authority)	vs.	Collectivist thinking
Pluralism	vs.	Tolerance
Minority rights	vs.	Majority rule
Liberty	vs.	Democracy
Secularism and the "Republic"	vs.	Theocracy
Democracy	vs.	Autocracy
Rule of law	vs.	Martial law
Government as protector of the individual	vs.	Government as protector of morality and God
Nationalism	vs.	Theocratic (Islamist) states
Reverence for religion	vs.	Reverence for past glory of religion and the desire to revive this glory
Truth	vs.	Corruption
Sanctity of life and humanitarianism	vs.	Dehumanization and lack of respect for life
Gender and racial equality	vs.	Misogyny and racism
Cognitive reactions	vs.	Visceral reactions
Faith (relationship with God)	vs.	Religion (relationship as a community with God)
Constitutional law (derived from natural law)	vs.	*Sharia* law (derived solely from particular interpretations of the Quran and God's law)
Free speech and religion	vs.	Blasphemy and apostasy laws

Each of these conflicts could give rise to a full discussion on the challenges before us, looking at both their historical and philosophical ramifications; however, what matters most for the next generation is how we begin to resolve these conflicts and establish an American Islam, which honors the ideas on the left column of this table, and relegates to history the ideas in the right column. The understanding of the dynamics of how exactly Islamism spreads in the Muslim community is so far only superficial; there has hardly been any discernible response from non-Islamists.

We need to promote the ideas of freedom, liberty, and equal respect for all individuals, over a blind allegiance to the tribe or a fear of "authority" or the "mob-ocracy" if there is to be any lasting change or victory over Islamism. To be sure, the secular dictatorships of the Muslim world are some of the worst ever seen, with constant human rights abuses. It may be palatable to some, and even seem preferable, to help supposedly "democratic" Islamists replace the Arab dictators. But I truly believe that the majority of Muslims and non-Muslims alike in the Muslim world have the same dreams and aspiration for freedom that my family had.

At the core of a "real Islamic practice," as with any faith, is the ability to choose or reject the faith. If, according to Islam, faith is a choice, then our societies, whether Muslims are a minority or a majority, need to be a laboratory of complete freedom so that any faith practice can truly be a personal choice. This negates the Islamist justification for Islamic governance and Islamization of society; the more space society gives individuals to live in freedom, the more their faith practices are genuine and not coerced. Until Muslims understand that their faith is not threatened by the Enlightenment and respect for the individual, we cannot win this war.

Sometimes, when I discuss these ideas, my detractors insist that I am advocating American exceptionalism and a blind patriotism. In fact, American Islamist organizations such as Council on American-Islamic Relations (CAIR), Islamic Society of North America (ISNA), Muslim Public Affairs Council (MPAC), Islamic Circle of North America (ICNA), and Muslim American Society (MAS), to name a few that purport to represent Muslims, also advocate a form of American patriotism. But their patriotism involves taking the American flag and adding a little crescent—and, of course, turning America into an Islamic state. They may dismiss this as fear-mongering, but if we asked them what type of government they advocate in Muslim-majority nations, or how they run their own organizations, then their core ideals of Islamism would become obvious. In my experience, as someone active in the Muslim community throughout my life, it has always been easy to discern Islamist from non-Islamist Muslims with only a brief analysis of ideology.

Firsthand Experience with Islamism in America

In the early 1990s, I was asked by my supervisor at Bethesda Naval Hospital to present a paper on hormonal regulation and endocrinology at the Islamic Medical Association meeting, which was held in conjunction with the Islamic Society of North America's annual conference. I had never been to a meeting of ISNA, the largest Muslim organization in America, whose annual meetings are attended by over 40,000 Muslim activists. The keynote address that year was given by Siraj Wahhaj, the imam of al-Taqwa Mosque in Brooklyn, New York, who was originally part of the Nation of Islam before converting to Sunni Islam. He is still today affiliated with CAIR and a frequent mosque speaker for many Islamist organizations. He was an unindicted co-conspirator in the 1993 bombing of the World Trade Center and provided character witness for the "blind sheikh," Omar Abdel Rahman, who is serving a life sentence in federal prison for this crime. In his keynote address, Wahhaj covered the struggle for American Islam and then began talking about the U.S. Constitution. He picked up the Qur'an and said, "I was on an airplane, and imagine, a Jewish passenger sitting next to me asked me about the Qur'an I was reading—she asked me if Muslims became a majority in America, would we replace the U.S. Constitution with the Qur'an?" He laughed and said, "Can you imagine someone wondering if a document made by humans would be superior to a document like the Qur'an, made by God?"

I felt ill listening to this, and after he was done, I went to the Q&A microphone and said, "I'm not sure if you understand American law, but you have just violated the Sedition Act as I understand it. You're free to disagree with foreign and domestic policy, but you cannot talk about the overthrow of the U.S. Constitution and its replacement by another document." I then encouraged other military personnel in the audience to actively walk out because by being members of this Islamist organization they were violating their oath to the U.S. Constitution.

This incident was emblematic of my struggle as I realized that the majority of America's Muslim organizations were blatantly Islamist. Their funding, and their ideological fuel from the Islamist clerics in the Middle East, were making them anathema to the majority of American Muslims and to America's founding principles.

Today almost two generations after their founding, these American Muslim organizations continue their Islamist mission in America, and are beginning to fulfill the stated goals of the original meeting of the *Ikhwan* (the Brotherhood) in the United States in 1991.[6] Rather than developing an American Islam rooted in the values of Western liberal democracy and the separation of mosque and state, American Islamists continue their project of imposing the theocratic values of Islamism upon the West. It is becoming more and more obvious that as anti-Islamist Muslims remain asleep, the "unaffiliated" Muslim will have nowhere to turn but toward Islamist groups. Similarly, government and much of the mainstream media continue to seek one point of view—the Islamist one—in their search for "Muslim" opinion. Sadly, this propagates the deep misconception that Muslims are monolithic, and that Islamists speak for all American Muslims.

Effectively Countering the Muslim Brotherhood Project in the West

In 1964, Sayyid Qutb, the leading theoretician of Egypt's Muslim Brotherhood, published *Ma'alim fi al-Tariq* (*Milestones*), in which he laid out steps to achieve an Islamic state and defeat the West. He described a multigenerational process to ensure the victory of Islamism over Western liberal society. This gave birth over the next forty-five years to what has become an extraordinarily potent transnational movement of political Islam claiming hundreds of brethren organizations united by one thing—the ideology of political Islam. Liberal and traditional non-Islamist Muslims have yet to wage an effective counter-jihad against their Islamist brethren. There is not yet a liberal Muslim intellectual work equivalent to *Milestones* that can lay the groundwork for defeating Islamism and ensure the creation of integrationist, tolerant American Muslim institutions.

More than eight years after 9/11 Americans are finally beginning to understand that terrorism is only a tactic. The tactic has a goal, a mission, and a dream: the establishment of an Islamic state. The only way to defeat a tactic is to defeat the source of this tactic completely. It is time for us to make this discussion public, and to stand up for American beliefs.

We do honor the Jeffersonian belief in religious freedom, and especially the First Amendment, but it is one thing to give Muslims and others the freedom to practice their faith, and quite another to allow unabated and un-debated growth of a politico-religious movement that for all practical purposes is an ideological insurgency. Islamists believe, like Zaid Shakir of the deceptively moderate Zaytuna Institute, that "[e]very Muslim who is honest would say, I would like to see America become a Muslim country," as he told the *New York Times* in 2006.[7] This Islamist ideology, which "tolerates" American liberty and lives here seeking to ultimately Islamize it, must be countered and marginalized. For, as Justice Robert Jackson stated in 1949, "the Constitution is not a suicide pact."[8] If a political and ideological threat to our way of life cloaks itself in religion, it deserves the same scrutiny as every other political ideology.

The American Islamic Forum for Democracy (AIFD), an organization I founded to counter political Islam, is launching a "Jefferson Project," based on the premise that before we move toward democracy and elections in the Middle East, the ideas of liberty must penetrate the culture.[9] Ultimately, just as the Brotherhood has spread its Islamist poison into the West through books, tapes, and viral media, so too can we anti-Islamists spread the ideas of liberty and universal religious freedom through similar means. It is imperative that we liberalize the education of Muslim youth and expose them to the Enlightenment thinkers and those who created the intellectual fabric of what became the religio-political movement to displace the Church of England from government in the New World. This same movement can happen within the Muslim consciousness.

History has demonstrated that "democracy" can become a *"mob-ocracy"* when a simple 51 percent majority is not legally constrained with a separation and balance of powers, and protection of minority rights, free speech, assembly, and religion. James Madison, Thomas Jefferson, and the other framers of our Constitution were mindful of this danger when they established the United States as a representative democracy with a system of checks and balances; they cherished the right of the people to govern themselves, yet created a republic that was and remains *a refuge* from unlimited "democracy."

It is time to change the primary terms used in our contest of ideas with the Muslim world. Members of the international community engaging with countries such as Iran, Pakistan, Saudi Arabia, Syria, Egypt, Iran, and the UAE should be constantly reminded that the citizens of these countries want to live in republics enjoying universal individual freedoms, in contrast to a simple "democracy" in which the majority rules by mob-ocracy. This is not about America imposing our values, but rather about the humanitarian need to give every citizen of every nation the chance to live in real freedom as a universal right. If our government officials cannot even employ the terms "Islamism" or "Salafism" in their discourse, it remains entirely unclear how they will be able to facilitate this contest of ideas.[10]

Settling for "democratization" movements alone will not bring stability for future generations. Islamism can operate quite well within an elective process that many people wrongly equate with democracy. The Islamist state's global vision is different from that of Western liberal democracies: Islamist society is not guided by the preservation of individual freedom above all else, but is focused on the tribe, the right of the collective to invoke "Islamic laws," no matter how harshly or moderately they are interpreted. Ultimately, Islamism is about transnational Islamic hegemony, by peaceful or violent means, and thus will always remain at odds with the West. Islamist regimes arising out of secular and monarchical dictatorships in the Muslim world will have this same goal, as exemplified in the MB, Iran, or the Taliban. This would continue to mean future conflicts.

It is in our interest as Americans and the interests of Muslims everywhere that we in the West help provide the intellectual stimuli in Muslim-majority nations for indigenous movements that support liberty. The spread of the language of liberty through efforts such as the Jefferson

Project will allow Muslims to develop a culture of democracy that can ultimately help them establish genuine liberty through a government that respects and balances the rights of all its citizens. Given the opportunity to enjoy such universal human rights and freedoms, Muslims around the world will choose such a democratic system over the profound limitations of the Islamic state and *sharia* law. Movements led by Muslims that tap into the principles of the UN Declaration of Human Rights can succeed if we give them the same attention that Islamists give to the spread of Islamism in those same nations. In the same way that the ubiquitous tapes and DVDs of Yusuf al-Qaradawi, Ayatollah Khomeini, and Tariq Ramadan have so influenced a generation, Muslims in the United States can influence their brethren by shipping tapes to the Muslim world preaching non-Islamist values of "Islamic humanism," freedom, and liberty. What would happen if the works of Thomas Jefferson, James Madison, or John Locke were translated into Arabic and shipped to the Muslim world, along with the works of reformist Muslim anti-Islamist scholars such as Mohammed al-Ashmawy and Abdullah an-Na'im to name a few. Without ideas, we cannot expect the Muslim world to realize modernity.

The "Jefferson Project" will start with a systematic countering of the Qutb plan to defeat the West, in which Muslim leaders would acknowledge the following ten points:

- An Islamic narrative should not conflict with established universal human principles.
- Mosques should support the separation of mosque and state, even as they take stands on social or political issues.
- An egalitarian approach to faith is needed that goes beyond simple tolerance. Tolerance implies superiority, while pluralism implies equality.
- If government enacts the literal laws of God rather than natural law or human law, then government becomes God, and abrogates religion and the personal nature of the relationship with God. Governmental law should be based on and debated in reason, not from scriptural exegesis.
- Separation of mosque and state will include the abrogation of all blasphemy and apostasy laws.
- Women's liberation and advocacy for equality with men, currently absent in many Muslim-majority, misogynistic cultures, are imperative.
- *Ijtihad*, the critical interpretation of Islamic scripture and jurisprudence in the light of modern day circumstances, should outline the steps toward the separation of mosque and state. Nowhere in the Qur'an does God tell Muslims to mix politics and religion, or instruct them as to what document(s) should guide governments.
- Muslim movements and organizations must be created that are specifically and openly opposed to such radical or terrorism-supporting

groups as al-Qaeda, Hamas, Hezbollah, Hizb ut-Tahrir, Jamaat al-Islamiya, and al-Muhajiroun, to name a few, rather than simply being against undefined, generic notions of terrorism.

- Leaders of Muslim-majority countries who are dictators and despots should be publicly identified and critiqued without apologetics. Muslims enjoying freedom in the West have yet to create mass movements to liberate their motherlands from dictatorship and theocracy, and to move them toward becoming secular democracies founded on individual liberties for all based in natural law.
- Classical liberal Muslim institutions and think tanks should be established to educate Muslims and non-Muslims concerning the aforementioned principles within an Islamic context to counter the Islamist movements. Muslim youth must be taught that individual liberty and freedom and Muslim theology need not be mutually exclusive.

Countering Islamism, and combating Islamist terrorism, should be a far greater focus for our Muslim community and leadership than the Islamist organizations' current obsessive focus on minority rights and victimization. Americans living in fear for their security are looking to moderate, traditional Muslims to lead this fight. The credibility of the Muslim community suffers because of groups such as CAIR, ISNA, and MPAC, which deny the interplay between Islamism and terrorism.

Non-Muslims also have a role to play. The U.S. government and mainstream media should recognize the diversity of thought within the Muslim population and give all a platform to debate while none are allowed to "speak on behalf of American Muslims." Reform will never happen if the reformists are ignored.

We should not allow Muslim organizations to simply circle their wagons and rally themselves around claims of victimization. We should rather engage them in debates so that we can determine whether they are Islamists, and whether they will help in the battle to win the hearts and minds of Muslims against political Islam. Most Muslims living in America practice an Islam that they have reconciled with American values. Most Islamic legal codes and commentaries are based on fourteenth-century models at the latest; others are drawn from twelfth-, eleventh-, or even seventh-century law. This is why corporal punishment (e.g., the severing of hands for theft, laws against blasphemy or apostasy, and the stoning of women for violation of marital laws) is still part of Saudi law. Real academic reform from learned Islamic jurists will need new institutions based in American ideals—an American Islam.

A Uniquely Western Islamic Narrative

It is up to American and European Muslims to change the global narrative on how Islam is taught and practiced in the twentieth century.

Currently the Islamist narrative is mostly unchallenged. We need to establish a tight-knit group of Muslims across the globe who believe in the Jeffersonian principles and are anti-Islamist. These Muslims need to believe in the mission and principles of organizations that openly counter Islamism and oppose the ascendancy of political Islam. However, it is also important that those of us who believe in instilling Islamic values in our children, and in living the faith of Islam, retain a strong Islamic spiritual identity. The majority of Muslims, who have remained silent against the Islamists, need to be awakened to join the battle.

Thus, to be Muslim in America is not to advocate for Islamism (a narrowly interpreted supremacist, theocratic, and societal construct), but to be personally pious while living in a land that is a laboratory of freedom and equality for all, whether Muslim or not.

If Muslims can show how "Islamic" we can be while living in a society guided by a U.S. Constitution that has an "establishment clause" that protects the equality of minorities, women, and all faiths, we will be able to spread freedom faster than they spread Islamism, and faster than they spread conspiracy theories.

As Muslim youth acquire knowledge of Islam and *sharia* that counters Islamist and Wahhabi interpretations that undermine individual freedom, the Internet—especially sites such as YouTube, Facebook, and MySpace—can generate a public discourse on "freedom versus Islamism." Few imams in the United States today are non-Islamist. We first need to teach the youth the ideas of the Enlightenment, and then empower them with enough knowledge about Islam so that they can begin forming new schools of legal thought that do not conflict with modernity and Enlightenment principles.

Americanism alone is not an antidote to Islamism, because Islamists use expressions of patriotism to advance their theocratic goals. Americanism can defeat Islamism only if it also takes back the issue of faith from the Islamists. With the growth of a moral, spiritual Islam, we can combat the immorality of terrorism in a jihad against jihad from within our American nation, under God.

Notes

1. "An Explanatory Memorandum: On the General Strategic Goal for the Group in North America" (1991). This Muslim Brotherhood document can be accessed at http://www.nefafoundation. org/hlfdocs.html (last accessed June 3, 2009).
2. Alexis de Tocqueville, *Democracy in America vol. I*, trans. and annotated by Stephen Grant (Indianapolis: Hackett Publishing Company, 2000), p. 308.
3. Pew Research Center, "Muslim Americans: Middle Class and Mostly Mainstream," 2007.
4. Ibid.
5. William Dalrymple, "Democracy, not Terror, Is the Engine of Political Islam," *The Guardian*, September 21, 2007.
6. http://www1.nefafoundation.org/hlfdocs.html (last accessed June 3, 2009).

7. Laurie Goodstein, "U.S. Muslim Clerics Seek a Modern Middle Ground," *New York Times*, June 18, 2006.

8. *Terminiello v. Chicago*, 337 U.S. 1 (1949).

9. For more information on the American Islamic Forum for Democracy visit http://www.aifdemocracy.org.

10. Zuhdi M. Jasser, "What War of Ideas," *Family Security Matters* (2008), http://www.familysecuritymatters.org/about.

ABOUT THE CONTRIBUTORS

Zeyno Baran

Born and raised in Turkey and partly in Greece, Baran was educated at Stanford University. She is currently a senior fellow at Hudson Institute's Center for Islam, Democracy and the Future of the Muslim World as well as the director of the Center for Eurasian Policy.

In 2006, she co-authored a "Muslim Manifesto" to denounce violence and extremism in the name of Islam. Baran promotes the fusion of tolerant faith and critical thinking to thwart the spread of radical Islamist ideology. She has testified repeatedly before the U.S. Congress on these issues, and briefed the president and vice president of the United States, as well as a range of European leaders.

Baran is the author of numerous articles and policy studies, including a major research monograph entitled *Hizb ut-Tahrir: Islam's Political Insurgency* (published by the Nixon Center in 2004). Her earliest work on Islam is "Turkey in the post-1980s: Can Islam and Democracy be Compatible?" for which she received the Firestone Medal for Stanford University's most outstanding political science/international relations honors thesis in 1996.

Her work has appeared in a variety of publications, including *Foreign Affairs*, the *National Interest Newsweek*, the *Washington Post*, the *Wall Street Journal*, and the *International Herald Tribune;* she also regularly appears on major American and international radio and television programs.

Ghaleb Bencheikh

Ghaleb Bencheikh has a background both in science (holding a Ph.D. in physics) and in humanities. He was educated at the *Institut des Hautes Études de Défense Nationale* (The Institute of Higher National Defense Studies, IHEDN) in Paris. He is a professor at the International Institute of Islamic Thought, having previously taught at *l'École Laïque des Religions* (Secular School of Religion) in Paris. He also teaches at the *Institut Français de Journalisme* (French Institute of Journalism), part of the *Faculté Libre de Droit, d'Économie et de Gestion* (University of Law, Economics, and Management).

For over ten years, he has been the host of a television program devoted to Islam on the public station France 2. He also has served as the French chairman of the World Conference of Religions for Peace.

A writer and an essayist, Bencheikh has published numerous works on Islam and interfaith dialogue, including "Secularism as Seen by the Qur'an" and "An Open Letter to Islamists." He is a regular speaker at international conferences on topics concerning religion, the relationship between science and faith, and the dialogue among cultures and civilizations.

Mostafa Hilali

Mostafa Hilali was born in Meknes, Morocco, and moved as a child to the Netherlands with his parents and siblings. He serves in the Royal Netherlands Army and holds the rank of Major of Infantry. He is a volunteer with organizations active in the anti-radicalization field in Amsterdam. Hilali is also an active member of the Moroccan community in the Netherlands and helps organize the annual celebrations of the War Remembrance Day and Liberation Day (May 4 and 5, respectively). In addition, he is an active participant in interfaith dialogue, particularly between the Jewish and Moroccan Muslim communities, and is part of the Multicultural Network of the Dutch Department of Defense.

Hilali studied Military History and Islamic Studies at the University of Leiden; he continues to study history with a particular focus on the Middle East and on radicalism and extremism within Islam. In his military career, Hilali has been deployed to a variety of conflict zones around the world.

M. Zuhdi Jasser

Dr. M. Zuhdi Jasser is the chairman of the American Islamic Forum for Democracy (AIFD) based in Phoenix, Arizona. Jasser was born in Wisconsin into a family of Muslim immigrants from Syria. He served in the U.S. Navy as an internist and is currently in private practice of internal medicine and nuclear cardiology in Phoenix. He is the immediate past president of the Arizona Medical Association (ARMA) and also chairs the Bioethics Committee for Banner Good Samaritan Regional Medical Center.

As a devout practicing Muslim, Jasser has always been very active in the study of Islam and its intersections with American culture. He has been active in multiple local efforts at interfaith work. In 2000 he and a leading local rabbi founded the Children of Abraham, an active Muslim-Jewish dialogue group in Scottsdale, Arizona. Jasser has also served as the Muslim representative on the Board of the Arizona Interfaith Movement since December 2001.

In 2002, as a result of what he felt to be a paucity of Muslim scholarship demonstrating the synergy of American democracy and its founding principles with the religion of Islam, Jasser set out to form AIFD. AIFD was formed in order to begin constructing a body of Islamic scholarship on the synergy between American principles of pluralism and Islamic principles of faith. Jasser has continued to work to organize Muslims, particularly those in the United States, to take a lead in the global effort to combat Islamism and the ideologies that facilitate the commission of terrorist acts in the name of Islam.

Samia Labidi

Samia Labidi is a feminist, a community activist, and an author who resides in Paris. She is the president of AIME (D'Ailleurs ou d'Ici Mais Ensemble, or "From There or Here, but Together"), an organization founded to educate people about—and to fight the spread of—Islamist ideology.

Labidi was born into a moderate family in Tunisia at a time when Islamist movements struggled to take over her country. She witnessed firsthand how political Islam infiltrated her family through her brother-in-law and led to its breakup. Believing the Islamist rhetoric that the *hijab* frees women and brings them emancipation, Labidi started wearing the veil for her before puberty. However, it did not take her long to realize that wearing the veild for her was not much different from "living in a prison." The psychological pressure she felt from her community discouraged her from removing it completely until the veil was banned in Tunisia in 1981.

Drawing from her personal experience, Labidi has fervently and frequently argued that a secular, integrated Muslim community is the only solid barrier against Islamism, which in Labidi's words "spreads like wildfire." To share her experience with others, in 1998 Labidi authored *Karim mon frère ex-intégriste terroriste* (Karim, My Brother the Ex-Fundamentalist Terrorist).

Fouad Laroui

Fouad Laroui is an economist, writer and a research fellow at the University of Amsterdam. Born in Oujda, Morocco, he moved to France to study at the École Nationale des Ponts et Chaussées, where he received a degree in civil engineering. Laroui then lived in Morocco and Great Britain, where he obtained a Ph.D. in economics and taught as a research fellow. He subsequently moved to Amsterdam, where he has taught econometrics and environmental science.

During this time, he published several novels dealing with his Moroccan heritage and the complexities of identity. After seeing many Muslim youth around him turn to Islamism at the end of the 1990s, Laroui soon became aware that his own interpretation of Islam was not represented in the public realm. Feeling ashamed of his fellow Moroccans, he began actively participating in the public debate on Islamism and integration. However, the highly polarized public environment in the Netherlands did not make it easy for reasonable voices to be heard. As a consequence, Laroui turned to writing; he took a sabbatical from his teaching position and published a book called *On Islamism: A Personal Refutation of Religious Totalitarianism* (2006).

Hedieh Mirahmadi

An attorney by profession, Hedieh Mirahmadi serves as legal counsel and consultant for several multinational non-governmental organizations. Together, these organizations form WORDE (the World Organization for Resource Development and Education), an international network of support and expertise in the struggle to stop the spread of Islamist extremism. She travels extensively (e.g., to Indonesia, Malaysia, Lebanon, Africa, Egypt, and the United Kingdom) on behalf of member organizations in order to share and gain knowledge about the methodology, ideology, infrastructure, and recruitment of Islamist extremist movements.

Mirahmadi draws from this wealth of knowledge to brief law-enforcement agencies, government policymakers, and counterterrorism experts on how to ultimately succeed in the long-term struggle against religious radicalism. Her expertise earned her an appointment to the U.S. Embassy in Afghanistan as senior advisor for civil society infrastructure. Recently, she was also appointed to the Heritage Council of the Office of the Director of National Intelligence.

Her current projects include extensive consultations and partnering with British Muslim NGOs to "rehabilitate" Muslim youth exposed to radical ideologies; she is also the cochair of the first-ever all-female Islamic Law Council that will reexamine the current standing of women's rights in Muslim societies and provide new verdicts on the most pressing issues. She is the author of *Islam and Civil Society* and *The Healing Power of Sufi Meditation* (both available from Ingram Publications) as well as various newspaper and magazine articles.

Cosh Omar

Cosh Omar is a British actor and playwright. His family belongs to the Turkish Cypriot community; in contrast to this relatively secular grouping, his family was particularly religious due to his father's role as imam. Omar was therefore caught between Islam and secularism throughout his childhood.

During the Yugoslav War, however, Omar became entranced by what he saw as the empowering message of Islam and the bond that connected Muslims worldwide, from Bangladesh to Bosnia. Overcome with this feeling, he was involved with the Islamist movement Hizb ut-Tahrir (HT)—although he did not find out until much later that it was in fact the group that had chosen him, not the other way around, due to his potential as a bridgehead within the Turkish Cypriot community.

Omar's passion for acting and playwriting as a platform for his views conflicted with Hizb ut-Tahrir's strict interpretation of Islam. As a consequence, he fell out with HT and soon learned all about the group's hypocrisy and narrow ideological horizons. In the wake of this personal turmoil, Omar brought his play *The Battle of Green Lanes* to the stage in 2004. Set in the London Cypriot community, it addresses the conflict between the Greek and Turkish Cypriots and the identity crisis faced by a young man within this community.

Yunis Qandil

Yunis Qandil is a public lecturer on Islamic studies, Middle Eastern politics, and Muslim minorities in the West at the Institute of Contemporary Intellectual Studies in Beirut. While serving as a senior researcher, he is also completing his doctoral dissertation entitled "Ambivalences of Islamist Concepts of Multiculturality and the Limits of the Theo-Political Foundations of Euro-Islam."

Born in Amman, Jordan, Qandil is the son of Palestinian refugees. Though his parents raised him in the oral religious tradition common among Palestinians, in his later youth he became closely involved with a fundamentalist Salafi mosque for five years before turning to the Muslim Brotherhood, with which Qandil was active for another four years. Yet, his comprehensive and methodical studies of religious discourses, his familial education, and his interest in poetry and literature outside of religious texts prevented him from being drawn entirely into Islamism.

After studying French and German, he moved to Germany in 1995, where he began his education in Political Science and Islamic Studies. Throughout his studies, Qandil has sought to combine his spirituality with a secular stance regarding politics. His cross-cultural experience has helped him to develop a reform-oriented understanding of Islam compatible with respect for fundamental human rights, individual dignity, and the welfare of all citizens.

Bassam Tibi

Bassam Tibi retired in 2009 after a long and productive career as a political scientist. He was Professor of International Relations at the University of Göttingen in Germany. He also was the A. D. White Professor-at-Large at Cornell University (2004–2010).

Tibi has held eighteen visiting professorships including fellowships at Princeton University, the University of California at Berkeley, the University of Michigan, and most recently (in 2008) at the Center for Advanced Holocaust Studies in Washington, D.C. He was a senior research fellow at Yale University in the academic year 2008–2009.

Born in Damascus, Tibi is a practicing Muslim who descends from the centuries-old noble family known as the *Banu al-Tibi*. He moved to Germany in 1962 to study social sciences, philosophy, and history at the Wolfgang von Goethe University of Frankfurt am Main, where he received his first Ph.D. In 1971, his second doctoral degree, known in German as the *Habilitation*, was granted by the University of Hamburg.

Tibi is a staunch critic of Islamism and an advocate of reform within Islam, with a focus on Islamism and Islam in Europe. In academic circles, he is perhaps best known for introducing the concepts of *Leitkultur* (leading culture) and "Euro-Islam."

In 1995, Tibi was decorated by German President Roman Herzog with the country's highest state medal (the Cross of Merit, First Class); he later received the annual prize of the Swiss Foundation for European Awareness in Zurich in 2003.

Tibi's books include *Islam's Predicament with Modernity: Religious Reform and Cultural Change* (Routledge, 2009); *Political Islam, World Politics and Europe* (Routledge, 2008); *The Challenge of Fundamentalism* (University of California Press, 2002); *Islam between Culture and Politics* (Palgrave, 2005), and *Europa ohne Identität?* ("Europe without an Identity?"; Siedler Verlag, 1998).

Ahmad Gianpiero Vincenzo

Ahmad Gianpiero Vincenzo teaches Islamic Law at the University of Naples. Raised in a Catholic family, he studied history, philosophy, and communications. During his undergraduate days, he joined a group of intellectuals in Milan that was united in search of a religious spirituality that its members did not find in Christianity. As a result, Vincenzo, along with the majority of its members, converted to Islam.

In the 1990s, an organization affiliated with the Islamist Muslim Brotherhood tried to gain state recognition as the sole representative for Muslims in Italy. The organization catered to the widespread desire of the political elites to have an institutional contact with regard to Muslim issues. Appalled by initial successes of the Brotherhood group, Vincenzo and like-minded Muslims created an opposing organization that success-fully halted the process of official recognition.

Following an unsuccessful election bid for the Italian Senate, he has nevertheless become a consultant in the Senate for issues concerning immigration and urban ghettos. He is responsible for intercultural and interfaith dialogue, and organizes conferences about Islamic and religious values in civil society. In addition, Vincenzo is the president of the orga-nization, Muslim Italian Intellectuals.

INDEX